THE NATIONAL
GEOGRAPHIC TRAVELER
FLORIDA

THE NATIONAL GEOGRAPHIC TRAVELER

FLORIDA

Kathy Arnold and Paul Wade

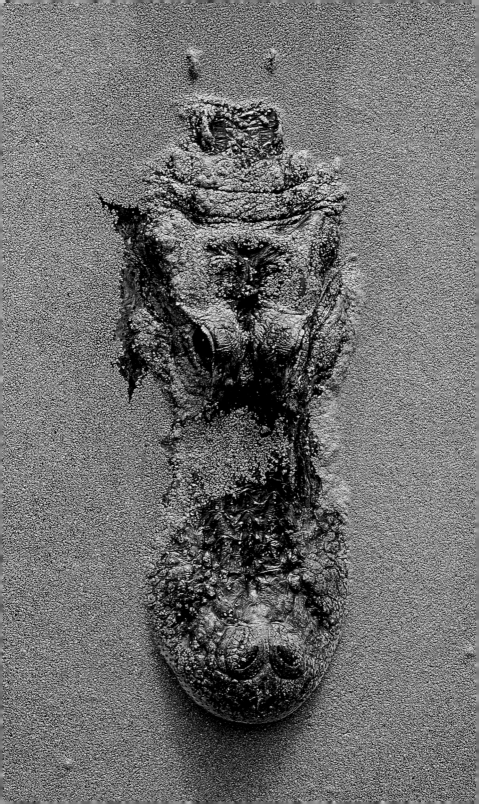

Contents

How to use this guide 6–7 About the authors 8
Florida's regions 43–230 Travelwise 231–64
Index 265–69 Credits 270–71

Page 1: Fun in the sun on a Florida beach
Pages 2–3: Relaxing at the end of a Florida jetty
Left: American alligator

How to use this guide

See back flap for keys to text and map symbols

The *National Geographic Traveler* brings you the best of Florida in text, pictures, and maps. Divided into three main sections, the guide begins with an overview of history and culture. Following are nine regional chapters with sites selected by the author for their particular interest and treated in depth. Each chapter opens with its own contents list for easy reference.

The regions, and sites within the regions, are arranged geographically. Some regions are further divided into two or three smaller areas. A map introduces each region, highlighting the featured sites.

Walks and drives, all plotted on their own maps, suggest routes for discovering an area. Features and sidebars offer detail on history, culture, or contemporary life. A More Places to Visit page rounds off some regional chapters.

The final section, Travelwise, lists essential information for the traveler—pre-trip planning, getting around, useful websites, and emergencies—plus a selection of hotels, restaurants, shops, and activities.

To the best of our knowledge, site information is accurate as of the press date. However, it's always advisable to call ahead.

92

Color coding

Each region is color coded for easy reference. Find the region you want on the map on the front flap, and look for the color flash at the top of the pages of the relevant chapter. Information in **Travelwise** is also color coded to each region.

Historical Museum of Southern Florida
- 🗺 45 D2
- ✉ 101 Flagler St.
- ☎ 305/375-1492
- 🕐 Closed Sun. a.m..
- 💲 $

Visitor information

Practical information is given in the side column by each major site (see key to symbols on back flap). The map reference gives the page number where the site is shown on a map, followed by the grid reference.

Further details include the site's address, telephone number, entrance charge in a range from $ (under $4) to $$$$$ (over $25), and days closed. Other sites have visitor information in italics and parentheses in the text.

TRAVELWISE

EVERGLADES & THE KEYS — Color-coded region name

KEY WEST — Town name

🏨 **BANANA BAY RESORT AND MARINA** — Hotel name,
$ — price range

2319 N. ROOSEVELT BLVD. — Address, telephone & fax numbers
TEL 305/296-6925
FAX 305/296-2004

The emphasis is on sports activities in this small modern resort a short drive from the historic district of Key West. — Brief description of hotel

🛏 30 📶 🏊 🏧 🅰 AE, DC, MC, V — Hotel facilities & credit card details

🍴 **MANGOES** — Restaurant name & price range
$$

700 DUVAL ST. — Address & telephone number
TEL 305/292-4606

Modern food in one of the prime spots for people-watching on Key West's main thoroughfare. With tables in two gardens and one indoor room, this does not feel like a large restaurant. — Brief description of restaurant

🍽 300 🅰 All major cards — Restaurant facilities & credit card details

Hotel and restaurant prices

An explanation of the price ranges used in entries is given in the Hotels & Restaurants section (see pp. 234–48).

REGIONAL MAPS

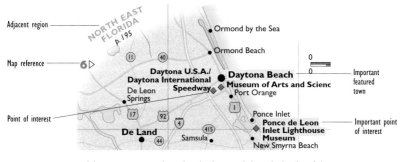

Adjacent region

Map reference

Point of interest

Important featured town

Important point of interest

- A locator map accompanies each regional map and shows the location of that region in the country.
- Adjacent regions are shown, each with a page reference.

WALKING & BIKING TOURS

Walk or bike route

Direction of route

Point of interest not on route

Building outline

Red numbered bullets link sites on map to descriptions in the text

Featured site (in bold) on route

Starting point

- An information box gives the starting and ending points, time and length of walk, and places not to be missed along the route.

DRIVING TOURS

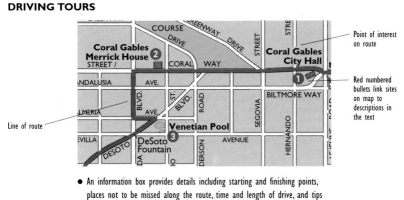

Line of route

Point of interest on route

Red numbered bullets link sites on map to descriptions in the text

- An information box provides details including starting and finishing points, places not to be missed along the route, time and length of drive, and tips on terrain.

THE NATIONAL GEOGRAPHIC TRAVELER
FLORIDA

About the authors

Kathy Arnold and Paul Wade are an Anglo-American couple based in London, England. Both are freelance writers and broadcasters, with some 25 books on travel and sports to their names. Since they prefer back roads to major highways, and family-run inns to high-rise hotels, they visited parts of Florida that many Floridians have yet to discover when they researched and wrote their first book on the Sunshine State, *Charming Small Hotel Guides: Florida.*

As contributing writers to *Gourmet* magazine, they have also written in-depth articles on Florida, from sailing among Lee County's barrier islands to eating at Miami's exciting new restaurants. As reporters, their experiences in Florida have been broadcast on the BBC. In the U.K., they write for national newspapers (*The Daily Telegraph* and *The Daily Express*) and magazines such as *Essentially America.* Winners of major writing and broadcasting awards, Kathy and Paul specialize in reporting on France and Great Britain, as well as the United States.

Additional contribution by Emma Stanford, co-author of *National Geographic Traveler The Caribbean* and author of *Essential Florida* and *Essential Orlando.*

History & culture

Ponce de León (1460–1521), discoverer of Florida

Florida today

IN HIS BOOK, *THE TRUTH ABOUT FLORIDA*, CHARLES D. FOX WROTE "HER [Florida's] assets are nature's own gift. They are enduring, and include a pleasant climate, a floral beauty of sufficient grandeur to delight the most exacting eye, and a soil so productive that it could support almost twenty times her present population." That prediction, made in 1925, has come true. The fourth most populous state attracts over 800 new residents every day of the year.

The Sunshine State

Most people sum up Florida in just one word: vacation. That is not a new attitude. A century ago, steamboats and then railroads brought northerners to the land of sunshine. If there is one individual's name that crops up time and again, on road names as well as in history books, it is that of Henry Flagler (see pp. 104–107). His determination and vision transformed Florida from a wilderness into a 20th-century state in a matter of years. By driving a railroad down the eastern coast of the state, he provided thousands with easy access to areas where handfuls of people had previously struggled to live in isolated communities.

Today, jumbo jets carry millions of visitors to enjoy the sun, sand, golf, water sports, and, of course, the world's top tourist attraction of Walt Disney World in Orlando. In 1995, over 5 million of the state's 41 million holiday visitors were from overseas. That figure increases year by year. Some vacationers are content with recreation; others are delighted to discover that Florida is much more than just one large playground.

Florida is a land of surprising variety. The Keys are tropical, with a relaxed, "anything goes" atmosphere. Miami is an international city, buzzing with Latin flair, while fast-growing Jacksonville provides a small city alternative to Atlanta. Contrasts are everywhere. The National Aeronautics and Space Administration is a center for cutting-edge technology, yet the NASA complex on Merritt Island is in the middle of one of the most important wildlife refuges in the United States. Rare and endangered wildlife lives and breeds just yards away from launch pads where rockets thunder their way into space.

Confusingly, Floridians will tell you that the farther north you go, the more southern Florida becomes. That is not just because the capital, Tallahassee, has the charm of a southern city. Out in the countryside, Spanish moss drips from enormous live oaks, there are old southern-style mansions, and villages that can still, justifiably, be called sleepy.

As the rural population shrinks, cities such as Orlando, Bradenton, Fort Myers, and Daytona are at the heart of some of the fastest growing metropolitan areas in the United States. A Louis Harris poll in 1997 reflected Florida's magnetic attraction. Those polled said that if they had to change states, Florida would be at the top of their list of preferred residences. Having doubled in the past three decades, the population is projected to reach 19 million by 2020; the pressure to build ever more houses, shopping malls, and golf courses is immense.

In response to this drive to develop, conservation movements thrive all over the state. Small towns once considered old-fashioned and dull have spruced up their main streets, restored historic buildings, and opened

Above: The original 1868 state seal
Right: Sun, sand, and sea are the basis of Florida's booming tourism industry.

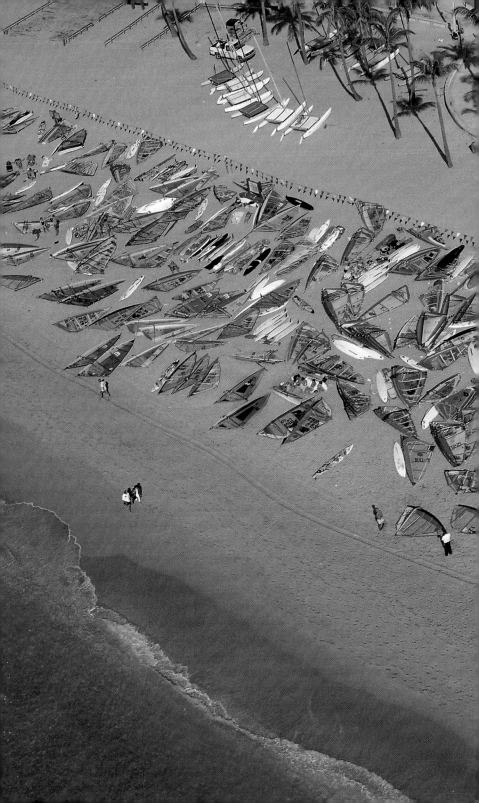

museums of local history. They have also created nature centers dedicated to preserving the local environment. The unexpected bonus of this passion for preservation is tourism. Attracted by what is labeled as heritage tourism and ecotourism, visitors enjoy these alternatives to beaches and theme parks.

To understand the Florida of today, you have to understand Miami. The city stands at the crossroads of trade in the Western Hemisphere. With Latin America in second place among the fastest growing markets for the United States, commerce is second only to tourism as the state's most lucrative industry. Miami's geographical position, its communications infrastructure, and, of course, its linguistic advantages, give the city a head start in its drive to win out over New York as the headquarters for the proposed Free Trade Area. This is due to link the 30 or so nations of the Western Hemisphere by the year 2005.

Miami, or more specifically South Beach, has been dubbed the coolest city on the planet, and is regularly featured in glossy magazines. British, German, and French fashion directors led the renaissance. British record producers joined the invasion: Chris Blackwell of Island Records set up the legendary South Beach Studios in one of his own hotels, The Marlin. Hip New Yorkers added the nickname "SoBe," a sultry version of Manhattan's SoHo. Hotelier Ian Schrager pinpointed Miami's appeal as

Venetian Pool in Miami's Coral Gables was created from a stone quarry.

"…a tropical destination that didn't require a passport or three changes of aircraft." The late Italian designer Gianni Versace compared the trendy square mile of South Beach to St. Tropez in the 1960s, while designer Barbara Hulanicki compares it with her experiences in London's Swinging Sixties. Whatever the analogy, Miami is a magnet with as many as

Reading at the News Café on Ocean Drive, South Beach

50 crews doing fashion shoots at 7 a.m. all along Ocean Drive.

Florida's New World cuisine

Despite the early arrival of the French and Spanish, there is no heritage of Floridian cooking. In the old days, white immigrants ate southern favorites such as grits, hush puppies, and corn pone. According to the *American Heritage Cookbook,* Florida's only culinary invention is key lime pie. Variations on the theme of eggs, condensed milk, sugar, and, of course, key lime juice have been popular ever since.

If, as ever, we are what we eat, then Florida's increasing ascendancy as a culinary center reflects the rich cooking pot of nationalities that now live and work in the state. The arrival of Latin American and Caribbean immigrants resulted in inexpensive ethnic restaurants catering to homesick workers from Nicaragua, Haiti, Cuba, and Jamaica. As foreign food found a wider audience, so little cafés and *loncherías* filled with curious gourmets. Not surprisingly, Miami now

offers some of the most innovative cooking in the United States.

In the past decade, chefs such as Norman van Aken, Douglas Rodriguez, Allan Susser, and Mark Militello revolutionized attitudes to food in southern Florida. Their "New World cuisine," reflecting the influx of Caribbean, Latin American, and even Far Eastern influences, has spread across the state.

Van Aken and his friends had all come from the northern states. In Florida, they were excited by the exotic fruits and vegetables, and fish caught just offshore. They were also intrigued by the bewildering range of spices and herbs used by the Cubans, Jamaicans, Peruvians, and Brazilians who worked in their kitchens. Soon they were experimenting with the produce and flavors, cooking in tune with the region. Their efforts have boosted interest in growing exotic fruits. Now orchards in Homestead, southwest of Miami, grow and ship everything from familiar mangoes, limes, avocados, and star fruit to yucca, tamarind, sapodilla, and passion fruit.

The best place to live

As Miami's influence grows so too does Florida's prosperity. The result is seen

A friendly smile at one of the art deco hotels on South Beach, Miami

everywhere. The Greater Miami area has more international and domestic banks than any other city on the East Coast south of New York, with over 48 billion dollars in total deposits. Commerce demands financiers, lawyers, and accountants. They, in turn, demand a pleasant lifestyle. No wonder Coral Gables, with its attractive Mediterranean Revival atmosphere and proximity to Miami's international airport, is now home to more than a hundred multinational companies.

Rival Florida cities such as Orlando are battling for a piece of the action, and Jacksonville has opened a trade office in Miami. Palm Beach and Fort Lauderdale have upgraded their ports to take advantage of increased foreign trade. Indeed, Port Everglades is twice the size of busy Miami, with containerized cargo volumes rising steadily. Miami, with three million passengers each year, is the world's leading cruise port; Fort Lauderdale is just behind.

A 1995 survey in *Money* magazine confirmed what many Floridians already knew: Their home towns and cities are some of the "best places to live in America." Top of the heap was Gainesville, followed by Jacksonville (3), Ocala (5), Fort Lauderdale (6), and Naples (10). Businessmen and women who were transferred to Florida by their companies have stayed. Former "snowbirds" live here year-round. They have become involved in their local communities and put down roots.

Sports are another mirror of today's success-oriented Sunshine State. With four professional football teams, as well as powerful representatives in baseball, basketball, and ice hockey, the state is a major player in the major leagues. There is considerable pride that the state is hosting virtually back-to-back Super Bowls in 1999 (Miami) and 2001 (Tampa). What is more, the state's colleges are attracting top-class sportsmen and women from across the nation. The dream of hosting the Olympic Games could come a step closer when Florida hosts the Pan-American Games early in the 21st century.

What of the future? Surely the questions for Floridians are not just "how much development" and "where," but also "what kind of development?" ■

History of the land

FLORIDA WAS A LATE ARRIVAL ON THE NORTH AMERICAN SCENE. WHILE the rest of the continent was forming, the peninsula was still at the bottom of the ocean, buried under sediment. Some 20 million years ago, the Floridian Plateau, a thick wedge of limestone, was the last American landmass to emerge from the ocean. As the ice ages came and went, so the peninsula waxed and waned. The valleys of northern Florida filled with debris washed down from Appalachia in the meltwater of the glaciers. To the south, a bed of limestone provided a base for the 10,000-year-old Everglades. And, like a tail curling into the Straits of Florida, the Keys combine limestone islets and fossilized coral reef, still covered in a few places with subtropical forest.

Although the north of the state is temperate and the south subtropical, they share Florida's greatest asset: sunshine. Between 1967 and 1969, St. Petersburg, on the west coast, recorded 768 consecutive days of sunshine. However, although on the same latitude as the Arabian and Saharan deserts, the average rainfall is 53 inches per year, with less in the Keys and more in the northwest. The rainy season is in the summertime, when there is a good chance of a daily shower. Not for nothing is Florida known as the "thunderstorm capital of America," with the "lightning belt" that girds Orlando and Lake Okeechobee the most turbulent region of all. Two-hour storms are commonplace here while the Tampa area averages well over one hundred a year. No wonder the ice hockey team is called the Tampa Bay Lightning. Even more severe are the hurricanes and tornadoes that are also part of Florida life (see pp. 118–19). Yet even here winter frosts can strike, and when they do the citrus industry can be devastated, as it was in 1894–95, 1962, 1985, and 1989.

The adjective most often used to describe Florida is flat. The highest point, in the hills near the Georgia border, stands a mere 345 feet above sea level. Once carpeted with trees, the state remains only about half forested, though that includes the national forests of Apalachicola, Osceola, and Ocala. Florida is a land of water—with oceans on three sides, home to 300 springs producing eight billion gallons a day, and nearly 8,000 lakes. Of the 12,000 miles of streams and rivers, the largest are the north-flowing St. Johns (273 miles) and the Suwannee (177 miles), made famous by the Stephen Foster song about the old folks at home, "way down upon the Swannee River."

Farther south, the Everglades and Big Cypress Swamp cover much of the tip of the peninsula.

Yet increasing demands for development, along with pollution, have damaged the fragile ecosystems. In 1968, the new state constitution included a commitment to the environment: "It shall be the policy of the state to conserve and protect its natural resources and scenic beauty." Since 1970, the amount of land owned and protected by the state has increased fivefold. Add in the areas under local and federal control, and the total is more than 20 percent of the entire peninsula. Some lands have been saved by off-site mitigation projects, such as the Disney Wilderness Preserve, created as compensation for expansion at Disney, the Orlando Airport, and Universal Studios Escape.

But the problem of balancing development and economic growth with preserving the natural beauty of Florida is continuous. As campaigning journalist Carl Hiaasen asks by way of Skip Wiley, one of his antiheroes:

…Are you blind?…maybe you can't understand because you weren't here thirty years ago, when it was paradise. Before they put parking meters on the beach. Before the beach disappeared…don't tell me you're like the rest of the migratory loons. They think it's heaven down here as long as the sun's out, long as they don't have to put chains on the tires, it's marvelous. They think it's really paradise, because, compared to Buffalo, it is. But…compared to paradise…
—*Tourist Season* (1986) Carl Hiaasen.

Preservation of the Everglades is vital to Florida's delicate ecosystem.

VEGETATION & WILDLIFE

Florida is a land of the exotic. Thanks to its combination of temperate and subtropical climate, there are more than 3,500 species of plants and 300 species of trees. It is like a huge hothouse, where species imported for private gardens have spread into the wild and propagated. Where else do you find roseate spoonbills, ospreys, alligators, and manatees?

The official state reptile is the alligator. Growing to 15 feet, it moves quite slowly on land, but once it gets its teeth into something, it bites with a force of 3,200 pounds per square inch, nearly double that of a great white shark. Most of the million or so alligators live in swamps, rivers, and canals, although a few turn up as unexpected guests in backyards and on golf courses.

By contrast, the extremely rare American crocodile, which lives in seawater on the edge of the Everglades, is smaller, more agile, and has a pointed snout. It is one of the state's

endangered species. Others include the Florida panther, a relative of the puma, of whom only about 50 survive. Also threatened are the tiny Key deer (see p. 85), manatees (see p. 148), and sea turtles (see p. 189).

Due to its situation on the main north–south migratory route, the bird life in Florida is spectacular. A huge variety of birds pass this way, including songbirds such as finches and larks, vireos and warblers. Thanks to stringent protection, herons, wood storks, woodpeckers,

Florida is the home of spectacular and unusual plants such as these scarlet hurricane lilies in the Panhandle.

ospreys, and the bald eagle, America's symbol, are making a comeback. There are numerous wildlife conservation areas, such as the J.N. "Ding" Darling National Wildlife Refuge (see p. 124), where dawn and dusk are good times to spy on the eccentric-looking roseate spoonbill sweeping the water for food.

Florida has more species of snakes than any other state. Most, like the scary-looking scarlet king snake, are harmless, but among the poisonous are the coral, the water-loving cottonmouth, and three types of rattlesnakes —the diamondback, pygmy, and canebrake. The humid climate also attracts a variety of bugs, as well as mosquitoes and chiggers, "no see ums," ticks, and spiders that abound in

**Above: Gulf fritillary butterfly
Right: The Florida panther is highly
endangered, the few survivors living in the
Everglades and Big Cypress Swamp.**

thick woods. Cockroaches, which can be two inches long, are politely referred to as palmetto bugs, because palms are their preferred habitat.

The claim that most of the flowering plants of the world can be grown in Florida is a bold one, yet horticulturists here try anything—and often succeed. As a result, you can see azaleas, camellias, orchids, and birds-of-paradise in botanical gardens. Even the commonest plants have their uses: The pawpaw shrub, which flourishes in Florida's pineland, was used to make medicinal tea by the Seminole.

The fast-growing slash pine tree, harvested both for its wood and turpentine, has long been prized for commercial lumber. By contrast, the live oak grows slowly, producing a natural umbrella of shade. Mangroves abound, as do palm trees, from the native sabal to the elegant Cuban royal palm, which reaches to 120 feet.

But it is Florida's flowering trees that catch the eye. With its lavender blue blooms, one of the most popular is the Brazilian jacaranda. At its peak in spring, the jacaranda sheds its flowers to create a purple carpet beneath its boughs. Despite its origins in South America, the red, pink, orange, or yellow bougainvillea is often associated with Florida, where it is at its best in late winter and early spring. The thorny vine thrives, either trimmed into shrubs and hedges, or clambering up walls and trees. The equally distinctive golden shower tree, with its bunches of golden-yellow flowers, comes from India. Also called the

pudding pipe tree or Indian laburnum, it grows to about 30 feet and develops long, sausage-shape seed pods.

STATE PARKS, GREENWAYS, & THE FLORIDA NATIONAL SCENIC TRAIL

Some call it ecotourism and some call it getting away from it all, but more and more visitors are enjoying the natural beauty of Florida through its state parks, its innovative greenways, and the Florida National Scenic Trail.

State parks

The 150 or so state parks are Florida's undiscovered gems. As well as numerous wildlife preserves, botanical gardens, archaeological sites, and recreation areas with some of the nation's best beaches, the state also cares for historic sites such as author Marjorie Kinnan Rawlings' home and the Ybor City museum,

dedicated to local Cuban heritage. For information on entrance passes, brochures, and maps, contact the Department of Environmental Protection (*Tel 850/488-9872*).

Greenways

The 1993 Florida Greenways Commission plans to coordinate trails all over the state, labeling them greenways. Some follow a river, others may be recycled railroad tracks. They might be paths suitable for cycling and hiking, or waterways with canoe access. A few are even in urban areas. The 32-mile-long Pinellas Trail from St. Petersburg to Tarpon Springs pulled in more than a million out-of-area visitors in 1996. The most popular cycle trail in Florida is St. Mark's Trail from Tallahassee to St. Mark's on the coast.

Of the 38 marked canoe trails, many are little more than a gentle paddle. The proposed Cross Florida Greenway follows the line of the Cross Florida Barge Canal, which was

Visitors taking an airboat trip through Florida's Everglades

abandoned in 1990. Now the 110 miles between Palatka on the St. Johns River and Yankeetown on the Gulf form one continuous recreation area, offering everything from camping and canoeing to fishing and horseback riding.

Florida National Scenic Trail
Snaking down through Florida, from the Apalachicola National Forest to Lake Okeechobee, the Florida National Scenic Trail was included in the national trails system in 1983. Gradually other segments are being added, to make an unbroken 1,300-mile hike from the Gulf Islands National Seashore in the Panhandle to Big Cypress National Preserve in the southwest. The best time to walk the trail is from late fall through early spring, when the weather is cool, insects less obnoxious, and migrating birds are passing through. ■

History of Florida

AFTER CHRISTOPHER COLUMBUS HAD ARRIVED IN THE NEW WORLD, SPAIN, with the support of Pope Alexander VI, claimed all the territory in the Western Hemisphere, with the exception of Brazil. Florida had the least to offer the Spanish, however, who wanted gold and silver to fill their coffers and fertile land to plant.

FROM SPANISH CONQUEST TO BRITISH COLONY

Early explorers included the Italian John Cabot in 1498 and Ponce de León from Spain, who first sighted land near St. Augustine on April 2, 1513, the Feast of Flowers (also known as the Feast of Easter)—Pascua Florida—which gave the state its name. In 1521 de León returned, landing on the west coast near present-day Fort Myers with 200 men, aiming to set up a colony. Driven off by the Indians, he was injured and his men took him to Cuba where he died.

Further attempts at settlement also failed: Pánfilo de Narváez (Tampa Bay, 1528), Hernando de Soto (Tampa Bay, 1539), and Tristán de Luna (Pensacola, 1559–1561).

Spain's main interest in Florida, however, was defensive: To prevent rival European nations from using it as a base and then raiding the route used by treasure galleons from Central America, South America, and the

Caribbean on their way home to Spain. The heavily laden wooden ships would round southern Florida and join up with the Gulf Stream or Bahama Channel which helped propel them across the Atlantic. After 50 years of unsuccessful colonization, Spain was goaded into action

Between 1562 and 1565, persecuted Huguenots (Protestants) from France tried to build a new life in the New World. Under the leadership of Jean de Ribault, the religious refugees built Fort Caroline and a village near present-day St. Augustine. When news of this

Lured by tales of gold, the Spanish made little attempt to make friends with the native population. Here, Ponce de León is depicted in battle against Florida's native Indians.

French enclave reached Spain, Pedro Menéndez de Avilés was sent to rout out the intruders who were not only illegally on Spanish soil, but as Protestants were also considered heretics.

The Spanish admiral landed south of Fort Caroline on August 28, 1565 (St. Augustine's Day). The French ships sailing south to intercept them ran ashore in a storm, leaving Menéndez free to march on the fort, where his troops killed all but the women and children. He then returned to find the shipwrecked French, whom he slaughtered; the site is still called Matanzas (slaughters). Determined to succeed where his fellow Spaniards had failed, Menéndez established St. Augustine, creating the oldest settlement in North America.

For the next 200 years, St. Augustine was a target for raiders from France and England, yet, thanks to its star-shaped fortress, Castillo de San Marcos (see pp. 204– 205), it survived as the main European toehold in Florida. Spanish priests busied themselves with converting the Indians to Catholicism, but the tribes died out, devastated by imported diseases. As Europe's warring nations battled for supremacy in the Caribbean and North America, Florida was a strategic pawn.

By 1763, thanks to their resounding successes in the French and Indian Wars, the British were dominant in North America. When they captured Cuba, Spain's capital in the New World, Spain insisted on the return of their headquarters in the Caribbean. The two countries agreed on a trade: Cuba for Florida—prompting most of the population of St. Augustine to flee to Cuba.

For the next 20 years, the British flag flew over Florida, which was divided into two jurisdictions. East Florida, governed from St. Augustine, was, in effect, the 14th Colony, while West Florida, stretching across the Panhandle to the Mississippi, was under Pensacola's administration. The land belonging to Florida's original Indians had been handed over to the Seminole from Georgia, with whom the new British governor, Gen. James Grant, had a good relationship. Opting for cooperation rather than conflict, and unhampered by the Spanish passion for religious conversion, British settlers and entrepreneurs moved in.

FROM EUROPEAN PAWN TO AMERICAN STATE

The years from 1763 to 1783 were turbulent times in the 13 Colonies. Although Florida was a British possession, it did not join the rebels; so, in the aftermath of the Revolution, many supporters of King George III fled south to start a new life. Florida experienced the first of many booms, its population

Two years later, in exchange for peace in Texas, Spain handed over Florida and its European inhabitants to the infant United States.

Florida was difficult to govern. In those days, ships were the primary means of communication between the two chief towns St. Augustine and Pensacola, and it could take ten days to make the 800-mile journey. In 1824, to establish a new, central headquarters

growing from 5,000 to 18,000 in a matter of months.

The newly independent southern states had long regarded northern Florida as a buffer against foreign aggression and were alarmed when, in 1783, Britain and Spain again swapped territory. Britain took the Bahamas, while Spain regained Florida.

By now, however, the Spanish Empire was on its last legs, with no real authority in the peninsula, especially over the Seminole. The neighboring Americans took advantage of this absence of a Spanish presence by making preemptive strikes against the Indians. These cross-border raids were later labeled as the First Seminole War when, in 1817, Andrew "Old Hickory" Jackson ignored diplomacy with his aggressive tactics from Georgia.

Left: Gen. Andrew Jackson, Florida's first Territorial Governor (Thomas Sully, 1845) Above: Pvt. Walter Parker, 1st Florida Calvary, one of 15,000 Floridians who fought for the Confederacy

for the new territory, two Florida officials were asked to find a mutually acceptable halfway point. Dr. William Simmons set out from St. Augustine, and John Lee Williams from Pensacola. They met at Tallahassee, which was deemed the state's new capital.

Most of Florida's inhabitants lived in the northern part of the state, and by 1830, when the population of the United States had tripled to 13 million in just 40 years, the census registered only 517 residents in the whole of southern Florida.

As more planters moved into the territory, clearing land for sugarcane and cotton, they came into conflict with the Seminole. Congress approved the Removal Bill, empowering President Andrew Jackson, an avowed Indian hater, to transfer any eastern tribe to trans-Mississippi areas. Most Seminole took the infamous Trail of Tears to Oklahoma, but a few remained. In 1835 Maj. Francis Dade

80,000 consisted of slaves of African origin, it entered the Union hand-in-hand with Iowa.

The new state thrived. By 1860, when the total population had risen to 140,000, there were 61,000 slaves. It was no surprise, therefore, when, on January 10, 1861, Florida became the third state to secede from the Union. Despite being one of the remoter Confederate states, Florida contributed

In 1864, Confederate troops defeated Union forces in the Battle of Olustee.

and 139 troops were massacred near Tampa, and the Second Seminole War lurched into seven years of guerrilla warfare. Chief Osceola, whose mother was white, was an inspirational tribal leader, but when he was treacherously seized under a flag of truce on Christmas Day 1837, the main resistance faltered. Some Seminole disappeared into the back country, and it was only in 1934 that a treaty was finally signed between their descendants and the United States government.

In 1845, Florida became the 27th state to be admitted to the Union. Under the Missouri Compromise of 1821, slave-owning states could only be admitted in tandem with a free state. Since half of Florida's population of

generously, sending supplies of both men and food. Its contingent of 15,000 soldiers (one in ten of the population) was the highest proportion of any member of the Confederacy. Florida cattle and cotton fed and clothed troops from Shiloh to Bull Run. Although forts at St. Augustine, Pensacola, and Key West remained Union strongholds, the only two battles on Florida soil (Olustee and Natural Bridge) were Southern victories. Moreover, Tallahassee was proud to be the only Confederate capital in the east to escape capture by Union forces.

In 1868, Florida was readmitted to the Union, having abolished slavery and given the vote to adult black males, as specified in the 13th and 14th Amendments.

An 1870s engraving of a paddle-steamer
plowing through the Florida Everglades

FROM POSTWAR BUST
TO POSTWAR BOOM

Once the last Federal troops had left Florida
in 1877, the white conservative businessmen
and plantation owners, who ran the Demo-
cratic Party under the banner of "Growth
and Prosperity," conspired to suppress
reforms and legal equality for the recently
freed slaves. By the 1880s, the state was deep
in debt. With one transaction, Gov. William
Bloxham, nicknamed "Slippery Bill," balanced
the books: He persuaded wealthy Philadelphia
industrialist, Hamilton Disston, to buy four
million acres of swamp for 25 cents an acre.
Disston sold half to a British land company,
and started to clear and drain the land in the
Caloosahatchee and Kissimmee Valleys of
central Florida, setting up the sugarcane
industry that still thrives today.

At that time, most of the railroads were
local, and confined to the north of the state.
The rest of the peninsula relied on steamboats
for transportation, though shifting sandbars
and lagoons along the coast made navigation
treacherous. It took the dynamism and
wealth of two men to revolutionize Florida
by building railroads down the east and west
coasts. Henry Plant's Atlantic Coastline
Railway began in Richmond, Virginia, and
ended at the deepwater port of Tampa, where
it linked up with his steamships which traded
with Cuba. The other Henry, Henry Flagler,
built the Florida East Coast Railroad. This
reached Miami in 1896 and Key West in 1912.
As well as dealing in freight, both men built
luxury hotels along their routes to house
affluent travelers from the North.

The end of the century saw the unlocking
of Florida's potential, with lumber and
mining industries exploiting the copious
timber and valuable phosphate deposits in
the center of the state.

In contrast to the Civil War, the 1898
Spanish-American War gave Florida's
economy a boost, particularly in Tampa,
where contingents of Federal troops gathered
before sailing off to Cuba. There were
difficulties, however, for citrus farmers; two
disastrous frosts devastated the crops,
forcing the industry south to warmer, frost-
free groves.

Florida was propelled forward by dynamic state governors, typified by the gloriously named Napoleon Bonaparte Broward, who set up a proper network of roads, regulated the railroads, introduced a full educational structure, and overhauled the electoral and prison systems. Florida's 500,000 residents had an efficient state government for the first time.

As Americans in the north of the country grew more affluent, increasing numbers dreamed of wintering in the south. In 1912, Indianapolis millionaire Carl Fisher created Miami Beach out of a mangrove swamp, and George Merrick planned Coral Gables, his "City Beautiful." Others saw the agricultural potential of the rich soil inland, draining the Everglades to create profitable farmland.

Once again, a war boosted Florida's economy. World War I helped everything from farm production to ship building. The guaranteed fine weather in Pensacola, Arcadia, east of Sarasota, and Miami allowed pilots flying the new airplane to train year-round, a tradition Pensacola still enjoys. At the end of the war, military personnel returning home sang the praises of the pleasures of life in the Sunshine State.

Once the railroads had opened up in Florida, winter vacations in the sun were available to thousands. These sunseekers, gathered on the sands in front of the fashionable Breakers Hotel in Palm Beach, were photographed in January 1928.

Florida's expanding economy continued to be dependent upon inexpensive black labor. As the North also boomed in the postwar United States, these workers were attracted to better-paid industrial jobs in Detroit, Pittsburgh, and Chicago. At the same time, what had been a predominantly rural state was moving toward a more urban lifestyle, fueled by innovations such as the telephone, electricity, and the mobility afforded by the car. Field labor was suddenly in short supply and farm prices plunged, sending even more workers into the towns to take jobs on real estate developments. The ensuing tension erupted into violence.

Politics only emphasized the racial problems. The Democrats were in control; they banned nonwhite party membership, ensuring white-only votes in the primaries. Only in 1944 did a Supreme Court decision halt this bias.

FROM ART DECO TO DISNEY

During the early 20th century, wealthy socialites who spent the summer in Newport, Rhode Island, or Bar Harbor, Maine, visited Palm Beach and Miami in winter. Sarasota, on the Gulf Coast, began to develop as a resort, but instead of relying on hotels, the rich put up their own vacation homes. Where they went, others followed.

During the 1920s, the speculation that fueled the rise in the New York Stock Exchange also affected Florida, and thousands of Northerners bought land, sight unseen. Speculators sold land that was under water at high tide, and some plots changed hands dozens of times in a matter of weeks. In Miami, the local paper printed a 500-page section devoted solely to property ads. But a major hurricane burst the bubble in 1926, and land prices plummeted. Citrus farmers who thought they had sold too cheaply were able to buy back their groves at about the same price, with nothing worse than bruised egos. Any thoughts of a revival vanished when another hurricane struck in 1928, causing Lake Okeechobee to overflow. More than 2,000 people drowned in one of the greatest natural disasters in United States history.

Although the 1929 Stock Exchange crash should have been the final straw, the rich soon returned to Palm Beach. Tourism figures dropped to 500,000 in 1933, but they climbed back to two million as developers took advantage of low costs for construction projects, such as the small art deco hotels along the southern end of Miami Beach.

War was again Florida's salvation. During World War II, hotels were turned into barracks, and the seven military airfields multiplied to 40 by 1945. Key West was revived as a submarine base to repel German U-boats, which daringly sank tankers off the United States coast in full view of Miami Beach. The war also generated new technology, such as better air-conditioning and frozen orange juice. As before, military personnel returned after the war, and by 1950 the population had increased by 50 percent. By 1960 it had nearly doubled again, reaching five million.

The biggest influx was in the south, a region that had been practically empty a century before. During the war, the patenting of the insecticide DDT allowed man to conquer vast tracts of the state at the expense of hordes of mosquitoes, as well as more innocent wildlife. Despite the push for ever-greater expansion, a few voices called for conservation. A wildlife refuge on the island of Sanibel (now the J.N. "Ding" Darling National Wildlife Refuge) was established in 1945, and in 1947, President Truman signed the bill establishing Everglades National Park.

America's postwar issues of racial equality were reflected in Florida. Jackie Robinson's barrier-breaking baseball exploits may have begun in Daytona, but it took the 1954 United States Supreme Court case of *Brown* v. *Board of Education* to end segregation in schools and to begin the dismantling of institutionalized racism.

If domestic politics were heated, the international forum focused on the Cold War. In the 1950s, competition between the United States and the Soviet Union expanded into space. The first American rocket, a version of the German V2 from World War II, blasted off from Cape Canaveral in 1950. Only 19 years later, in 1969, Neil Armstrong walked on the moon. The Space Race added hi-tech industries to Florida's economy, for so long based on tourism and agriculture.

And then came Disney. Just as Flagler and Plant opened Florida to the United States, so Walt Disney's theme parks opened it to the world. The launch in 1971 of Walt Disney World coincided with the development of the jumbo jet, which expanded mass tourism even further.

Recent U.S. Department of Commerce statistics placed Florida as the top destination for all visitors to the United States. Of 22 million travelers, about one-quarter headed for Florida, pushing California into second place. Among cities, although New York claimed 4.2 million visitors and Los Angeles 3.3 million, Miami and Orlando pulled in 2.6 million each. Tourism, now the state's largest industry, employs about one million people and generates more than 30 billion dollars a year.

The downside of Florida's profitable tourism industry is clear for all to see in the scars of uncontrolled development in the Sunshine State.

The arts

FLORIDA'S CULTURAL HERITAGE HAS LONG BEEN OVERSHADOWED; vacationers headed south only for sun, sand, surf, and golf. But gradually there has been a change, and the Florida of today has carved out a place for itself on the cultural map of the United States.

The progression started with the wealthy, who retired to the Sunshine State and decided to leave their considerable treasures to their new communities. The earliest donors were John and Mable Ringling, whose Museum of Art in Sarasota (see pp. 128–31) revolves around its well-publicized collection of works by Peter Paul Rubens (1577–1640).

Often the foundation of a museum has acted as a catalyst, attracting generous support. A superlative example is the Norton Museum of Art in Palm Beach (see pp. 108–109), which began with a priceless collection of contemporary American works and Impressionists, and now acquires equally impressive works each year. Like many museums around the state, it has a handsome new extension.

St. Petersburg received the world's largest private collection of the Spanish eccentric Salvador Dalí (see p. 144), while in Winter Park, outside Orlando, the Charles Hosmer Morse Museum of American Art (see p. 154) is the home of a comprehensive display of Louis Comfort Tiffany glass. Visit the Cummer Gallery of Art in Jacksonville (see p. 199) and you will discover the priceless Wark Collection of Meissen porcelain; and drop by the Tampa Museum of Art (see pp. 138–39) to see a rare collection of Greek and Roman vases. In Daytona, the Museum of Arts and Sciences (see p. 193) has two collections that are as much about heritage as art. The Cuban Museum is an important assembly of paintings from pre-Castro times, while the Dow Gallery shows the evolution of a distinctly American style in art, furniture, and silver.

Not all collectors are historically minded. In Miami, the Rubell Family Collection (see pp. 48–49) showcases art from the 1980s and 1990s, and the Martin Z. Margulies Family Collection (see pp. 71–72) focuses on contemporary sculpture. It is displayed on the campus of Florida International University, one of many Florida institutions that play a role in the cultural world, as well as the educational.

The University of Miami has the Lowe Museum (see p. 56), with American and European paintings, as well as a fine display of Native American art. The Seminole's own impressive Ah-Tah-Thi-Ki Museum (see p. 100), which opened in 1997, has on loan rare tribal works from the Smithsonian Institution in Washington, D.C.

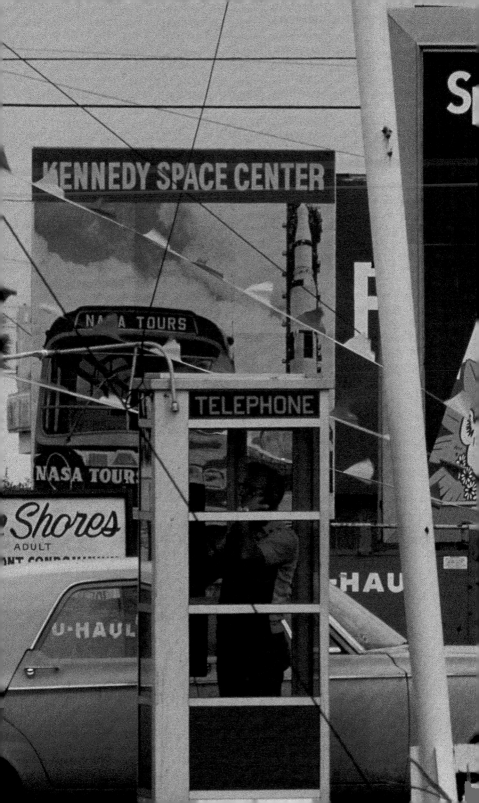

Florida's year-round tourist industry produces a rash of festivals celebrating everything from jazz to modern dance, and cinema to theater. Broadway shows and international rock tours make regular stopovers and are guaranteed good audiences. Major-league stars are matched by major-league culture. Robert Heuer, general manager of the Florida Grand Opera, explains "Northerners who once came down just for the winter season still tended to support the arts back home. Now that Miami is their year-round home, they are demanding a full program here." The opera, the seventh oldest in the nation, gave one Luciano Pavarotti his United States debut back in 1965.

The multinational Miami City Ballet is just one strand in Florida's rich, new cultural tapestry.

Classical music lovers have been supporting the New World Symphony, under the baton of Michael Tilson Thomas, since 1987. The conductor coaxes the best out of America's brightest young musicians, graduates of the country's best music schools and conservatories. They are complemented by the equally dynamic Miami City Ballet, which, under the artistic direction of Edward Villella, also performs in Fort Lauderdale.

In Palm Beach, large audiences support ballet and classical music, with Ballet Florida and the Florida Philharmonic Orchestra. Formed when the Boca Raton Symphony merged with the Fort Lauderdale Symphony in 1984, the orchestra has grown in stature under music director James Judd. They also perform in West Palm Beach, Fort Lauderdale, Boca Raton, West Broward, and Coral Springs.

ARCHITECTURE

Those who know Florida only from the freeways and main streets could be forgiven for thinking that the state lacks a fine architectural heritage. Yet there are handsome buildings all over the peninsula, ranging from 100-year-old New England look-alikes, complete with gables and porches, to grandiose old courthouses in DeLand, Madison, and Bartow. Styles range from Creole to Folk Victorian, and shotgun to vernacular. The renovations in St. Augustine give a good idea of what the Spanish settlement looked like 300 years ago, and no doubt inspired Henry Flagler to build his first Florida hotel, now Flagler College, in extravagant Spanish-Renaissance style.

Some buildings have been moved to historic villages. Downtown Pensacola, for example, has a collection of early 19th-century cottages as well as the suitably impressive original city hall from 1907, now the Wentworth Museum. In Key West, a Caribbean-influenced tropical style evolved, with airy verandas and windows carefully placed to catch any breeze. A century ago, northerners who spent winters in Florida built in styles that were familiar to them: Mount Dora, northwest of Orlando, has a New England feel.

It is the grand hotels and mansions of the early 20th century, however, that are the most impressive. Miami's mock-Renaissance Vizcaya (1916) was considered a catalyst for Floridian design by architect Russell T. Pancoast, who claimed: "Although the architectural inspiration of Vizcaya was derived from Italy, it introduced and suggested to many the rich, relatively untapped sources of design inspiration available in all Mediterranean countries…." When the flamboyant society architect Addison Mizner built the Everglades Club in Palm Beach in 1918, he aimed simply "to turn Spanish inside out like a glove." His exclusive shopping lane, Via Mizner, off Worth Avenue, shows off the "picturesqueness of Old Spain—the narrow streets of Granada. Characteristics are the light stucco walls in pastel tints, topped with tile roofs, weathered cypress woodwork, and the inevitable coconut tree." Down in Miami, George Merrick's Coral Gables was another, more tightly controlled vision of romantic Spanish-Mediterranean flair.

The 1929 Wall Street crash, followed by the Depression, changed everything. Out went the elegant and ornate; in came what we now call art deco. The clean, streamlined outlines were complemented by details such as flamingos, fish, and palm trees incorporated into murals, etched glass, fountains, and sculptures.

After World War II, a parade of huge hotels lined up on Miami Beach. Before the war,

Opposite: Florida's architectural heritage boasts outstanding art deco on South Beach.
Above: The Donnelly House, Mount Dora

architect Morris Lapidus had designed department stores; in the early 1950s, he turned to hotels and built the Fontainebleau, Eden Roc, and Americana. Each gave vacationers the feeling of living in a mansion.

When Frank Lloyd Wright came for a look in 1955, he was shocked by the gigantism. "You have all these exquisite, lovely, beautiful things with such charm. Why don't you do something down here that belongs?" he asked a convention of designers. His own buildings certainly do belong. At Lakeland, Wright's "Child of the Sun" collection, the largest assembly of his buildings in the world, stands on the campus of Florida Southern College (see p. 176).

WRITE ON!

Many authors have lived in, written about, and been inspired by Florida, but no one has had the effect of Ernest Hemingway, whose stormy lifestyle in Key West produced as much comment as did his books (see p. 94). Yet the Nobel Prize winner was only one of many writers who have made Key West a literary enclave (also see pp. 94–95).

Renaissance. Born in Eatonville, near Orlando, Hurston is best loved for her storytelling and memories of Florida. One of the first African Americans to graduate from Barnard College, she won awards for her 1943 autobiography *Dust Tracks on a Road*. Interest in her work has been sparked by novelist Alice Walker, who placed a memorial stone on Hurston's grave in Fort Pierce.

Harriet Beecher Stowe (1811–1896)

Zora Neale Hurston (1901–1960)

Controversial in her time was Harriet Beecher Stowe, labeled "the most hated woman in the South" for *Uncle Tom's Cabin*. Her 1852 novel was suppressed in Florida, but after the Civil War, Stowe still wintered on her orange plantation near Mandarin, south of Jacksonville. Here, she wrote books such as *Palmetto Leaves* (1873) and was a tourist attraction for passing steamboats on the St. Johns River.

Black writer Zora Neale Hurston (1901–1960) died penniless but is recognized today as a significant member of the Harlem

Florida inspired Marjorie Kinnan Rawlings' lyrical descriptions of rural life:

Enchantment lies in different things for each of us. For me, it is in this: To step out of the bright sunlight into the shade of orange trees; to walk under the arched canopy of their jadelike leaves; to see the long aisles of lich-ened trunks stretch ahead in a geometric rhythm; to feel the mystery of a seclusion that yet has shafts of light striking through it….
—*The Yearling* (1938)

Marjorie Kinnan Rawlings (1896–1953) is considered a Floridian, although she moved from Washington, D.C., to Cross Creek, south of Gainesville, in 1928.

Some authors spent only a limited time in Florida, although even this could provide inspiration. Henry James, the acid observer of American and European high society, describes his 1904 visit to Florida in *The American Scene*.

and recommended by historian Thomas Carlyle to his friend, Ralph Waldo Emerson. It also inspired romantic poets such as Samuel T. Coleridge and William Wordsworth.

Similar inspiration from afar can be found in Jules Verne's *In Voyage from the Earth to the Moon*. The Frenchman never set foot on Florida soil, but in 1865 he launched his fanciful space flight from Tampa Bay. By contrast, Tom Wolfe's

Marjory Stoneman Douglas (1890–1998), environmentalist and author

Altogether calmer and more introspective was poet Anne Morrow Lindbergh. Captiva Island, near Fort Myers, makes much of its connection with Charles Lindbergh's wife, who wrote *Gift from the Sea* (1955).

Sometimes the Florida environment itself has inspired books. *The Everglades: River of Grass* (1947), by Marjory Stoneman Douglas, spearheaded the campaign to preserve Florida's wetlands. An earlier work, *The Travels of William Bartram,* records the Florida landscape of 1773–78. Written by a botanist from Philadelphia, it was popular in Europe

1979 bestseller *The Right Stuff* detailed the lives of the real astronauts at Cape Canaveral.

However, it is thriller writing that thrives in the Sunshine State. In the 1930s, Anna Maria Island was a retreat for Dashiell Hammett, Raymond Chandler, and Edgar Rice Burroughs. John D. MacDonald created sleuth Travis McGee, and now every airport newsstand is filled with exciting tales set in Florida: Elmore Leonard (*Gold Coast Swag*), Carl Hiaasen (*Skin Tight*), Charles Willeford (*Miami Blues*), James W. Hall (*Hard Aground, BuzzCut*), and Edna Buchanan (*Miami, It's Murder*).

LIGHTS, CAMERA, ACTION!

With its sunshine and hip lifestyle, Florida has long been a backdrop for popular movies, from the 1929 Marx Brothers' debut film *The Cocoanuts* to the James Bond trio of *Dr. No, Goldfinger,* and *Live and Let Die.* Orlando serves as the location for both Disney-MGM and Universal Studios.

A less well-known fact is that Florida, or more specifically Jacksonville, rather than Hollywood, could have been the home of the industry. In 1908, New York, then the center of the infant movie business, suffered a hard winter that forced producers to search for sunshine in Florida or California. Kalem Studios shot *A Florida Feud,* the first feature to be made in the state, and, producing movies at the astonishing rate of two a week, went on to film 18 movies in Jacksonville in their first season.

From 1909 to 1921, the city was nicknamed the "Winter Film Capital of the World," with some 300 feature movies made in the northeast

of Florida. Among the 30 production companies with studios in or near Jacksonville were Edison and Biography, Klutho, and Lubin Manufacturing Co. At one stage, there were more movie crews working in Jacksonville than Los Angeles. But despite the boost to the local economy, local bankers and tradesmen lost their initial enthusiasm for the movie industry because of safety problems on the sets and worries about the fast lifestyle of the stars. Slowly but surely, the studios headed

In the 1920s, Florida's beaches doubled as the Arabian desert.

west to California, and just 20 years after its birth, Jacksonville's film industry died.

In the 1960s, moviemakers returned to the Sunshine State. This time, Florida, with its sun, sand, and fun, was the star of the show. The publicity value of hosting a movie was never demonstrated better than when college students flocked to Fort Lauderdale's beaches, ready to replicate the antics of Annette Funicello and Frankie Avalon in half-a-dozen mildly titillating Beach Party movies. It has taken years and a calculated publicity campaign for Fort Lauderdale to shed its image as the spring break capital of the United States.

The 1990s saw a revival in Jacksonville, thanks to its varied urban landscape. In

Above: South Beach provided the perfect location for the exotic night club in the 1996 comedy, *The Birdcage*.
Right: Jim Carrey finally escaped from Seaside (the fictional Seahaven Island), his hometown in *The Truman Show* (1998).

GI Jane (starring Demi Moore), Huguenot Park was the beach base for naval operations and nearby Camp Blanding doubled as a Navy Seal obstacle course. Cecil Air Field (the helicopter base), Dunns Fish camp (the rustic bar), and Big Talbot Island (the wartime training area) showed the versatility of backdrops available in the northeast.

Down in Miami, the Miami-Dade Film Office is one of the busiest locations in the United States. In 1994, for example, movie producers invested 200 million dollars in 11 major feature films. A year later, their expenditure had jumped to 500 million dollars, as they shot 17 major feature films, as well as hundreds of documentaries, music videos, and commercials. Recent movies include *The Birdcage* with Robin Williams, Eddie Murphy's *Holy Man*, *There's Something About Mary* (Cameron Diaz), *Blood and Wine* (Jack Nicholson and Michael Caine),

Ace Ventura (Jim Carrey), and *Up Close and Personal* (Robert Redford and Michelle Pfeiffer). Not surprisingly, the region has also become a major player in the Spanish-language TV and moviemaking industry.

In addition to the Miami-Dade Office of Film and Entertainment, three other cities have their own such offices. With special sales tax rebate incentives by the state on items such as recording equipment, tax-free property rental, and a relaxed attitude toward union and nonunion workers, Florida bends over backward to attract movie companies. The University of Florida at Gainesville stands in for Ivy League colleges, while the directors of *My Girl* (McCaulay Caulkin) decided that Bartow in central Florida epitomized small-town America. Up in the Panhandle, the pastel-colored town of Seaside took on the role of Seahaven Island for the 1998 Jim Carrey movie, *The Truman Show*.

In Orlando, Universal Studios bills itself as "the largest production facility outside Hollywood," shooting movies as well as the Nickelodeon Studios television shows for children. Over at Disney-MGM, 1998 productions included *From the Earth to the Moon*, the TV mini-series about the Apollo space program, and the full-length cartoon feature, *Mulan*. ∎

Miami is one of North America's most vibrant and multiracial communities. The downtown skyscrapers proclaim the city's wealth; in areas such as Miami Beach and Coral Gables, individual affluence is equally apparent.

Miami & Miami Beach

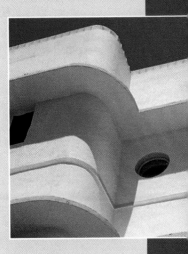

Art deco detail, Miami Beach

Miami & Miami Beach

MIAMI CELEBRATED ITS 100TH birthday in 1996, and what was once a mosquito-ridden outpost at the mouth of the Miami River is now a booming economic intersection.

Few homesteaders moved to southern Florida during the 19th century because of the swampy conditions and constant threat of Indian raids. In 1875, Julia Tuttle (known as the "Mother of Miami") arrived, bought a square mile of land, and was determined to put Miami on the map. Tuttle saw railroads as the only potential lifeline, but railroad magnate Henry Plant was not interested. In 1893, Tuttle tried to persuade Henry Flagler to extend his East Coast line beyond Palm Beach, but he, too, was not interested. To change Flagler's mind, legend has it that Tuttle sent him a branch of orange blossom. On April 15, 1896, the first train puffed in, carrying building materials. Miami was up and running.

Apart from tourism, the major influence of the past century was the influx of affluent Cubans in the 1960s. These refugees have transformed the city into a Latin-American power base on the U.S. mainland.

To see how the city has grown, start downtown before going off to explore Coconut Grove, with its gardens and Italian-style villa. Next door is affluent and elegant Coral Gables, a classic example of sensitive urban development. Then it's off to Miami Beach and the highly publicized South Beach district. Finish your tour on Key Biscayne, the southernmost barrier island off Miami. ∎

Area of map detail

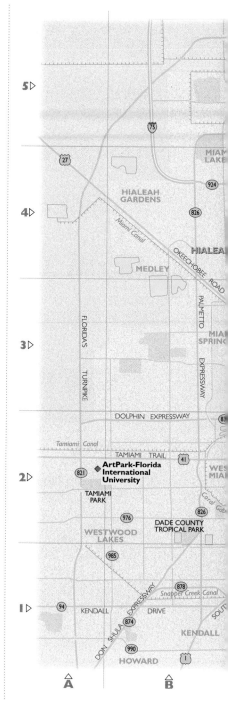

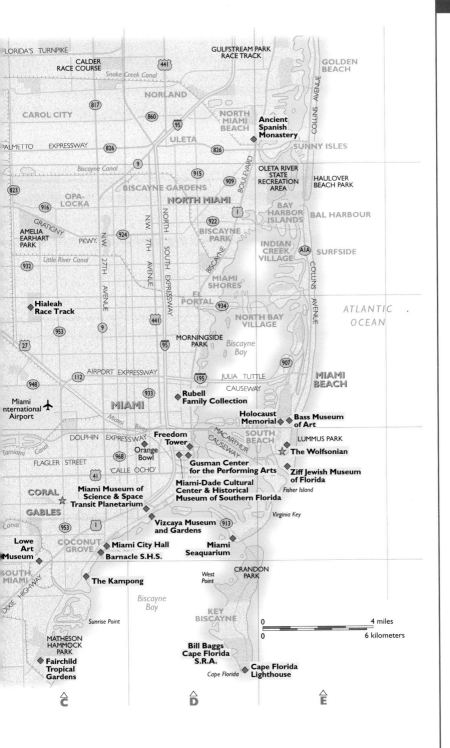

FLORIDA'S TURNPIKE

GULFSTREAM PARK RACE TRACK

CALDER RACE COURSE

441

Snake Creek Canal

GOLDEN BEACH

NORLAND

COLLINS AVENUE

CAROL CITY

817

860

95

NORTH MIAMI BEACH

Ancient Spanish Monastery

ULETA

SUNNY ISLES

PALMETTO EXPRESSWAY

826

826

Biscayne Canal

9

915

909

OLETA RIVER STATE RECREATION AREA

HAULOVER BEACH PARK

BISCAYNE GARDENS

BOULEVARD

823

OPA-LOCKA

916

NORTH MIAMI

BAY HARBOR ISLANDS

BAL HARBOUR

GRATIGNY

924

922

BISCAYNE PARK

INDIAN CREEK VILLAGE

A1A

SURFSIDE

AMELIA EARHART PARK

PKWY.

N.W. 27TH AVENUE

N.W. 7TH AVENUE

BISCAYNE

MIAMI SHORES

COLLINS AVENUE

Little River Canal

932

NORTH - SOUTH EXPRESSWAY

EL PORTAL

934

ATLANTIC OCEAN

Hialeah Race Track

9

441

NORTH BAY VILLAGE

953

95

MORNINGSIDE PARK

Biscayne Bay

27

907

AIRPORT EXPRESSWAY

112

195

JULIA TUTTLE CAUSEWAY

MIAMI BEACH

948

933

Rubell Family Collection

Miami International Airport

MIAMI

Miami River

Holocaust Memorial

Bass Museum of Art

DOLPHIN EXPRESSWAY

Freedom Tower

MACARTHUR CAUSEWAY

SOUTH BEACH

LUMMUS PARK

Tamiami Canal

968

Orange Bowl

The Wolfsonian

FLAGLER STREET

Gusman Center for the Performing Arts

Ziff Jewish Museum of Florida

41

'CALLE OCHO'

CORAL

Miami Museum of Science & Space Transit Planetarium

Miami-Dade Cultural Center & Historical Museum of Southern Florida

Fisher Island

GABLES

953

US 1

Vizcaya Museum and Gardens

913

Virginia Key

Canal

Lowe Art Museum

COCONUT GROVE

Miami City Hall

Barnacle S.H.S.

Miami Seaquarium

SOUTH MIAMI

DIXIE HIGHWAY

The Kampong

West Point

CRANDON PARK

Biscayne Bay

KEY BISCAYNE

Sunrise Point

0   4 miles

0   6 kilometers

MATHESON HAMMOCK PARK

Fairchild Tropical Gardens

Bill Baggs Cape Florida S.R.A.

Cape Florida

Cape Florida Lighthouse

C

D

E

Downtown Miami

**Historical
Museum of
Southern Florida**

🗺 45 D2
✉ 101 Flagler St.
☎ 305/375-1492
🕐 Closed Sun. a.m.
💲 $

THANKS TO THE BUSINESS BOOM OF RECENT YEARS, Miami's downtown now boasts a classic American skyline, spiked with skyscrapers, magically lit at night. Winding through the buildings on an elevated trackway supported by giant stilts is the quiet, pollution-free MetroMover—worth a ride just for the views across the city. Down at street level, the reality of dull shopfronts and office entrances is less stimulating. There are, however, a handful of landmarks and museums that make a short visit worthwhile.

**Seminole
Indian artifacts
at the Historical
Museum of
Southern Florida**

Since 1984 the **Historical Museum of Southern Florida** has faced the huge plaza that is the focus of the downtown Miami-Dade Cultural Center. Its permanent exhibit, "Tropical Dreams: A People's History of Southern Florida," provides a who, what,

when, where, and why look at a region whose past has long been overlooked. Discover how the ingenious Tequesta tribe turned shells, stones, and bones into everyday tools 2,000 years ago. See how the Spanish kept track of their treasure, transported over thousands of miles from the colonies to the Old World. The tarnished silver bars in the sturdy glass case need a good polish, but you can still make out the markings that show the purity, tax code, shipper, and mint.

Wherever the Spanish went, they took their priests. Conversion was part of colonization, and the host press for embossing communion wafers and found on the Gulf Coast, dates back more than 400 years.

In the revamped "Gateway of the Americas" exhibit, covering 1950 to 2000, the most sobering artifact is the 19-foot raft that carried 70 desperate economic refugees to the United States from Haiti. This frighteningly fragile craft amounts to just a few logs tied together, topped with a hand-sewn cotton sail on a hand-carved mast.

If there is a must-see, it has to be the regularly changing display of Audubon prints at the bottom of the Grand Staircase, since the museum boasts the only complete set of *The Birds of America* in the whole of Florida.

Near the museum, you can step into the **Gusman Center for the Performing Arts** and be

taken back to a time when movie theaters were entertainment centers, pulling in crowds not just for movies but for live shows as well. Used today by the Miami City Ballet and the New World Symphony, the Gusman also hosts a wide range of cultural events, including the annual film festival.

Built in 1926, this was one of about 16 movie houses opened by Paramount Studios to welcome in the new era of the talkies. Changing every Tuesday, there were six daily showings of the latest movie as well as six live stage shows. A cavalcade of stars has trodden the stage, from Rudy Vallee and Mae West to Frank Sinatra, Elvis Presley, and Luciano Pavarotti. The pipe organ, the only one of its kind south of Atlanta, is no museum piece, but a mighty 1,035-pipe Wurlitzer that thunders into action for special concerts.

While the lobby is ornate, with hand-painted decorations and gilded lamps, the auditorium is astonishing. Referred to as an environmental theater because of its sense of being in the open air, the interior of the Gusman is like

the courtyard of a Spanish nobleman's house. The 70-foot-high blue ceiling is adorned with moving clouds and twinkling stars, all worked with the original mechanisms. On all sides are gilded statues and secretive alcoves, with trompe l'oeil *doñas* with fans leaning over the balustrade.

The theater has often been threatened with demolition. In the 1970s, plans to turn it into a parking lot were thwarted, thanks to philanthropist Maurice Gusman. In 1995, Sylvester Stallone helped a second rescue campaign.

Two blocks to the east, the former rundown area alongside Biscayne Bay has been cleaned up and revived. **Bayfront Park** has a monument dedicated to those who died in the disastrous Challenger space mission, while the nearby **Bayside Marketplace** (*401 Biscayne Blvd., Tel 305/377-4091*) is a lively, Bahamian-style, open-air shopping area. This market is particularly popular with passengers using the busy cruise port; the shops and restaurants overlook boats in Miamarina.

Thanks to careful restoration, the Gusman Center for the Performing Arts provides a glamorous setting for Miami's thriving arts scene.

Gusman Center for the Performing Arts

⬛ 45 D2

✉ 174 E. Flagler St.

☎ 305/930-1812 (tickets), 305/372-0925 (administration)

Freedom Tower is a downtown Miami landmark.

Traveling northward a little to the junction of Biscayne Boulevard and Northeast Sixth Street you cannot miss **Freedom Tower**.

Anyone who has seen the Giralda in Seville, Spain, will recognize the inspiration for this fine example of the New World's love affair with Mediterranean Revival. New York architects Schultze and Weaver, who designed the Biltmore Hotel, built newspaper offices here for 1920 presidential candidate James Cox. Innovations, such as the floodlighting, could be seen 50 miles out to sea. After losing to Warren Harding, Cox bought the *Miami Metropolis* and renamed it the *Miami Daily News*. Its first ever edition, on July 26, 1925, was the biggest newspaper of all time. It weighed in at 7½ pounds, with 504 pages in 22 sections. When the newspaper offices moved out after 32 years, the building was left vacant and decaying—until 1962, when thousands of Cubans anxious to escape the Castro regime flooded into Miami. The government took over the tower, converting it into an Ellis Island-like processing office. This Cuban Refugee Center, soon nicknamed the Freedom Tower, was kept busy for 12 years, welcoming 650,000 Cubans. When Fidel Castro halted the airlift, the downtown landmark was left empty again.

Once a secret known only to the cognoscenti of the art world, the **Rubell Family Collection** took a more prominent place on the cultural stage in 1998. Despite being off the beaten track, in a down-at-heel residential area north of downtown, security is not a problem: The building was formerly the warehouse for the Drug Enforcement Agency. What once housed confiscated cars, weapons, and drugs now showcases a fascinating collection of contemporary art.

"My parents began buying art when they got married 30 years ago," says Jennifer Rubell. "As a boy, my father had a stamp collection; I suppose he has an acquisitive nature." What marks out the Rubells from other collectors is their passion for cutting-edge, contemporary art. "Oh Charlie! Charlie! Charlie!" by Charles Ray, for example, is sent out on loan, and always causes controversy. A sexually explicit orgy of male mannequins, all casts of the artist himself, it is a powerful and disturbing piece.

Not all the sculptures, paintings, and collages here are as shocking, although all are thought provoking. David Hammons' "Portrait of John Henry" combines red hair, a rusty rail, and a head-shaped stone for a symbolic representation of the African-American hero.

Art for all

Standing in the Miami-Dade Cultural Center is Miami's best-known outdoor sculpture, "Dropped Bowl with scattered Slices and Peels" by Coosje Van Bruggen and Claus Oldenburg. The city has commissioned many public works, including a giant red "M" at the entrance to the Riverwalk MetroMover station (where Julia Tuttle, founder of Miami, once lived).

Out at Miami International Airport stands the "36th Street Wall." This mile-long concrete sound barrier is enlivened with colored glass disks.

Inside the airport is the interactive "Harmonic Runway" at Concourse A. As passengers pass the rainbow-colored glass screens, they trigger the sounds of birds, frogs, and crickets. ■

The Metro-Dade Cultural Center boasts Van Bruggen's "Dropped Bowl with scattered Slices and Peels."

The RFC is unlike any other gallery in Florida. There is none of the formality of so many museums of fine art; the enormous, high-ceilinged rooms have the ambience of an artist's studio. Be careful where you walk, since many works are on the floor.

Art is, of course, a matter of personal preference; you may or may not like what you see here. But for anyone interested in what artists from the United States and abroad have produced in the last 20 years, it is a valuable place and worth a visit. ■

The Rubell Family Collection includes thought-provoking modern works.

Ethnic Miami

From the moment visitors arrive at Miami's international airport, there is a feel of Latin America: Signs are in Spanish as well as English, voices speak Spanish and English with a Spanish lilt.

Although Miami's much-publicized Hispanic population has swelled to constitute about 50 percent of Dade County, Spanish-speakers are just one ethnic grouping in a city that is today truly multinational. In bars, cafés, shops, and offices you'll also hear conversations in French, German, and Portuguese.

Surprisingly, Brazil is now Miami's top trading partner. "Latins come to Miami because they find it simpatico," according to the marketing manager of a Miami company, "We have the North American efficiency and work ethic, with a Latin culture and flavor." The Hispanic influence spreads throughout the metropolitan area, but the heart of this community is Little Havana.

"Republic Bank Welcomes You to Little Havana USA" proclaims a sign on a corner of Southwest Eighth Street, known to locals, and now visitors, as Calle Ocho. Here, cafés advertise *comida Cubana* (Cuban food) and serve *batidos* (shakes) and *churros* (similar to a doughnut). In Máximo Gómez Park, named for a 19th-century hero of the Cuban fight for liberation from Spain, the Domino Club is a social center. Under the shade of two gazebos, the older generation of men (with only the occasional woman) play dominoes, chess, and cards, and discuss the old days. A mural portrays the political leaders from some 30 North and South American nations who gathered in Miami in 1994 for the Summit of the Americas. A few blocks away, the eternal flame on Cuban Memorial Boulevard honors the soldiers who died in the failed Bay of Pigs invasion of Cuba in 1961.

After Fidel Castro took over in 1959, the 300,000 Cubans who fled the island between 1966 and 1973 were mainly businessmen, doctors, and lawyers. Having rebuilt successful careers and new lives—and adding immeasurably to the city's growth and prosperity—some still dream of returning to their homeland; others harbor only feelings of nostalgia. Gloria Estefan's 1993 album *Mi Tierra* (My Country) may tug at their heartstrings, but they, and their American-born children, are staying put—most even after Castro falls. Gloria Estefan, like her husband-manager, Emilio, exemplifies the second-generation Cubans who have integrated into the United States in general, and South Florida in particular.

Outsiders can rarely differentiate between these ambitious middle-class Cubans and the

International leaders look on as Cuban Americans play dominoes, their favorite game, in Parque Máximo Gómez in Miami's Little Havana.

flood of poorer Cubans triggered by the Mariel boatlift of 1980. This wave of 125,000 people included not only economic refugees, but also criminals released from Cuban jails by Fidel Castro.

Although Cubans may be in the majority, there are also Spanish-speaking immigrants from South and Central America, as well as the Caribbean. Along Calle Ocho, there are Nicaraguan restaurants and even an automobile dealership that exports cars to Honduras and Guatemala. And who needs Havana-made cigars when some 40 factories in Miami still make them the traditional way—by hand?

The Hispanic immigration is only a recent phenomenon. Some of Miami's other ethnic communities have a longer history. In Coconut Grove, for example, beyond the side-walk cafés and neon lights, are the simple

homes of the Bahamian community, many of whom arrived in the 1880s to work at the Peacock Inn, Miami's first hotel. Bahamian Ebenezer Stirrup invested his wages in land, built houses, and rented them to fellow Bahamians—in some cases their descendants still live in them.

North of downtown, Overtown was known as Colored Town in 1896, and until integration during the 1950s, African Americans were forced to live here. Today, the heritage of this once thriving small town is being rediscovered. No wonder Miami-Dade Community College history professor Dr. Paul George points out that "from its earliest days, Miami hasn't been a traditional American city. Today it is unlike any major city in the country. It's an incredible array of people and cultures." ■

Coconut Grove & beyond

Vizcaya Museum and Gardens

🅰 45 D2

✉ 3251 S. Miami Ave.

☎ 305/250-9133

🕐 Call for details of special events, such as moonlight garden tours.

💲 $$

NOT SO LONG AGO, COCONUT GROVE HAD A SLIGHTLY hippy reputation. Despite its current fashionable image, "The Grove" retains a feel of community, with a post office, thrift shop, and small mom-and-pop businesses. Single-story houses are surrounded by lush greenery. At night, in and around the CocoWalk shopping development, sidewalk cafés are abuzz with visitors from all over the world. Few people realize that several special gardens are close at hand.

If imitation is the sincerest form of flattery, then James Deering should be very pleased. Villa Vizcaya, the winter home of the co-founder of International Harvester (the world's biggest manufacturer of combine harvesters), plays a special role in Florida's architectural history.

Deering's mock Renaissance palazzo, now called **Vizcaya Museum and Gardens,** inspired the Mediterranean Revival style that is so characteristic of South Florida in general, and Miami in particular. Built between 1914 and 1916, it was designed to copy a 16th-century Italian villa. Even the furnishings, bought from all over Europe, were supposed to give the impression that the same

family had lived there for more than 400 years, with each generation leaving their furniture and decorations to their descendants. Examples therefore abound of the best of the Italian Renaissance, baroque, rococo, and neoclassical periods.

With 34 rooms overlooking a central courtyard, this is grandeur on a scale that is hard to credit today. During construction, more than 1,000 men (10 percent of Miami's population) worked on the estate. While architect F. Burrall Hoffman was responsible for the reinforced concrete design, cleverly masked with stucco and limestone, it was New York painter Paul Chalfin who ensured that Vizcaya

VIZCAYA
The name Vizcaya comes from the Basque language. It translates as "elevated place," even though the house is at sea level. ∎

would be truly memorable. European antiques dealers supplied rugs, tapestries, mantelpieces, and furniture, wrought-iron grille work, and door handles, while valuable paintings and statues added the final touch. Carefully concealed, however, were hi-tech inventions of the day, such as the elevators, a central vacuuming system, refrigeration, and telephones.

Not a square inch of wall, floor, or ceiling was left plain, while the roll call of furnishings would make a Sotheby's auctioneer covetous. Inside are a second-century Roman marble basin in the **Loggia;** a ceiling from the Rossi Palace in Venice in the **Louis XV Reception Room;** and in the dining room, 16th-century tapestries once owned by the 19th-century English poets Robert Browning and his wife Elizabeth Barrett Browning.

Upstairs, the bedrooms are equally splendid, each with a different theme. In the **Lady Hamilton Room,** the gold headboard may well have been used on the bed of the mistress of Lord Nelson. Ironically, the British admiral's

old enemy, Napoleon, was the inspiration for the **Master Bedroom.** Here, the Napoleonic eagle supports the drapery on the bed and the industrious bee, another Napoleonic symbol, is embroidered on the bedspread. The bathroom, too, has Napoleonic references, with a canopied ceiling, like a battlefield tent. Even the French emperor, however, would not have had the choice of three faucets for his bath: providing hot, cold, and salt water. James Deering never married; the portrait downstairs shows a thin-lipped man, who even in the heat of southern Florida always wore starched linen suits.

Surprisingly, the main kitchen was on the upper floor, next to the breakfast room. Here, when the sliding doors were opened, guests could feel as if they were eating on an outdoor terrace. This is the best view of the formal gardens, designed by Colombian Diego Suarez. After some neglect, the landscaping has been restored, with shrubs clipped and parterres looking like oriental carpet patterns. Note that local live oak and jasmine are used instead of

Vizcaya (opposite), an Italianate mansion, is a treasure trove of European art and antiques. The restored gardens (above) are equally impressive.

"Must we be so grand?" —Owner James Deering to the interior designer of Vizcaya.

Noted landscape architect William Lyman Phillips (1885–1966) transformed swampland into elegant vistas at the Fairchild Tropical Gardens (right). Orchids are among the exotic blooms (below).

Miami Museum of Science and Space Transit Planetarium

🅰 45 D2

✉ 3280 S. Miami Ave.

☎ 305/854-4247 or 305/854-4242

🕐 Observatory open Sat. evenings.

💲 $$

Miami City Hall

🅰 45 C2

✉ 3500 Pan American Dr.

🕐 Lobby open to the public during office hours

ilex and boxwood. A huge, heavily carved stone copy of a Venetian barge doubles as a breakwater. Guests for daytime entertainments often arrived by water. Deering did not indulge in evening events.

Across the street from the entrance to Vizcaya is the **Miami Museum of Science and Space Transit Planetarium.** In partnership with the Smithsonian Institution, this museum will expand dramatically over the next few years into the Science Center of the Americas, reflecting the civilizations of the ancient Americas, the story of the Caribbean, and the latest developments in science and technology.

When President Franklin D. Roosevelt flew to Casablanca to meet Winston Churchill in 1943, he left from the Pan American Airways terminal—what is now **Miami City Hall,** north of Vizcaya.

Pan Am inaugurated the world's first international air service from Key West to Havana, then moved its operation to Dinner Key in 1931. Originally on an island, called Dinner Key by picnickers, the terminal building has been Miami's City Hall since 1954.

After national hero Charles Lindbergh flew nonstop from New York to Paris, Pan Am signed him up as a consultant. From Miami, the airline connected with 32 foreign destinations from the Bahamas to South America, with their well-known Clipper flying boats taking off from the waterway now used by yachts and fishing boats.

The ten-foot globe of the world made by cartographers at Rand McNally, showing all Pan Am's routes, once stood in the entrance hall, but today it's at Miami's Museum of Science (see this page).

Dr. David Fairchild

In 1898 the "Columbus of American horticulture" Dr. David Fairchild (1869–1954) began a new department of the United States Department of Agriculture, dedicated to introducing new seeds and plants to America from around the world.

Over the next decades, he brought in 75,000 plants, including the flowering cherry (in 1902) and the soy bean from Japan (now a 20-billion-dollar industry), plus mangoes from Indonesia, dates from Egypt, and seedless grapes from Italy. In1912, when he first visited southern Florida, he dubbed it "the entrance to the Garden of Eden," because it was an ideal spot for propagation. A frequent contributor to NATIONAL GEOGRAPHIC magazine, his memorials are appropriate: The Kampong and Fairchild Tropical Gardens. ■

One of Coconut Grove's best-kept secrets, **The Barnacle State Historic Site,** hides behind a tangled wall of trees. Built in 1891, with a square-hipped roof, The Barnacle is the oldest house in the area and gives a glimpse back to the days before Miami existed. This was the home of Commodore Ralph Munroe.

Munroe had taken just one class in mechanical drawing at college, but went on to be a successful boat designer. He also advocated the use of septic tanks, and seawalls, and tried to propagate sponges. As well as touring the house, with its ingenious air-conditioning system, visitors can see Munroe's workshop. At the end of a broad lawn, floating at anchor in the bay is a reproduction of his best-selling boat, the 28-foot, 3-inch-long, shallow-drafted *Egret*. Drawing a mere eight inches of water, it was ideal for exploring the shallow Florida shores.

Farther south in Coconut Grove, **The Kampong** was the home of Dr. David Fairchild. Guests included Thomas Edison, Henry Ford, and his father-in-law, Alexander Graham Bell, whose solar-powered device for extracting fresh water from seawater is still on show.

Fairchild's backyard on Biscayne Bay was an open-air laboratory where Larry Schokman, the garden's director of horticulture, continues the work. Explaining that this is an "edible garden," he tempts visitors to bite into berries tasting of peanut butter, to chew curry-flavored leaves, and to admire 57 varieties of mango.

The philosophy at **Fairchild Tropical Gardens** is true to Fairchild's dedication speech in 1938: "This garden should become a place where everyone…can see and touch the beautiful, the strange, the interesting forms of tropical plants that characterize the vegetation of the tropics."

Among the 5,000 types of plants in these 83 acres is the world's finest collection of palm trees, while the landscaping balances the best of Italian, French, and English traditions with the demands of a world-class botanical collection. Join a tour to hear enthusiastic guides who believe in the hands-on approach suggest: "Crush these and smell them." ■

The Barnacle State Historic Site

🅰 45 C2
✉ 3485 Main Hwy.
☎ 305/448-9445
🕐 Closed Mon.–Thurs. Tours 10 & 11:30 a.m., 1 & 2:30 p.m.
💲 $

The Kampong
🅰 45 C1
✉ 4013 Douglas Rd.
☎ 305/445-8076
🕐 Call for days and times of tours.
💲 $–$$

Fairchild Tropical Gardens
🅰 45 C1
✉ 10901 Old Cutler Rd.
☎ 305/667-1651
💲 $$

Coral Gables

Lowe Art Museum
🖼 45 C2
✉ University of Miami, 1301 Stanford Dr.
☎ 305/284-3535
🕐 Closed Mon.
💲 $

GEORGE MERRICK, FOUNDER OF CORAL GABLES, BELIEVED that "natural beauty is a community's greatest asset" when he developed what was wilderness earlier this century. Today, this is the most beautiful suburb of Miami. The small business district, with its multinational companies, has long had a reputation for fine restaurants. But it is the homogeneous design of the comfortable houses that makes this such a sought-after residential area. On the southern side of "The Gables" is the sprawling campus of the University of Miami.

On the campus, **Lowe Art Museum** is well worth half a day's visit. Among the highlights is the **Kress Collection of Renaissance and Baroque Art,** with paintings by old masters such as Guardi, Tintoretto, and Cranach the Elder. Lippo Vanni's triptych of the "Madonna with Child" is particularly beautiful.

Spain's Golden Age is represented by the **Oscar B. Cintas** donation of 17 works by great artists such as Goya, Murillo, and El Greco. Fans of French art should seek out "The Barge and the Boat" by Paul Gauguin, which typifies his scenes of rural French life, and "Waterloo Bridge" by Claude Monet.

The **Art of the Americas** ranges from early 19th-century portraits to big, bold, and colorful statements by Roy Lichtenstein and Frank Stella, which can be seen clearly thanks to the high ceiling in the new gallery. "Le Neveu de Rameau" by Frank Stella teases the eye, with the vibrancy of its concentric squares of color, while in "Modular Painting in Four Panels, No. 5," Lichtenstein takes an art-moderne design from the 1930s and gives it his pop art treatment. By contrast, the 1826 portrait of Julcee Mathla by Charles Bird King emphasizes the intelligence and pride of this Seminole chief.

Pottery, textiles, and carvings allow you to take a closer look at the artistic skills of Native American tribes. The extensive collection here focuses on the Navajo, Pueblo, and Rio Grande from the Southwest, but also includes an intricately beaded bandolier bag (big holster) that was part of the ceremonial dress of the Seminole.

Continuing south to the rest of the Americas, the model of a coastal Peruvian tomb provides an insight into ancient customs. One of the most important pieces in the collection is the Chimu Disc from Peru. The silver circle is a complex design of fruits, stylized animals, and heads. But what was it used for and what do the symbols mean? The mystery dates back more than 500 years. ∎

Lowe Art Museum's "Le Neveu de Rameau" (1974), a large acrylic on canvas by Frank Stella.

A Spanish Colonial house exemplifies the Mediterranean Revival architecture of Coral Gables.

George E. Merrick (1887–1942)

The developer who created Coral Gables came to Florida as a 12-year-old boy in 1899. The son of a Congregational minister, he had nothing in his background to explain where he got his grand vision of a new planned community.

His dream was to build "Miami's master suburb," turning 3,000 acres into plazas, wide boulevards, green spaces, and handsome houses. Design was paramount, and Merrick insisted that stores and banks, even schools, the library, and the town hall, had to be designed in the same Mediterranean Revival style. In just six months, some 600 houses were built, along with 65 miles of roads, embellished with 50,000 trees, bushes, and plants. He raised 100 million dollars for the buildings and spent a further five million dollars on promotion, advertising in magazines and on billboards in Times Square.

Everything went well until September 1926, when a hurricane burst the bubble of southern Florida land speculation. By April 1929, Merrick had filed for bankruptcy. The final two years of his life were spent working as postmaster for the City of Miami. Although only a quarter of his dream became reality, Merrick's legacy remains one of the finest planned communities in the United States, as well as one of the most beautiful. There are avenues shaded by mature mahogany, balsa, poinciana, and kapok trees, and gardens overflowing with oleanders, hibiscus, bougainvillea, and jasmine. ■

Drive through Coral Gables

This tour shows the scope of Merrick's vision. His plans for the "City Beautiful" included public buildings, decorative gates, fountains, and a range of innovative housing designs, all surrounded by trees and flowering shrubs. Allow about 30 minutes. Start at City Hall, at the intersection of Le Jeune Road and Miracle Mile/Coral Way.

Coral Gables' Merrick House on Coral Way. The attractive gardens retain many of the original trees.

City Hall ❶ (*Tel 305/446-6800*), with its tower, tile roof, and columns, typifies Merrick's adaptation of Mediterranean architecture. Note the small, triangular park with a simple memorial to G.E. Merrick, "dreamer, writer, poet, philosopher, lover of the beautiful." Keeping City Hall on your left, drive down Miracle Mile/Coral Way past the Granada Golf Course. Continue to No. 907, **Coral Gables Merrick House ❷** (*Tel 305/460-5361. Closed Mon.–Tues.; Wed. & Sun. a.m.*). The Merrick family bought this house in 1899 and in 1906 they named their home after its building materials: Coral Gables. After his father's death in 1911, George continued to buy land, and his 3,000-acre estate was the basis for his dream of a brand-new city.

Continue on Coral Way, turn left on the gated Granada Boulevard, then left again on Almeria Avenue. Under a canopy of dramatic banyan trees, this leads to DeSoto Boulevard. Opposite is the **Venetian Pool ❸** (*Tel 305/460-5356, closed Mon.*). The quarry where Merrick's men excavated coral rock now looks like Venice without the gondolas. This spring-fed 820,000-gallon pool is the only municipal swimming pool on the National Register of Historic Places. Turn right on DeSoto Boulevard, and at the fountain go straight across the rotary, following the banyans down the extension of DeSoto. Merrick not only worshiped at the **Coral Gables Congregational Church ❹**, but also donated the land for this building, which was inspired by a church in Barcelona, Spain. Inside, the beams were deliberately aged to make the building look older. The first service was held in 1925. DeSoto Boulevard dead-ends at Anastasia Avenue. Ever since January 1926, the **Biltmore Hotel ❺** (*1200 Anastasia Ave., Tel 305/445-1926*) has entertained the rich and famous. Johnny Weissmuller (alias Tarzan) swam in the enormous swimming pool, and the Duke and Duchess of Windsor were regular guests. During World War II and on into the late 1960s, this was a hospital. Now it is once again a luxury hotel.

Turn left on Anastasia Avenue, then take the first right on Granada Boulevard and continue across Bird Road, which passes alongside and across canals that were designed to connect to Biscayne Bay. Turn left on Blue Road, then right on Biltmore Drive and, soon after, it becomes Riviera Drive. Cross US 1. Ahead is a gold and red house, part of the **Chinese Village ❻**. Turn left on Castania Avenue and drive around the block. Although 20 themed villages were planned within the city, only seven were built. More distinctive than the Italian or French Country Villages, the Chinese houses sport dragons and

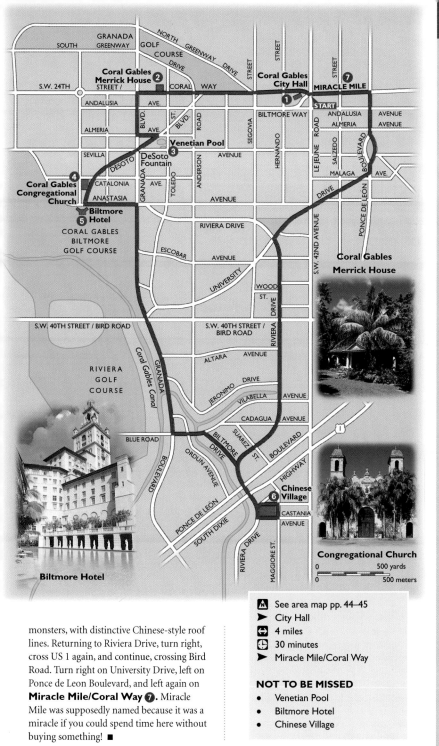

Coral Gables
Merrick House

Coral Gables
Congregational Church

Biltmore Hotel

	See area map pp. 44–45
►	City Hall
↔	4 miles
⏱	30 minutes
►	Miracle Mile/Coral Way

NOT TO BE MISSED
- Venetian Pool
- Biltmore Hotel
- Chinese Village

monsters, with distinctive Chinese-style roof lines. Returning to Riviera Drive, turn right, cross US 1 again, and continue, crossing Bird Road. Turn right on University Drive, left on Ponce de Leon Boulevard, and left again on **Miracle Mile/Coral Way ❼**. Miracle Mile was supposedly named because it was a miracle if you could spend time here without buying something! ■

Sportscity, U.S.A.

When it comes to sport, Miami is strictly major league. Professional sport may have been a long time coming, but today the thrill of competition is on offer year-round. America's four major league sports—football, baseball, hockey, and basketball—all have teams in Miami, while the world's top tennis and golf stars are regular visitors. At New Year's, sports are the driving force behind many of the year-end celebrations.

Local fans had to wait until 1966 for their first professional team, when the American Football League awarded Joe Robbie's Dolphins the ninth franchise. A mere six years after their first pro game, the aqua-and-orange-clad Dolphins made it to the Super Bowl, only to lose to Dallas. In 1972 they set a record that has never been approached, with a 17–0 season as they beat Washington in Super Bowl VII. They won again a year later, beating Minnesota.

The success of the Dolphins has rubbed off on college football. In the 1980s, the University of Miami Hurricanes grew into a powerhouse, winning the national title four times in a decade (three times on home ground, at the Orange Bowl) thanks to fine players such as Heisman Trophy winner Vinnie Testaverde. The legendary Orange Bowl, which features top college teams in post-season action, is second only to the Rose Bowl of Pasadena in seniority.

For 20 years Miami had just one professional team, but now it is represented by basketball's Miami Heat, the Florida Panthers ice-hockey team, and the club that has produced a modern fairy tale, the Florida Marlins baseball team. On October 27, 1997, the Marlins clinched the World Series by

Left: Florida Marlins victory parade
Above: Florida Panther Rhett Warrener
Below: Miami Dolphins take on the Colts.

beating the Cleveland Indians 3–2 over 11 innings. They had only been in existence since April 5, 1993. They were not only the first club to win the World Series without winning their own division, they were also the southernmost team to reach the World Series, with four games of the Fall Classic played in the damp warmth of the Pro Player Stadium. At 22, Cuban defector Livan Hernandez was the youngest pitcher to win Game 1, and went on to become M.V.P. (Most Valuable Player) of the World Series, yet only the year before he had been playing Double-A ball in the minor league.

Although many of America's leading golfers have moved to Florida in recent years, the game has been played in Florida for more than a century. When he brought in the railroad, Henry Flagler also installed a six-hole course at his sumptuous Royal Palm Hotel. The sport was so popular with his affluent visitors that he built an 18-hole course in 1898, triggering the game's popularity statewide. Eager to compete, the Biltmore Hotel signed up America's leading architect, Donald Ross, to build them the 18-hole course that still graces Coral Gables. Since 1960, members of the United States professional golf tour have headed for Miami in early March, and Alfred L. Kaskel, owner of the Doral Golf Resort and Spa, put up $50,000 for what is now the Doral-Ryder Open, where the world's top players have tackled the challenging Blue Monster course.

Played out on breezy Key Biscayne since 1987, the Lipton International Players Championship was established as the fifth Grand Slam in tennis, with both the men and the women of the professional tours playing here each March/April. Over 200,000 spectators support the event. Add in the downtown motor race, the Marlboro Grand Prix, game fishing, jai alai, and three horse-racing tracks (Gulfstream Park, Calder Race Course, and Hialeah), and sports are always just around the corner in Miami. ∎

Miami Beach

THERE ARE TWO PARTS TO MIAMI BEACH, THE LONG THIN barrier island off Miami. The northern part, with its big hotels right on the beach, has been eclipsed in the last two decades by South Beach, with its Art Deco District, down at the southern end. Here, Ocean Drive is thronged with visitors from all over the world intent on having a good time, often until late into the night. But away from the ocean, the year-round community has a strong cultural life.

Just off Dade Boulevard, in the middle of Miami Beach, the renovated **Bass Museum of Art** is part of a grand plan to create a "Cultural Campus" between 21st and 23rd Streets. Neighboring buildings will include a new library and rehearsal rooms for the Miami City Ballet. Standing behind the original 1930s structure of the museum is the 1999 wing, allowing more display space, particularly for works from the core collection given to the city of Miami Beach by Austrian-born John and Johanna Bass.

Bass Museum of Art

- 45 E3
- 2121 Park Ave.
- 305/673-7530
- Closed Mon. & Sun. a.m.
- $

Of the 500 paintings covering five centuries of European art, many carry the apology of "follower of" or "style of." The imposing 15th-century altarpiece depicting the coronation of the Virgin is, however, attributed to Sandro Botticelli and Domenico Ghirlandaio, who worked together on several projects including the decoration of the walls of the Sistine Chapel. From England come three late 18th- to early 19th-century portraits by George Romney, Thomas Lawrence, and the American-born artist, Benjamin West, a founder member of London's Royal Academy. "The Tournament" is a meticulously restored tapestry woven from a silk and wool mixture in Brussels in the early part of the 16th century. The Camelot-like panorama (about 14 by 22 feet) shows two knights just before they meet in the lists.

Recent acquisitions include Korean art, contemporary American paintings, and the archives of Morris Lapidus, the architect who designed the Fontainebleau Hotel and who is now generally considered to be the father of postmodernism in the United States.

In the 1930s, when the houses of the rich and famous were closed up at the end of the winter season, the contents were moved to the Washington Storage Company. Today, this building, a classic 1927 example of Mediterranean Revival style, is still chock-full of beautiful objects, but they are all part of the Mitchell Wolfson, Jr., Collection of Decorative and Propaganda Arts, known as **The Wolfsonian.** Fascinated by the power of

design in the influential period between 1885 and 1945, Wolfson collected furniture, glass, and sculpture, as well as useful everyday objects.

From a stylish 1930s art deco toaster to "The Wrestler," a massive statue from the 1932 Olympic Games in Los Angeles, this collection of more than 70,000 pieces represents a cross section of design movements, from surrealist and Italian futurist, to Dutch nieuwe kunst and Czech constructivist.

The Wolfsonian (Mitchell Wolfson, Jr., Collection of Decorative and Propaganda Arts)

 45 E2

✉ 1001 Washington Ave.

☎ 305/531-1001

🕐 Closed Mon. & Sun a.m.

💲 $, free Thurs. 6–9 p.m.

The Midas Touch—Carl Fisher

Henry Flagler, Julia Tuttle, and John Collins may have their boulevards, but Carl F. Fisher is commemorated by exclusive, residential Fisher Island, just off Miami Beach and reached by ferry.

His contribution to Miami's development was considerable. In 1913, by piling sand from Biscayne Bay onto this swampy barrier island, his workers created Miami Beach. He spearheaded the Dixie Highway Association, which built a road from Chicago to South Florida—towns vied for the privilege of being alongside it—and in 1915 led a motorcade from his native Midwest into Miami.

His advertising campaign included billboards in Times Square bearing the simple message for freezing New Yorkers: "It's June in Miami." When they arrived, Fisher used circus elephants to promote his lots on Miami Beach: In 1926, he sold six million dollars' worth. ∎

The Wolfsonian is generally regarded as a specialist museum for students of design, but the eclectic collection has something of interest for everyone.

A stained-glass window in the art deco building housing the Ziff Jewish Museum of Florida

Since 1995, the public has been welcome in the library, research center, and the small museum where the exhibits change regularly. You may perhaps see King Farouk's matchbooks, Hitler's *Mein Kampf* in Braille, or Giuseppe Verdi's barber chair; but whatever is on display represents the dramatic changes in popular design in the past century.

Many people assume that the Jewish connection with Florida started after World War II, when there was an influx of retired New Yorkers to Miami Beach. In fact, the roots of the third-largest Jewish community in the United States date back more than 200 years. Although Jewish people were banned from Florida under the Spanish, the British were more tolerant after they took over in 1763.

In central Florida, Moses Levy dreamed of starting a Jewish colony back in 1819. The idea failed, but

his son, David Levy Yulee, was the first Jewish person to take a seat in Congress.

The aim of the **Ziff Jewish Museum of Florida** is to create a memory bank of Jewish history in Florida for the younger generation. Originally a traveling exhibit, "MOSAIC: Jewish Life in Florida" now has a permanent home in a former synagogue. Designed in 1936 by Henry Hohauser, who also created the fine art deco Cardozo and Century Hotels, the building is at the southern tip of Miami Beach—the only place in the city where Jewish people were allowed to live before World War II.

Under the 80 stained-glass windows with their symbols of Jewish culture, memorabilia range from citrus labels in Yiddish to copies of the *Florida Jewish News,* founded in 1924. Enthusiastic docents love to fill in details. Take the Weinkle Torah. When the young

Ziff Jewish Museum of Florida
- 45 E2
- 301 Washington Ave.
- 305/672-5044
- Closed Mon.
- $, free on Sat.

Holocaust Memorial
- 45 E3
- 1933–45 Meridian Ave.
- 305/538-1663

Marcus Weinkle fled Tsarist Russia in the late 1800s, he took this Torah. Later, he settled in Florida to run a lumber business near Sarasota in 1908. Wherever he traveled along the Gulf Coast, he carried the Torah, conducting services.

In the sunshine and vacation atmosphere of Miami Beach, the Holocaust of World War II seems remote. However, the strong Jewish community has not forgotten the six million Jewish people who died at camps such as Belsen, Treblinka, and Buchenwald. Just to the west of Miami is the powerful **Holocaust Memorial.**

What you see from the street is a sculpted hand, clawing at the sky. Below, a tangle of emaciated, writhing bodies rises like a column, which becomes a wrist, which becomes that hand grasping for help. In the surrounding walkway are the names and photographs of victims such as Anne Frank, whose words are inscribed here. "…in spite of everything, I still believe that people are really good at heart…." ■

This moving sculpture, a tribute to victims of the Holocaust, contrasts starkly with the fun on the nearby beaches.

Miami Vice & the Versace effect

The 1980s TV series *Miami Vice* made the city both famous and infamous. Today's vibrant fashion industry, based on Miami's South Beach, descends directly from that show, which projected a new type of male: the stylish, macho man. As well as their scarlet Ferrari Testarossa, the wardrobes of policemen Crockett and Tubbs heralded the new look.

The creator behind it all was Gianni Versace. As Laurie Brookins wrote in *Ocean Drive* magazine in an obituary to the designer, murdered in 1997:"…he had South Florida on his mind when he worked with television producers to create the T-shirt-and-colorful-linen-jacket look that was *Miami Vice*, which for a decade defined Miami Style to an international audience." ■

Atlantis Building on Brickell Avenue, as seen in *Miami Vice*

Drive: South Beach past & present

There is more to South Beach than just art deco buildings. This drive covers history, entertainment, art, and architecture, and delves into some hidden corners of this fascinating community.

Start on Washington Avenue at the historic **Old City Hall**, near the circular **Old Post Office** (note its mural by artist Charles Hardin).

At 1443 Washington Avenue, the pink **Clay Hotel ❶** *(Tel 305/534-2988)*, now the International Youth Hostel, has a racy past. Clubbers wanting a wild night out in the 1930s could gamble at mobster Al Capone's casino or dance the new craze, the rumba, introduced to Florida by bandleader Desi Arnaz.

Turn left on Española Way. Designed as a "Spanish Village" in 1922, this enclave retains an unconventional ambience. Cafés, galleries, and off-beat shops line the tiny lane, overlooked by decorated buildings and brightened by palms and hibiscus. At Plaza de España, turn right on Drexel Avenue, right on 15th Street, right again on Washington Avenue, and proceed south. At 13th Street, turn left, then right onto Collins Avenue.

On the corner of 12th Street and Collins, the **Marlin Hotel ❷** (see p. 236), an L. Murray Dixon design, has the "eyebrows" and rounded corners typical of South Beach art deco. The frieze of underwater creatures is original; the sound studios in the basement (not open to the public) are not. They were installed by record producer Chris Blackwell of Island Records, who owns this and several other hotels on South Beach. Funky yet luxurious, this is a haunt of singers, musicians, and producers in the music industry.

Turn left on 12th Street, then right on Ocean Drive. Number 1114 is **Casa Casuarina ❸**. Today, flowers are left at the wrought-iron gate and photographs are taken of this building, the home of Gianni Versace from 1992 until he died in 1997. The copper-domed observatory is an original feature of the mansion, which was inspired by the 16th-century Dominican Republic house of Diego Columbus, son of Christopher.

Continue south to 10th Street. From the beach, the **Art Deco District Welcome Center ❹** *(1001 Ocean Dr., Tel 305/672-2014)*

looks like a stranded ocean liner, a favorite art deco design. The center is filled with art deco memorabilia inside; the clock outside, showing the temperature, month, day, and year, is a popular photo spot.

Turn right on Tenth Street, also signposted Barbara Capitman Way in honor of the New Yorker who spearheaded the campaign to save this historic district. Then turn right on Collins Avenue, past a parade of ever-larger hotels built at the end of the 1930s boom, and before you reach the Delano Hotel, look left on Lincoln Road toward the pedestrianized mall, which has become a fashionable area of stores, restaurants, and galleries.

Standing on the corner of 17th Street, and one of the star attractions on South Beach, the fashionable **Delano Hotel ❺** *(1685 Collins Ave., Tel 305/532-0099)* was renovated in 1995 by style gurus Ian Schrager and Philippe Starck. Note the small blue door facing the street; it is a fake. The real entrance, behind the hedge, is hung with the breezy white curtains that have become the hotel's trademark.

Turning on 17th Street, continue to Washington Avenue. On the northwest corner is the **Jackie Gleason Theater of the Performing Arts ❻** *(1700 Washington Ave., Tel 305/673-7300)*. Originally the Municipal Auditorium, this was designed (1950–51) by three of the most familiar names

---

▲ See area map pp. 44–45
► Old City Hall
◄► About 2 miles
🕐 30 minutes
► Jackie Gleason Theater of the Performing Arts

NOT TO BE MISSED
- Marlin Hotel
- Casa Casuarina
- Art Deco Welcome Center
- Delano Hotel

Jackie Gleason Theater of the Performing Arts

South Beach Post Office

Gleason Theater **6**

WASHINGTON

17TH STREET

Delano **5** Hotel

LINCOLN ROAD MALL

LINCOLN ROAD

DREXEL AVENUE

AVENUE

A1A 16TH ST.

15TH ST. ST.

15TH ST.

ESPAÑOLA WAY

PLAZA DE ESPAÑA

Clay Hotel 1

AVENUE

14TH ST.

DRIVE

Old Post Office

13TH ST.

LUMMUS

START 12TH ST.

2 **Marlin Hotel** PARK

Old City Hall

3 **Casa Casuarina**

11TH ST.

10TH ST.

4 **Art Deco Welcome Center**

9TH ST.

COLLINS

OCEAN

ALTON ROAD

LENOX

MICHIGAN

JEFFERSON

MERIDIAN

EUCLID

WASHINGTON

AVENUE

8TH ST.

7TH ST.

A1A

6TH ST.

ATLANTIC

907

A1A

5TH STREET

41

OCEAN

MACARTHUR CAUSEWAY

ALTON

AVENUE

AVENUE

AVENUE

AVENUE

Marina

0 500 yards

0 500 meters

Biscayne Bay

ROAD

among art deco architects: L. Murray Dixon, Henry Hohauser, and Russell Pancoast. In the garden facing 17th Street is a sculpture of Jackie Gleason with his signature straw boater hat. "Mermaid," the colorful sculpture by Roy Lichtenstein, is part of the Art in Public Places program in Miami. Take time to look at the Walk of the Stars in the adjacent area, noting the imprint of the size 8½ shoes of Miami Vice director Michael Mann and the strong toes of Edward Villella, the artistic director of the Miami City Ballet. ■

Art deco in Miami Beach

"The largest grouping of art deco buildings in the world" is the proud boast of Miami Beach's South Beach. Today, some 400 buildings, ranging from private homes to hotels, stores, and theaters, maintain a unity and continuity of design.

Over the past 60 years, the Art Deco District has survived careless owners, army occupation, retired folk from New York, and greedy developers. Fortunately, vigorous campaigning led by the late Barbara Capitman rescued this national treasure. In 1979 about a square mile became the first 20th-century historic district put on the National Register of Historic Places. The rescue work has paid off, bringing visitors to admire America's answer to the French Riviera.

Little is known about Henry Hohauser, L. Murray Dixon, Albert Anis, and Roy F. France, the men who left us this Busby Berkeley legacy of glitzy buildings. Although much was built quickly to deal with the boom in winter tourism, there is an individuality and attention to detail that can still be appreciated today: the jaunty nautical motifs, sexy smooth curves, and barrel-tile rooftops.

Under the broad label of art deco are a range of subheadings to describe the variety of influences: moderne, streamline moderne, even classical moderne and nautical moderne. Not surprisingly, nautical moderne reflects the great ocean liners of the 1930s. The tubular steel railings and porthole windows are easy to spot here, where architects called it simply streamline moderne. The futuristic smooth surfaces, rounded corners, and flat roofs contrast with the retro balustrades, barrel-tile roofs, and bracketed cornices of the Mediterranean Revival style that flourished in Coral Gables in the 1920s.

Although labeled art deco, experts prefer to call the more specific Miami Beach style "tropical deco," which reflects the fun-in-the-sun designs. Following up Capitman's crusade, local designer Leonard Horowitz used a palette of pastel colors such as flamingo pink, sea green, and sunshine yellow to highlight the art deco design features. Since the mid-1980s,

Above: Art deco interiors
Opposite: The Marlin Hotel, the ultimate in South Beach's art deco design

the combination of architecture and design has been a magnet for fashion photographers, moviemakers, and vacationers.

Many art deco buildings have been saved, and the best have also been sympathetically modernized. Where there were tiny bathrooms and noisy bedrooms, walls have been knocked through and modern soundproofing installed. Some have become design statements of our time. At the Delano Hotel, trendy designer Philippe Starck showed how the cool chic of the 1990s could blend with the 1930s: A swimming pool is a water salon and the lobby has a kitchen-cum-coffee shop.

The annual Art Deco Weekend festival in mid-January is organized by the Miami Design Preservation League, which also organizes year-round walking, biking, and audio tours (*Tel 305/672-2014*). ∎

Key Biscayne

SEPARATED FROM THE CITY BY THE RICKENBACKER Causeway, Key Biscayne is popular with Miami families who drive out to the peace and wide-open spaces of Crandon Park and Bill Baggs Cape Florida State Recreation Area. After their hammering by Hurricane Andrew, these parks have recovered remarkably well.

Cape Florida's historic lighthouse

Founded in the 1950s, **Miami Seaquarium's** TV stars—Lolita the Killer Whale and Salty the Sea Lion—are familiar to many. The TV series *Flipper* was filmed here. The stars of southern Florida's biggest marine center are undoubtedly crowd-pleasers. The shows have a mildly educational bias, but balance this with good fun.

There are regular shows in the 2,500-seat stadium (be warned, the first few rows are likely to be a wet zone), touch tanks, and shark feeding by divers. A shark channel is crossed by bridges allowing visitors to observe the sharks below. A manatee breeding program is underway, and the staff is actively engaged in coaxing back to health manatees that have been injured off Florida's coast (see p. 148).

As ever, the dolphins are a great attraction, and some special children have experienced healing benefits from the dolphins. Dr. David Nathanson, president of Dolphin

Human Therapy, dedicated to helping children with disabilities (*Tel 305/378-8670*), offers this treatment.

In the **Bill Baggs Cape Florida State Recreation Area,** trees are being replanted after Hurricane Andrew's destruction in 1992. Boardwalks and cycling and walking trails have been reopened or replaced.

The beach is excellent, and barbecue grills have been installed in special areas. Fishing is a popular pastime here, and a stall sells or rents all the equipment fishermen or fisherwomen might need.

In the preserve, at the tip of Key Biscayne, is the **Cape Florida Lighthouse** (*Tel 305/361-8779*). Visitors with energy can climb 95 feet to the top of the lighthouse on the spiral staircase. They will be rewarded with excellent views. Rangers give a colorful talk to the first ten visitors who sign up half an hour before the lighthouse tours at 10 a.m. and 1 p.m. Thursday to Monday.

The lighthouse was solid enough to withstand storms, but lacked any defensive capability, built as it was in 1825 to guide ships round the treacherous tip of Key Biscayne. On July 23, 1836, John Thompson, the assistant keeper, found himself 60 feet up with a bunch of very angry Seminole below. Thompson lit a fuse on a barrel of gunpowder and hurled it down the inside of the tower. Instead of blowing himself and the Seminole to pieces, the lighthouse belched out enough smoke to scare the intruders away. ■

Miami Seaquarium

45 D2
4400 Rickenbacker Causeway, Miami
305/361-5705
$$$

Bill Baggs Cape Florida State Recreation Area

45 D1
1200 S. Crandon Blvd., Key Biscayne
305/361-5811

The cloisters of the chapel of Saint Bernard de Clairvaux. The chapel itself is still in Spain.

More places to visit in Miami

ANCIENT SPANISH MONASTERY

Completed in 1141, after eight years in the making, the cloisters were part of the monastery of Sacramenia, located north of Madrid, Spain, for nearly 800 years. In 1925, newspaper mogul William Randolph Hearst bought them, supposedly to enclose a swimming pool on his San Simeon estate in California. One by one, the stones were taken down, packed in hay, and transported across the Atlantic.

On their arrival in the United States, the boxes were quarantined—and there they stayed until after Hearst's death. In the early 1950s, the 10,751 crates were shipped to this site, where the problem was how to put the 35,000 stones back together in the correct order. Well off the normal vacation circuit, the cloisters stand under huge trees overgrown with vines. On most days the serenity is broken only by the clicking of cameras as brides and grooms pose for formal wedding portraits.

Although many of the statues and decorative carvings, along with the baptismal font, came from the original monastery, the corbels did not. These carved-stone coats of arms, which represent noble families of 12th-century Spain, were added from Hearst's collection of art.

Now administered by the Episcopal Diocese of South Florida, the cloisters are best enjoyed during church services and especially at Christmastime. The original church remains where it always was—in Spain.
🅐 45 D5 ✉ 16711 W. Dixie Hwy., North Miami Beach ☎ 305/945-1462
🕐 Closed Sun. a.m. Ⓢ $

ARTPARK, FLORIDA INTERNATIONAL UNIVERSITY

Way out in West Miami, near the Florida Turnpike, is the modern campus of Florida International University. What makes it worth the drive is ArtPark, an outdoor display of contemporary sculpture that rivals the

"Argosy" (1980), a sculpture by Alexander Liberman, stands at the entrance to the campus of Florida International University.

better-known collections at Stanford, UCLA, or the University of Pennsylvania.

Based around the Martin Z. Margulies Family Collection, the 50 bronze, granite, and steel pieces, worth 30 million dollars, have been on show on the 342-acre campus since 1994. Marty Margulies was in the real estate business, but a visit to a New York studio in the 1970s triggered a hobby that turned into a passion.

Most students who walk past these monumental works on their way to class have a favorite, whether it is a representational work such as Barry Flanagan's "Large Leaping Hare," the 24-foot-tall mechanical "Hammering Man" by Jonathan Borofsky, or "Rocher du Diamant," a yellow stick insect-like work by John Henry. One of the most eye-catching sculptures is "Marty's Cube," Tony Rosenthal's 1983 tribute to Margulies. Students like to give the huge, black metal cube a spin as they pass, or to have their family picture taken in front of "The Rim," a massive metal circle by William Tucker.

The ArtPark catalog, featuring works of the past 50 years, reads like a Who's Who of sculptors from around the world: Willem De Kooning is represented by the powerful, twisting "Seated Woman on a Bench"; and Alexander Calder riveted together the bright red "Lion." Some works may look familiar to New Yorkers—Donald Judd's "Untitled" sculpture has a sibling in the Museum of Modern Art, while Sol LeWitt's gaunt, white "Eight Unit Cube" used to stand in the United Nations Plaza. ■

🄰 44 A2 ✉ Tamiami Trail at S.W. 107th Ave., Miami ☎ 305/348-2890 🕐 Call for information and narrated educational tours

HIALEAH PARK RACE TRACK

Two miles north of Miami International Airport to the west of downtown, the race track has had a roller-coaster existence ever since its glamorous opening, but its famous 400 flamingos still brighten the lake in the middle of the one-and-an-eighth-mile oval.

There is no end to man's ingenuity when it comes to placing a bet. In 1929, when the Florida-wide ban on betting was stringently enforced, the owners of Hialeah Park racetrack came up with a way to beat the ban. Instead of betting slips, bettors purchased postcards with a picture of a horse on it—if the horse on the postcard matched the horse that won the race, the lucky gambler collected. Seventeen thousand people turned out for the first race meeting on January 15, 1925, when Mose Goldblatt's Corinth won the $1,500 Miami Handicap.

Subsequent spectators included Winston Churchill and Harry Truman. Competitors included thoroughbreds that went on to win the Kentucky Derby: Seattle Slew, Northern Dancer, and Spectacular Bid. In the paddock area, a bronze statue pays tribute to Citation, the world's first million-dollar thoroughbred and winner of racing's Triple Crown in 1948. This all-time champion horse recorded 19 wins in 20 starts, including four wins here in 1948.

🄰 45 C3 ✉ 2200 E. 4th Ave., Hialeah, Miami ☎ 305/885-8000 🕐 Season: mid-March to late May ■

According to the United Nations, the Everglades are "a place to be cherished for all mankind; a place to preserve for all time." The Keys, a chain of islands, retain a Caribbean ambience.

Everglades & the Keys

American alligator

Everglades & the Keys

THE EVERGLADES AND THE KEYS ARE TWO OF FLORIDA'S GREATEST - attractions. Everglades National Park, dedicated to wildlife, still fits the description of a visiting reporter on the *New Orleans Times-Democrat* over a century ago. He decided that the Everglades were: "…a vast and useless marsh, and such will they remain for all time to come, in all probability." Unlike today's visitors, he did not have the help of national park rangers. The Keys have the feel of the Caribbean, laid-back and surrounded by a glistening cobalt sea. Activities include fishing, diving, and doing nothing; by the time you reach Key West, the sunsets are merely an excuse for another party.

EVERGLADES NATIONAL PARK

This is one park where you cannot drive in one side and out the other: Roads from all three entrances lead to dead ends. In any case, it is impossible to appreciate the subtlety of the landscape through a windshield. Several companies offer guided tours by boat and air-boat, and rent canoes and even bicycles. One of the most satisfying and least expensive ways to visit, however, is on foot, following one of the clearly marked and well-maintained walking trails (see pp. 80–81).

If you are starting from Miami, head south to Florida City and the Ernest F. Coe Visitor Center at the main park entrance. Here the slide shows and exhibition give a rapid insight into the flora, fauna, and diverse habitats within the Everglades. Because dawn and dusk are the best times to view wildlife, it is worth staying overnight in Flamingo, 38 miles farther west. Winter is the peak season for visitors: Undergrowth is less lush, and birds and animals are more visible. Visitors to Shark Valley, 30 miles west of Miami on US 41, can take the two-hour, narrated tram tour. If you are staying on the Gulf Coast, entry to the park is at Everglades City, where you see a different face of the park, best explored by boat or canoe.

THE KEYS

Trickling away from the peninsula of Florida is the 124-mile-long trail of 800 limestone and coral islets known as the Keys, bordered on the ocean side by the only living coral reef

Snowy egret on a pier at Islamorada

★ Tallahassee

Miami

Area of map detail

Dry Tortugas

Dry Tortugas National Park & Fort Jefferson

Marquesas Keys

Key West

Sugarl Key

in the United States. A flavor of romance has long spiced these islands, from the days of the Spanish who called them *los cayos* (islets), later corrupted to "keys," to the legendary pirates and wreckers whose haunts are now holiday resorts.

Starting in Florida City, green roadside signs, known as mile markers, provide a countdown from MM 126 to MM 00 (Mile Zero) in Key West. These are used to pinpoint the location of everything from hotels to wildlife refuges, and dive shops to restaurants.

At the end of the chain, Key West is closer to Havana than Miami, and has always welcomed a motley collection of peoples from the United States, the Caribbean, and Europe. Today, the small town known for its alternative lifestyle also has a wide array of museums. Driving down the Keys along the single lane highway, traffic can be slow. Then suddenly, you are up on one of the 43 bridges, looking across sapphire water to a distant smudge of an island. That's the magic of the Keys. ■

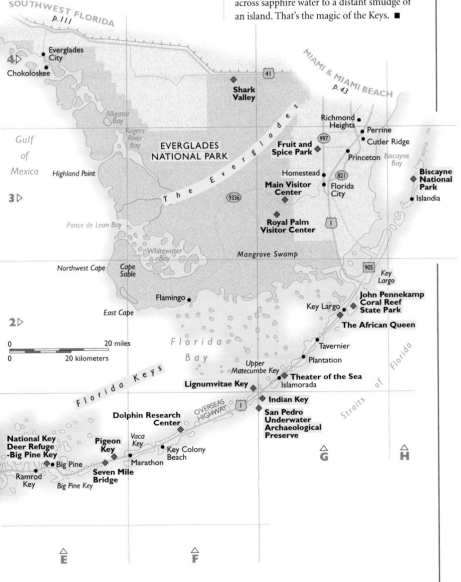

Homestead

NOWHERE ELSE IN THE UNITED STATES CAN BOAST A public park that grows and displays 500 varieties of exotic and tropical fruits, nuts, herbs, vegetables, and spices. As well as the Fruit and Spice Park, Homestead's historic downtown attracts visitors to its restaurants and antique shops.

Just two of the 500 varieties of fruit growing at Redland Fruit and Spice Park

Redland Fruit and Spice Park

🅰 75 G3

✉ 24801 S.W. 187th Ave.

☎ 305/247-5727

🕐 Guided tours Sat. & Sun., 1 & 3 p.m.

💲 $

Located 35 miles southwest of Miami in what the director, Chris Rollins, calls "the most intensive horticultural spot in the United States," **Redland Fruit and Spice Park** was totally redefined after the devastation of Hurricane Andrew in 1992. It is a work in progress. The 35 acres are being redesigned to reflect five warm areas of the world: Asia, Africa, Australia and the Pacific, Tropical America, and the Mediterranean. Instead of the traditional display found in botanic gardens, the park concentrates on showing who grows what, and how they do it. Each area has an arboretum of commercially grown trees, an example of a traditional, single-family farm, and a crop-growing plantation.

Visitors who are unfamiliar with tropical fruits should take one of the daily tours. Walk through a banana grove from the American tropics and see 80 varieties flourishing. Depending on what is in fruit and flower, you might see the ice-cream bean or learn that the gourdlike fruit of the calabash provides bowls and maracas. Some crops are worth more than others. Looking like a watermelon wrapped in an alligator skin, jackfruit is not the beauty queen of the fruit world, but it can sell for $2 per pound, making a well-laden tree worth more than $3,000.

Although the aim is to help private and commercial growers, as well as to show outsiders the vast range of tropical plants around the world, a visit to this park is more than educational. Local residents looking to plant something different take classes on plant propagation, or join one of the cookery demonstrations. Even chefs from Miami's enthusiastic new wave of restaurants turn up to check out what's new on the exotic fruit and vegetable scene. ■

Biscayne National Park

THE CHAIN THAT MAKES UP THE FLORIDA KEYS STARTS not at Key Largo, but here in what is essentially an underwater park. If it hadn't been for effective local protest back in the 1960s, these islands would now be like Miami Beach, built up with hotels, houses, and a major seaport. The bay itself would be scarred by a long causeway and gouged by a 40-foot-deep channel. Luckily, tropical fish still swim freely in the sapphire waters, while the string of 32 coral-reef islands is protected from development.

Colorful fish and beautiful corals are features of the park.

First conserved as a national monument in 1968, the park has been enlarged to cover 284 square miles, embracing the coral reef below the surface as well as the mangroves along the shore. In 1980, it was upgraded to a national park.

The gateway to the park is the visitor center, which opened in 1997. Don't expect to find a beach; the focus of this park is the water. Using a glass-bottom boat, the park rangers provide an insight into the profuse wildlife beneath the waves, pointing out the curious Atlantic bottle-nosed dolphins and shy manatees, the lumbering sea turtles and spotted eagle rays,

which can leap four feet out of the water. They also regale visitors with tales of pirate booty and sunken treasure, and there is a chance to go ashore on Boca Chita Key to see a 65-foot lighthouse. Built as a folly by the Honeywell family, who once owned the island, it is just ornamental and warns no ships. (It is best to visit the key in the winter months when there are few mosquitoes.)

Although there is plenty of room for snorkelers and scuba divers to explore the reef, there are two drawbacks: The only rental facilities are at the visitor center, and it takes about an hour to get out to the reef. ∎

Biscayne National Park

🅰 75 H3

✉ Entrance on N. Canal Dr. & S.W. 328th St., Homestead

☎ 305/230-7275, 305/230-1100 (rentals)

💲 Fees for snorkeling, scuba diving, & glass-bottom boat trips

The Everglades: more than a nature preserve

The Everglades are much more than a wilderness of swamp and saw grass, hammock and mangrove forest, and even more than an important breeding ground for a wide variety of wildlife. They also provide a vital commodity to humans: water.

Natural springs and rivers in the west and center of Florida feed the River of Grass, and today cities, sewage, cattle pastures, and citrus groves all add their detritus to the water as it seeps its way to the Everglades. In the 1950s, an arrow-straight canal, nicknamed the "Kissimmee Ditch," funneled wastewater and floodwater into Lake Okeechobee. The marshy margins of the Kissimmee River dried up, denying wildlife their breeding haunts, and the lake choked on the pollution. A combination of crusading by Marjory Stoneman Douglas and more enlightened water management is now reversing such a misguided scheme.

When rain falls on central Florida, some evaporates, some makes its way into streams and rivers, some stays in the wetlands and lakes, and some filters through the limestone to fill the aquifers, or underground reservoirs. Florida's climate makes water storage in open reservoirs impractical, so the state's burgeoning population relies on subterranean wells drilled into the sponge-like, porous limestone. What was until recently considered to be an inexhaustible source is now under severe pressure. Droughts have reduced availability, and low rainfall comes in the winter months, when vacationers' demand for water is at its highest. As over demand lowers the level of the groundwater, saltwater creeps in, polluting surficial (fresh water) aquifers. All this emphasizes the importance of maintaining the wetlands, which not only help to conserve water, but also act as a natural filter (capable of recycling treated wastewater), a climate stabilizer, and, of course, a fish and wildlife habitat.

Every link in the chain, as a drop of water makes its journey from a cloud high in the Florida sky to the ocean, is vital. Different forms of wildlife rely on different sorts of water, much of which is connected in some way with the Everglades. Rivers, for example, are a playground for animals such as the American river otter. In the impenetrable thickets that dot the saw grass marshes, turtles, frogs, and snakes hide from view, avoiding the ever-hungry American alligators that cruise the shallow waters. Meanwhile, the soggy dampness of branches and bogs supports exotic plants, such as the carnivorous pitcher plant and the fragile orchid.

Swamps of cypress trees, with their characteristic "knees," are home to birds, fish, reptiles, and amphibians. The islands of dry land, where shrubs, clambering vines, and hardwood trees flourish, are known as hammocks. High up in the canopy, these trees shelter birds such as the great horned owl, while box turtles and snakes lie low among the entangled roots.

In the estuaries where freshwater from the land meets the saltwater of the ocean, the briny environment is a fertile breeding ground. Here, the multirooted mangroves form a near impenetrable barrier, protecting the shoreline from tides, currents, and storms. Shellfish and juvenile fish, such as snook, mullet, and sea robins, can grow here, out of reach of predators. Fish that eventually go out to sea, such as the aptly named bonnet-head shark and the southern stingray also breed in among the roots of the mangrove. ■

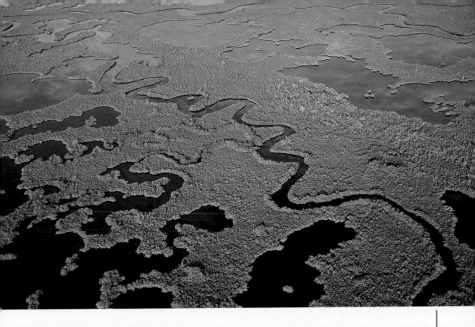

Above: Whitewater Bay, endangered by run-off from encroaching housing developments
Opposite: Environmentalists debate the long-term effects of the popular air boat tours.
Below: The American alligator, a familiar inhabitant of the Everglades

Walks in the Everglades

To appreciate the subtlety of the various ecosystems in the Everglades, walk the well-signed trails. The dry season (December to May) is best for wildlife, as summer heat drives animals into the shade and out of sight.

To follow these walks enter the park via the main entrance near Florida City (*Tel 305/242-7700*), where Fla. 9336 enters the park. The main road then winds for 38 miles through the park with lots of points of interest to stop along the way.

ANHINGA TRAIL

Begin at the Royal Palm Visitor Center, 4 miles from the park entrance
Half a mile; allow 30 minutes
The trail loops through a saw grass marsh, home to some 18 different grasses and flowering plants, as well as alligators and turtles. Easy to spot is the string or swamp lily, whose white flowers hang down in strands. The fruit of the pond apple tree looks like a Granny Smith apple but tastes of turpentine. The small, white clusters on the stalks of pickerelweed could be the eggs of the apple snail, a tasty treat for the endangered snail kite. High above, a great blue heron on top of a tree cools off by fluttering its throat, while in the water, the anhinga stalks its prey. With its body submerged, its head and ten-inch-long neck look like a snake cruising through the water, giving it the nickname "snakebird."

GUMBO LIMBO TRAIL

Begin at the Royal Palm Visitor Center
Half a mile; allow 30 minutes
Named for the tree with reddish bark (also called the tourist tree because it is red and peeling), this trail winds through a dense hammock, or wood. The resinlike gum of the gumbo limbo was used as a glue and as an antiseptic by both the Calusa Indians and the Spaniards. Tales are told of brewing a tea with the leaves, although the flavor of varnish made it a drink only for the desperate.

Other trees here include palms and the tamarind, whose soft bark allows the tree snail, once collected for its colorful shell, to climb up the trunk. Orchids stand out in the dense greenery, which was even more junglelike before Hurricane Andrew swept through in 1992. If you walk into a spider's web, see if the trap's owner is the golden orb weaver, recog-

Anhinga Trail: Wildlife is at its most visible in winter, when the weather is cooler and drier.

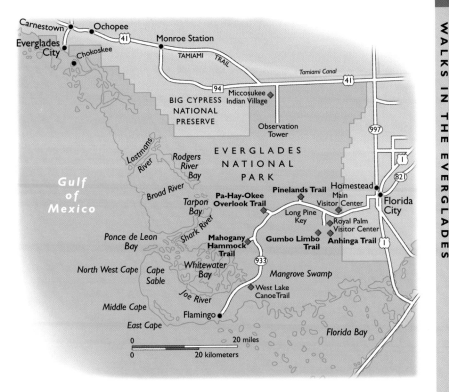

nized by the yellow head plate. The skunk-like smell? That's the white stopper bush.

PINELANDS TRAIL

7 miles from the park entrance
Half a mile; allow 30 minutes
Slash pine trees grow in the higher parts of the Everglades, 3 to 7 feet above sea level. To thrive they need fire to clean out the understory vegetation and fertilize the minimal soil cover. In this climate, plant life recovers quickly, while dead trees provide a rich pecking ground for pileated and red-bellied woodpeckers. The path starts in the open, moving into a thicketlike area and then the pine forest.

Flowers include the perky tickseed and the lusher looking purple blooms of the ruellia. In the summer, listen for the telltale clicking of yellow-and-black lubber grasshoppers mating.

PA-HAY-OKEE OVERLOOK TRAIL

13 miles from the park entrance
Quarter of a mile; allow 15–30 minutes
The shortest walk provides the broadest vista.

Stand on the observation platform and scan the northern horizon: The River of Grass stretches as far as the eye can see. Be careful touching a leaf of saw grass; the edges are razor sharp. The boardwalk leads through a hammock thick with ferns and ephiphytes. Look for huge vultures, smaller red-shouldered hawks, and herons, and listen for piglike snorts: That will be the pig frog!

MAHOGANY HAMMOCK

20 miles from the park entrance
Half a mile; allow 30 minutes
The tiny periphyton that live in the brown ooze below the boardwalk are the first link in the Everglades food chain. Wading birds such as ibises, egrets, and white herons feed on them at dawn and dusk. In the hammock, the play of light and shade through the trees looks almost familiar to those from northern climates—until they see the clamshell, cowhorn, and butterfly orchids, the strangler fig that hugs its host tree to death, and the largest surviving mahogany tree in the United States. ■

The Upper & Middle Keys

Key Largo
🗺 75 G2
Visitor information
✉ 10600 Overseas Hwy.
☎ 305/451-1414

John Pennekamp Coral Reef State Park
✉ Key Largo, MM 102.5
☎ 305/451-1202
💲 $

The African Queen
✉ Key Largo Holiday Inn Resort, Key Largo, MM 100
☎ 305/451-2121 (call for details of tours)
💲 Free; fee for tours ($–$$)

Pigeon Key National Historic District
🗺 75 E1
✉ Access from Pigeon Key Visitor Center, Knight's Island, Marathon, US 1, MM 47
☎ 305/289-0025
🕐 Tours on the hour
💲 $

"It is perfectly simple. All you have to do is build one concrete arch after another, and pretty soon you will find yourself in Key West."
—Henry Flagler, on the building of his Overseas Railway to Key West

THE ISLANDS FROM KEY LARGO TO LONG KEY ARE THE Upper Keys. To enjoy the underwater beauty of John Pennekamp park, just sign up for a snorkel trip. Movie fans should stop in Key Largo, while Pigeon Key in the Middle Keys (Long Key Viaduct to Spanish Harbor Key) is a memorial to those who built the railroad.

John Pennekamp Coral Reef State Park, on Key Largo, begins where its northern neighbor, Biscayne National Park, ends. These two sites, along with the Florida Keys National Marine Sanctuary to the east, help to protect the only living coral reef in the continental United States. Three miles deep and 25 miles long, covering 54,000 acres, Pennekamp was America's first undersea park. Owing to the scientific studies of Dr. Gilbert Voss, supported by journalist John Pennekamp's campaign, the area was protected in 1960. By then tourism was already damaging its fragile beauty, with coral, sponges, seashells, and sea horses scooped up and taken home as souvenirs.

Today, the park has a simple mission: to keep the area much as it was 400 years ago. Boats with engines are banned from certain areas to protect the sea grass meadows; as much as one-fifth of the park has suffered prop scars (furrows caused by propellers) that can take ten years to heal.

The sea grass meadows play a vital role in the balance of the environment as they trap sediment that would otherwise smother the nearby reef. Also, the soft mud is home to worms and crabs, while turtles and manatees browse on the grass itself, as do schools of surgeonfish and parrot fish. Queen conchs and sea stars nibble at the leaves.

The visitor center on Largo Sound has tanks full of tropical fish (with identification placards) and exhibits on the other flora and

Pigeon Key

Today this small island to the north of the modern Seven Mile Bridge is a peaceful spot, where researchers for Mote Marine Laboratory of Sarasota study coral and its potential for bone transplants. Between 1908 and 1912, however, it was a crowded construction camp, home to 400 workers and their families. They built the original Seven Mile Bridge with steam-driven tools and special concrete, impervious to saltwater, shipped all the way from Germany. Since there were no wells, fresh water had to be transported onto the island. The finished bridge was so narrow that passengers looking out of the train windows felt as if they were rolling on air. All they could see below was blue water and tropical fish. Only two buildings remain from that era. A small museum explains the massive project, with photographs, models, diagrams, and old postcards.

Today's traffic whizzes along a bridge built in the 1980s, after an explosion ripped a hole in the original. Nearly 90 years old, the original structure serves as a handy fishing pier and as a dramatic monument to Henry Flagler and the men who turned his vision into reality. ■

fauna, plus boat hire for fishing, scuba, and snorkeling.

The African Queen

Humphrey Bogart will be forever associated with the movie *Key Largo,* although he never filmed on the island. The hotel where he sat out the hurricane with Lauren Bacall and Edward G. Robinson was on a Hollywood set. However, some atmospheric scenes for the 1948 film hit were shot at Rock Harbor, and that was enough of a connection for locals to decide to change the name to Key Largo.

Another piece of Bogart memorabilia floats outside the Holiday Inn Key Largo Resort. Originally named *The Livingstone,* this 30-foot steamboat was built in England in 1912. While chugging along the rivers of East Africa, she was discovered and given a starring role in the 1952 movie, *The African Queen.* The venerable tub returned to transportation duty after filming in the Belgian Congo, but was later shipped to the United States, and was rotting away when hotelier James Hendricks found her in 1982. After careful restoration, he moored her outside his hotel in Key Largo, where she once more enjoys star status, particularly on the hour-long outings. *Thayer IV,* the boat in the movie *On Golden Pond,* is moored nearby. ■

The nine-foot-high "Christ of the Deep" is a popular dive destination in Pennekamp state park.

It is hard to imagine that the quiet, 11-acre Indian Key once had its own town, post office, resort hotel, and bowling alley.

Special parks on the Keys

INDIAN KEY HISTORIC SITE

Indian Key is accessible only by boat. Bought by professional wrecker Jacob Housman in 1831, the island became a busy port, and then, under physician-botanist Dr. Henry Perrine, an experimental farm for tropical plants and

fruits. In 1840, these dissimilar ventures were wiped out by a group of Seminole in a surprise attack. Only Dr. Perrine's plants, which are now growing wild, and a stone building survive above ground, but archaeologists are uncovering traces of a thriving ancient Indian community.

🗺 75 G1 ✉ Access from boat landing Upper Matecumbe Key, US 1, MM 78.5 ☎ 305/664-4815 🕐 Closed Tues.–Wed. Guided walks by reservation only, 9 a.m. & 1 p.m. 💲 $

LIGNUMVITAE KEY

This state botanical site is reached only by boat. In 1919, William J. Matheson, a Miami pharmacist, bought the island as a retreat. His house still stands, with its rainwater cistern and

Unique to the Keys, the toylike Key deer are related to the Virginian white-tailed deer family. Their size results from a restricted diet.

power-producing windmill. But it is the remnant of virgin forest that intrigues botanists: strangler fig, Jamaica dogwood, mastic, and lignumvitae—a tree with super-hard wood for which the island is named.

 75 F2 ✉ Access from the boat landing on Upper Matecumbe Key, US 1, MM 78.5 ☎ 305/664-4815 ⏲ Closed Tues.–Wed. Guided walks by reservation only, 10 a.m. & 2 p.m. 🛇 $

NATIONAL KEY DEER REFUGE
The Key deer stands only 24 to 28 inches tall. Numbering about 300, the Bambi-like creatures mate in the fall, giving birth to tiny fawns in spring. Feeding the deer is strictly prohibited. The ranger knows from day to day where is the best place to see them.

75 E1 ✉ US 1, MM 30.5. Heading south on Big Pine Key, go right at the light (only light); bear left onto Key Deer Blvd. and drive 0.25 mile. The refuge office is on the right, in the Winn Dixie Shopping Plaza, across from Winn Dixie. ☎ 305/872-2239 ⏲ Closed weekends

SAN PEDRO UNDERWATER ARCHAEOLOGICAL PRESERVE
In June 1733 a hurricane struck a convoy of treasure-laden galleons bound from Havana for Spain. The 100-foot *San Pedro* sank in shallow water, making it all too easy for souvenir hunters to strip it bare of Chinese porcelain and gold coins. The bones of the wreck, enhanced with reproduction Spanish cannon, remain a popular destination for scuba divers.

75 G1 ✉ 1 mile south of Indian Key. Access by boat ☎ 305/664-4815 ■

Encounters with dolphins

According to experts, dolphins are the only wild animals that interact with man of their own free will.

There are several programs in the Keys offering humans encounters with dolphins both in and out of the water. The programs teach dolphin biology and communication. Be sure to call ahead for days and times. Among the programs are :

Dolphin Cove Research & Education Center, US 1, MM 101.9, Key Largo, Tel 305/451-4060

Dolphins Plus, US 1, MM 99.5, Key Largo, Tel 305/451-1993

Theater of the Sea, US 1, MM 84, Islamorada, Tel 305/664-2431

Dolphin Research Center, US 1, MM 59, Grassy Key, Marathon, Tel 305/289-1121 ■

A dolphin interacts with a human underwater.

Underwater Florida

The warm waters that surround Florida are a paradise for underwater enthusiasts. Some use scuba equipment for exploration, but millions more use only a snorkel and mask to enjoy the beauty just beneath the waves.

Sad to say that beauty is under constant threat from human pollution in the form of sewage, fertilizers, even fishing lines and trash. In 1990, 2,800 square nautical miles of ocean were set aside for the Florida Keys National Marine Sanctuary. Stretching from Key Largo to the Dry Tortugas, this is the second largest marine sanctuary in the United States.

Running parallel to the Keys is America's only living coral reef, a haven for fish, lobsters, snails, sponges, jellyfish, and sea anemones. What surprises many is that the coral itself is alive, made up of millions of slow-growing polyps, which can be as small as a pinhead or up to a foot across. These combine to form the fantastic shapes of the stony and soft corals, while minute cells, zooxanthellae, give color to the reef.

Viewed through goggles, reefs are like a fantasy landscape: Staghorn, elkhorn, and finger corals form forests of giant branches; star, flower, and brain corals stand out like mountain boulders. Like leaves swaying on a tree, the purple sea fans, green Venus sea fans, and twiggy gorgonia gently wave. But there are nasty surprises lurking, such as the aptly named red fire sponge, which produces a burning sensation if you touch it, the long-spined sea urchin, and various stinging corals that leave the unwary itching and in pain. Coral reefs may look solid, but are easily damaged by an anchor from a boat, a clumsy diver standing on a branch or even by the detritus thrown overboard from a picnic.

Surrounded by the Gulf Stream, as well as the waters of the Gulf of Mexico and the Atlantic Ocean, Florida has as much natural variety underwater as it does on land; and plastic, fish-spotting booklets that can be read underwater are readily available.

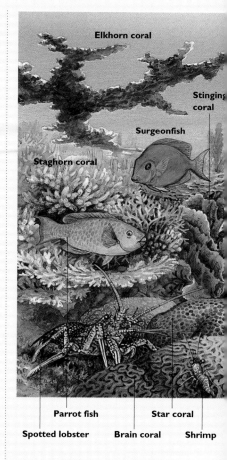

Elkhorn coral

Stinging coral

Surgeonfish

Staghorn coral

Parrot fish   Star coral

Spotted lobster   Brain coral   Shrimp

While sharks are common off the Florida coast, they prefer to avoid humans, as do the alarming, but usually harmless barracuda. Equally shy are the evil-looking but innocuous rays that like to snuggle down and hide in the sand.

On the reef itself, it is difficult to know who is most startled in a face-to-face confrontation between a swimmer and a moray eel. Protruding from the coral like a snake, the moray warns all comers to keep clear by opening wide its tooth-filled jaws. It's a message that's easy to understand.

More attractive are the fish that look like the underwater equivalent of a butterfly. The uninspiringly named butterfly fish flicker in and out of the reef, although it's the angelfish, with its gaudy colors, that is more like the

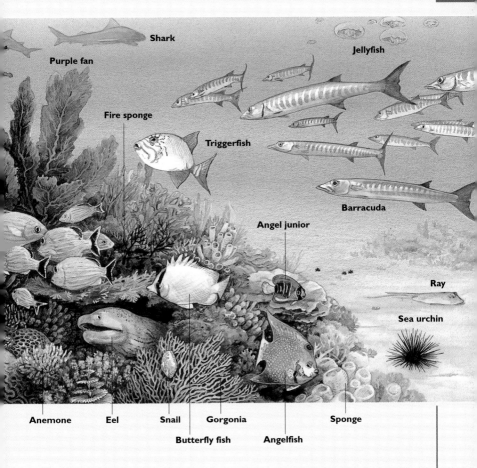

Shark

Jellyfish

Purple fan

Fire sponge

Triggerfish

Barracuda

Angel junior

Ray

Sea urchin

Anemone   Eel   Snail   Gorgonia   Sponge

Butterfly fish   Angelfish

butterfly. There is nothing busier than the parrot fish, with its rainbow plumage and beaklike mouth, used for grazing on the microscopic algae that grow on the coral. This constant nibbling ingests the coral and turns it into sand. Names are intriguing: The grunt actually grunts, surgeonfish conceal a scalpel-like spine near the tail, while the trigger fish has a triggerlike dorsal spine.

Only an expert can begin to explain the curious life of the bluehead wrasse, one of a host of gaudy tropical fish found in the park. This branch of the wrasse family is named for its "supermale" leader; females and lesser males are not only smaller but also a different color. If the tribe loses its leader, another male takes over, growing larger and changing color to blue. If all the males are eaten by predators,

Florida's delicate coral reef is inhabited by a variety of underwater life. Divers and snorkelers can find a tranquil world here, but thoughtless destruction is a problem.

then a female changes sex and takes on attributes of the supermale!

Even the bleak-looking "hardbottom" (bottom of the reef) plays an important role. This sediment-covered limestone is home to soft corals, sponges, shrimp, and crabs. If the hardbottom is not protected, then culinary delicacies, such as the spiny lobster, will vanish. The seemingly harmless activities that cause this destruction include boaters dragging anchors across the ocean floor and divers flipping over rocks on the seabed to see what's underneath. ■

Key West

UNTIL THE RAILROAD ARRIVED IN 1912, KEY WEST WAS accessible only by boat. Once the haunt of pirates and wreckers, its later, legitimate, industries included shipping, sponging, cigarmaking, and shrimping. Today, tourism is the main business. Many visitors do little more than stroll along the pretty streets of the Old Town, with their art galleries and cafés. Do not, however, miss the best collection of small museums in the state: There are shrines to wildlife artist John James Audubon and writer Ernest Hemingway, as well as reminders of Key West's past at the Heritage House, the Mel Fisher Museum, and the Little White House.

At the corner of Whitehead Street and Greene Street is **Audubon House,** where you will see antiques, Audubon prints, relics of 19th-century Key West life, and a botanic garden: There is something for everyone here.

In a small room upstairs, a portrait of artist John James Audubon fixes you with his piercing, observant eyes. While in the Keys to research his monumental work, *The Birds of America* (1827–1838), Audubon stayed with Dr. Strobel, who owned the property next door. Bowled over by the lush garden of what is now known as Audubon House, John Audubon received permission to work among the first exotic plants and flowers introduced to the Keys from Central and South America by the then owner, a roving sea captain named John Geiger.

During his stay, Audubon identified 18 new species of birds for his portfolio. Among the 28 original Audubon engravings on show, the great white heron and roseate spoonbill look more dramatic than the white-crowned pigeons, although the pigeons are perched on the yellow-flowering Geiger Tree, named for the captain.

Key West, the end of the line

The first harbor pilot to be licensed by the state, Geiger surveyed all dangers to shipping—but the cop turned robber, using his knowledge for the Key West hobby of wrecking. His family lived here for 120 years, and the house was saved from demolition in 1958 and transformed into a shrine to Audubon. The handsome European and Asian antique furnishings were purchased as part of the massive restoration of the house. As the first such project in Key West, this also triggered a general drive to conserve the historic district.

On Greene Street, across from Audubon House, is the **Mel Fisher Maritime Heritage Society Museum.** This could be your one chance to lift a solid gold bar. Displayed in a thief-proof case, with a hole just big enough for one hand, the bar weighs 74.5 ounces and is worth around $18,000. Over 200 of them were found off the Keys, aboard the *Santa Margarita* and *Nuestra Señora de Atocha,* two galleons that foundered in 1622.

Underwater treasure hunter Mel Fisher discovered them in 1969 and recovered a 400-million-dollar haul, of which he donated ten-million-dollars worth of treasure to this small but serious museum.

Behind the scenes, archaeologists are still researching valuable finds such as an intriguing gold cup, nicknamed "the poison chalice." "Some guy did not trust his closest friends or family. An insert in the cup actually reacts to arsenic, the favorite poison of the time," says director Dr. Madeleine Burnside. The museum has helped recover other wrecks, including the only surviving 18th-century slave ship, which tours the country.

Among the exhibits in the museum are an outline of the story of Fisher's quest, an explanation of how the Spanish administered the mining of metals and minting of coins in the New World, how the captains navigated the Caribbean and Atlantic, and just how unpleasant life on board a 17th-century sailing ship could be. The star attraction, however, is a 78-carat emerald, worth more than $500,000. Mined in the world's richest deposit of emeralds in Colombia, experts reckon it was probably being smuggled back to Spain, since it does not appear on the ship's manifest.

Much is made of the treasure that was lost during the mighty

Top: Hemingway would be amused to find that the descendants of his cats have become a tourist attraction in their own right. Above: Audubon's roseate spoonbill

A fire-eater entertains the crowd at Mallory Dock.

hurricane of 1622, but 550 passengers and crew also perished. On the lists recording those on board, the teenage page boys are not even named.

One block south, on Caroline Street, is the **Heritage House Museum.** "What a beautiful island it is. I wish it could be a little more isolated, though." So Robert Frost wrote to his friend Jessie Porter, whom he visited in Key West between 1944 and 1960. The poet stayed in the guest cottage in the garden, where he occasionally read his works to his fans.

Her friendship with Robert Frost is just one of many tales told of Key West native "Miss Jessie." A descendant of Commodore Porter, who arrived in the Keys in the mid-1830s to rid the waters of pirates, she knew everyone who was anyone in South Florida. Her 1834 house is crammed with family furniture and possessions. Everything has a story, from the matador costume, a gift from Hemingway's second wife, Pauline, to the shell box made by Dr. Mudd, the physician imprisoned at

Fort Jefferson for treating John Wilkes Booth after the shooting of Abraham Lincoln (see p. 96).

Jessie Porter traveled the world, collecting temple carvings, musical instruments, and an opium chair, but always returned to Key West, where she helped start the restoration of the Old Town.

Go west along Caroline Street and you will see the entrance to a residential community. Tell the guard you're visiting President Truman's **Little White House.** Although Dwight D. Eisenhower worked on his State of the Union address here in 1956 and John F. Kennedy held a summit meeting with British prime minister Harold Macmillan here in 1961, it is Harry S. Truman who will be forever associated with Key West.

In all, nine Presidents have visited the island, but Truman spent the most time here. His first vacation, in November 1946, was on doctor's orders. After leaving a cold, rainy Washington, D.C., he arrived at the United States naval base to find it basking in sunshine, with a temperature of 80°F. Tales of

Heritage House Museum

✉ 410 Caroline St.
☎ 305/296-3573
💲 $

Little White House

✉ 111 Front St.
☎ 305/294-9911
💲 $

his daily routine during 11 working vacations in Key West are told on the guided tour.

He would start early with an invigorating walk and a swim, using what he called "the famous Missouri dog-paddle," and end with a poker session, which made the south porch "smell like a saloon," according to his daughter. In between, he read official papers delivered daily from Washington, conducted meetings, and gave the occasional press conference. In 1947, he dedicated Everglades National Park, then drove the official automobile down to Key West.

In the 1990s, the naval quarters that surrounded the Little White House were sold and converted into a chic development of houses and condominiums, while the building itself has been restored. Although the re-created comforts were typical of a well-off family home in the post-World War II era, they look surprisingly simple today.

Several blocks farther south, still on Whitehead Street and located near the Lighthouse Museum (see p. 92), you will find the **Ernest Hemingway Home and Museum.** This house has been on the vacationer route since 1934, when Hemingway complained in *Esquire* magazine that it was one of "48 things for a tourist to see in Key West."

It is still one of the top attractions in town. Visitor numbers are boosted further each July during the annual Hemingway Days Festival, with readings and a look-alike contest. Guides show you photographs of Hemingway the big game hunter and of Hemingway the fisherman, and the study where he wrote.

Stories are told about the swimming pool, the first in Key West, and the urinal bought from his favorite bar, the original Sloppy Joe's, as a souvenir of his many drinking sessions there. As for the six-toed cats—some claim they are descendants of the Hemingway pets, others say cats only came into his life in Cuba.

Those searching for the romance of his writings may be disappointed; moreover, the comforts of the middle-class surroundings are at odds with the macho legend of Key West's most famous resident (see p. 94). ∎

Ernest Hemingway Home and Museum

✉ 907 Whitehead St.
☎ 305/294-1136
💲 $

"I've a notion to move the capital to Key West and just stay."
—President Harry S. Truman (1949)

The Conch Republic

In Key West, locals celebrate two independence days: July 4 and April 23. The second anniversary dates back to 1982, when zealous customs officials blocked US 1 near Florida City, causing a 20-mile traffic jam as they searched cars for smuggled drugs and illegal immigrants.

Worried about the impact on tourism, the inhabitants of Key West filed suit against the federal government. Virginia A. Panico was among the representatives who came out of Miami's federal courthouse to face a barrage of reporters. At that point, she recalls, they unfurled the flag of the Conch Republic and seceded from the Union.

Border passes, visas, and currency were issued, sticks of Cuban bread were taken up as weapons, and the mayor-turned-prime minister applied to the United States for foreign aid. Eventually the roadblock was dismantled and the Conchs recall their Revolution each April with parades, parties, and mock battles. ∎

The marker at Southernmost Point is a popular photography spot.

Bike ride around Key West

Although small and compact, the Old Town of Key West is bigger than you think, so cycling is the easiest and most efficient way to get around. This tour takes from 40 minutes to one hour, depending on heat, humidity, and leg muscles.

Start on Mallory Square, at the **Chamber of Commerce** (*402 Wall St., Tel 305/294-2587*). Adjacent is the **Historic Memorial Sculpture Garden,** telling the stories of those who made Key West what it is, from Henry Flagler, who brought the railroad, to 19th-century wrecker John Bartlum. Directly behind is **Mallory Dock ❶.** The setting for the daily celebration of the sunset was given a facelift in 1998. Named for Stephen Mallory, customs officer, United States senator, and secretary of the navy in the Confederacy, the enlarged piazza now provides more room for the crowds watching fire-eaters, sword-swallowers, and bagpipe players.

Return to the Chamber of Commerce and ride to Front Street. Turn right, then left almost immediately onto Whitehead Street. You can't get more official looking than the handsome brick-built 1891 **Custom House ❷.** After the sinking of the U.S.S. *Maine* in 1898 triggered the Spanish-American War, the Court of Inquiry sat here. When restoration is completed at the end of 2000, this will be the home of the new Museum of Art and History.

Continue down Whitehead Street, past Audubon House (see pp. 88–89) and the Mel Fisher Maritime Heritage Society Museum (see pp. 89–90). This is "Captains' Row," where the grand houses of ship captains showed off their wealth. On the corner of Caroline Street, Kelly's Restaurant is owned by actress Kelly McGillis. As the sign proclaims, the building housed the first offices of Pan-American Airways. At 321 Whitehead Street, part of the Banyan Resort, is the former **Cosgrove House ❸,** built by 19th-century wrecker, sponger, and Coast Guard veteran Capt. Phillip Cosgrove. His ship was the first to reach the U.S.S. *Maine* as it was sinking in Havana harbor.

Continue down Whitehead Street, where Mile Zero marks the start of US 1 at the intersection with Fleming Street. Number 702 is the **African Methodist Episcopalian Zion Church,** whose congregation was founded in 1865. Opposite the **Ernest Hemingway Home** (see p. 91) is the 1848 lighthouse, now the **Key West Lighthouse Museum ❹** (*938 Whitehead St., Tel 305/294-0012*). The first-order lens of this light was visible 15 miles away. Climb the 88 steps for the superb vista over historic Key West.

Continue on Whitehead Street to **Southernmost Point ❺** (*corner of Whitehead and South Sts.*). The bollard marking the most southerly point in the

Parking is never a problem in Old Town, Key West, when you travel by bicycle.

continental United States is one of the most photographed spots in Key West. From here, Cuba is 90 miles away to the south and Miami 160 miles to the northeast.

Take South Street to Duval Street and turn left. In the 1100 block, note the **Key West Cigar Store,** which recalls one of the major industries of the 19th century, and the **Cuban Club,** founded in 1900. Turn right on Angela Street, climbing Solares Hill, the highest point in town at just 16 feet above sea level. Angela Street becomes Windsor Lane, heading downhill to **Key West Cemetery ❻** (*Angela, Frances, Olivia, and Windsor Sts., Tel 305/292-6718*), in use since 1847. Some tombs are elaborate, with carved angels, others bear eccentric inscriptions, such as "I told you I was Sick." Return part way up Windsor Lane to William Street and turn right. Of the charming

19th-century houses, the most decorative is cigarmaker George Roberts' House (No. 313). William Street ends at Key West Bight, the old port. Newly renovated, **Key West Historic Seaport ❼** sheltered three-masted schooners. Today fishermen meet up for deep-sea fishing, and vacationers set off for day trips to the Dry Tortugas (see p. 96). There are stores, restaurants, and a market selling fresh fish and vegetables. ■

☒ See area map pp. 74–75
▶ Chamber of Commerce
↔ 2 miles
⏱ 40 minutes–1 hour
▶ Key West Historic Seaport

NOT TO BE MISSED
- Mallory Dock
- Key West Lighthouse Museum
- Southernmost Point
- Key West Cemetery

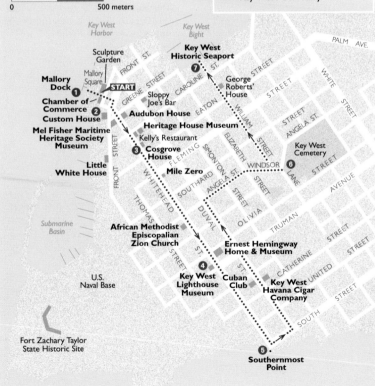

Key West & its authors

Ernest Hemingway (1899–1961) will forever be associated with Key West. Certainly his was the biggest ego, but there are other writers who also found inspiration in the sultry, bohemian town. In fact it was the novelist John Dos Passos (1896–1970) who introduced Hemingway to Key West, calling it the "St. Tropez of the Poor." Hemingway described it as "...the best place I've ever been anytime, anywhere, flowers, tamarind trees, guava trees, coconut palms."

Hemingway was an amateur boxer, as poet Wallace Stevens (1879–1955) found out. When he met Hemingway's sister at a party, Stevens made disparaging remarks about the novelist. Word got back to Hemingway, who met Stevens in the street and knocked him down three times. A well-known piece by Stevens, who spent his winters in Florida, is "The Idea of Order at Key West."

Playwright and novelist Tennessee Williams (1911–1983) also enjoyed what is coyly referred to as a "colorful lifestyle" during two decades in Key West, when it was still "a small time place." He wrote *The Night of the Iguana* and *The Rose Tattoo*, which was later filmed here. When Williams decided that the island had become "a big time place in a small way," he left.

So it is Hemingway, standing 6 feet 2 inches and weighing 225 pounds, who physically and psychologically overshadowed everyone. His boyhood inspiration was Theodore Roosevelt, with whom he shared a love of hunting and braggadocio. Both were clever and athletic, but Hemingway was nagged by self doubt, leading to heavy drinking in his final years. "He wanted to be more than Superman. He wanted to be Superman's older brother," said his brother Leicester after Ernest committed suicide in 1961.

When he arrived in Key West in April 1928, Hemingway settled in to a routine, writing for four or five hours each morning, often standing up. Then he would meet his three new chums who also enjoyed drinking and fishing. The foursome included Charles Thompson, the affluent son of a local businessman; Joe Russell, a part-time smuggler and owner of Sloppy Joe's bar; and Captain Bra Saunders, who ran deep-sea fishing charters. All were competitive game fishermen—indeed, Hemingway set records for trophy-size tuna, sailfish, and marlin.

Soon after his arrival in 1929, his novel *A Farewell to Arms* became a huge success, selling 50,000 copies. The only book Hemingway wrote about Key West is *To Have or Have Not*, all about smuggling between Cuba and the Keys.

In 1931 a rich uncle of Hemingway's wife bought the couple the restored 80-year-old house at 907 Whitehead Street, but in 1936 the marriage was wrecked when the author walked into Sloppy Joe's, saw 28-year-old Martha Gellhorn, and was smitten.

After ten years in Key West, Hemingway left in a huff, accusing locals of freeloading and taking advantage of government handouts after the devastating 1935 hurricane. His reputation for drinking by this time almost dwarfed his ability to write, and he ran a gamut of nicknames from "The Old Brute" to the more gentle "Papa" of his later days. He may be America's most well-known author, but the biggest hero he created was Ernest Hemingway himself.

The Key West literary tradition persists with Pulitzer Prize winners and other well-known authors who spend their winters on the island. Among the nationally acclaimed writers are Richard Wilbur, the former United States poet laureate, noted for his translations of Molière; Phyllis Rose, known for her biographies (*The Year of Reading Proust*); and popular novelists such as James Hall, Robert Stone, Ann Beattie, Annie Dillard (*Pilgrim at Tinker Creek*, Pulitzer Prize 1974), and Alison Lurie (*Foreign Affairs*, Pulitzer Prize 1984). Tom McGuane's book, *Ninety-two in the Shade*, is about fishing off Florida.

Each January, the distinguished Literary Seminars attract heavyweight names from the world of books. The Key West Literary Seminar also runs weekly Writer's Walks. For details call 888/293-9291. ∎

Above: There have been two Sloppy Joe's in Key West. Hemingway happily drank at both.
Below left: Tennessee Williams. Below right: Ernest Hemingway at work.

Built to house 1,500 soldiers and with 450 gun ports, Fort Jefferson never saw military action. It was abandoned in 1874.

Dry Tortugas National Park & Fort Jefferson

THE LARGEST BRICK-BUILT FORT IN THE UNITED STATES, Fort Jefferson has walls 8 feet thick and 50 feet high. Hexagonal and surrounded by a moat half a mile long, this defense against nothing in particular required a massive investment both in time and lives.

One of the United States' least-visited national parks, Dry Tortugas is well worth the hour by seaplane or four hours by boat from Key West, 68 miles to the east. With 250 wrecks, a coral reef, and tropical fish, the waters attract fishermen, snorkelers, and scuba divers. If you enjoy primitive camping you can stay the night, perhaps snorkeling in the moat with a flashlight to spy on sea stars and octopus foraging for food. The fortress stands on Garden Key, but there are six other islands in the group, named for the turtles and the lack of fresh water.

The fort looks enormous even from a distance. Once you are up close, the size is almost overwhelming. Started in 1846, it was obsolete almost as soon as it was completed.

During the Civil War it housed more than 2,000 Union soldiers charged with desertion and other crimes. In 1874 the fort was abandoned to the sooty terns that migrate through here to nest on Bush Key. It became a national park in 1992.

Its most famous prisoner was Samuel Mudd. In 1865, the doctor set the broken leg of John Wilkes Booth, assassinator of Abraham Lincoln. Mudd was convicted of aiding and abetting the assassin, and sentenced to life imprisonment. But when yellow fever rampaged through the fortress, killing the official doctor, Mudd was needed to treat the sick. In 1869, at the age of 36, he was freed by President Andrew Johnson. He was never pardoned. ∎

Dry Tortugas National Park

🏕 74 AI

☎ 305/242-7700

Administered by Everglades National Park, where rangers have a list of licensed air and sea operators that take visitors to the park.

The beaches north of Miami were labeled the Gold Coast, thanks to bullion washed up from wrecked Spanish galleons. Today, the opulence of cities such as Palm Beach makes the nickname equally appropriate.

North of Miami

Fort Lauderdale

A high-rise view of Palm Beach

North of Miami

IF YOU THINK FORT LAUDERDALE IS CROWDED WITH RAUCOUS COLLEGE
students on spring vacation, then you are showing your age. Of all the cities along this
stretch of Atlantic coast, Fort Lauderdale has jumped straight into the millennium.
Thanks to imaginative urban planning, a new riverfront, a new beachfront, numerous
marinas, and a revamped cultural district, this is now a lively, sophisticated year-round
resort. In 1996, a *Money* magazine poll rated it "the best big place to live" in America.

North of Fort Lauderdale is Palm Beach
County, the largest county in the state, boasting
mile upon mile of clean Atlantic beach. In just
20 years, the county's population has doubled
to one million, filling the cities that merge into
one another in a solid strip along the coast.
When it comes to restoration and renewal, all
these communities are learning from one
another. Boca Raton, Delray Beach, and Palm
Beach have all been revitalized to the benefit of
visitors and year-round residents alike.

Boca Raton is an affluent town retaining
many of the easy-on-the-eye Spanish
Revival buildings designed 75 years ago by
architect and developer Addison Mizner. To
appreciate his Mediterranean style, all pink
and pastels, head for Old Town Hall and the
Cloister Inn, part of the luxurious Boca Raton
Resort & Club. Neighboring Delray Beach is
another conservation-minded community,
where echoes of yesterday are louder than you
might expect. Barbara Hutton and Cary Grant
were regular visitors in the good old days

when Delray, rather than West Palm Beach,
was where the polo set came to play and party.

And then there is Palm Beach. Few places
in the world have attracted more wealth than
this long slim barrier island, 12 miles long and
a mere 400 yards wide. To appreciate the city's
affluence, stroll along Worth Avenue, whose
shops rival those of Fifth Avenue; take tea at
The Breakers, one of America's grandest
hotels. On the mainland, West Palm Beach
also reflects the wealth of the area. You can't
miss the imposing Raymond F. Kravis Center
for the Performing Arts, while the more
discreetly designed Norton Museum of Art has
one of the finest collections in the entire state.
Farther inland are the polo fields, where you
can watch international teams play.

Palm Beach County does not rely solely on
tourism for employment; computers and jet
engines are manufactured here. The dense population along the Atlantic shore contrasts with
the emptiness inland, beyond the Florida turnpike. Thousands of acres have been preserved

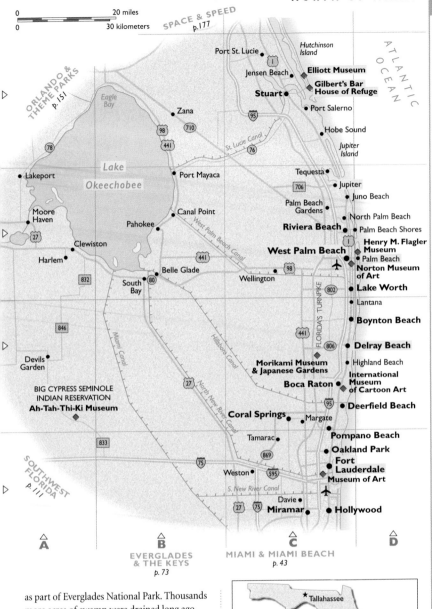

0 ____ 20 miles
0 ____ 30 kilometers

SPACE & SPEED p.177

ORLANDO & THEME PARKS p.151

ATLANTIC OCEAN

Port St. Lucie
Hutchinson Island
Jensen Beach
Elliott Museum
Gilbert's Bar House of Refuge
Stuart
Port Salerno
Zana
Hobe Sound
Jupiter Island

Eagle Bay

Lakeport

Lake Okeechobee

Port Mayaca

Tequesta
Jupiter
Juno Beach
Palm Beach Gardens
North Palm Beach
Riviera Beach
Palm Beach Shores
West Palm Beach
Henry M. Flagler Museum
Palm Beach
Norton Museum of Art
Lake Worth
Lantana
Boynton Beach
Delray Beach
Highland Beach
Morikami Museum & Japanese Gardens
International Museum of Cartoon Art
Boca Raton
Deerfield Beach
Coral Springs
Margate
Pompano Beach
Oakland Park
Fort Lauderdale Museum of Art
Tamarac
Weston
Davie
Miramar
Hollywood

Moore Haven
Clewiston
Harlem
Canal Point
Pahokee
Belle Glade
Wellington
South Bay
Devils Garden

BIG CYPRESS SEMINOLE INDIAN RESERVATION
Ah-Tah-Thi-Ki Museum

SOUTHWEST FLORIDA p.111

A **B** **C** **D**

EVERGLADES & THE KEYS p. 73

MIAMI & MIAMI BEACH p. 43

as part of Everglades National Park. Thousands more acres of swamp were drained long ago and converted into flat, featureless farmland, devoted to growing vegetables. The sugarcane industry still plays a major role in the local economy. Then there is Lake Okeechobee, so vast that locals compare it to an ocean. Some drive out to the eastern perimeter of the lake just to watch the sunset, "because it reminds us of the sun setting into the Pacific." ■

Tallahassee
Miami
Area of map detail

A display of artifacts at the Ah-Tah-Thi-Ki Museum.

Big Cypress Seminole Indian Reservation

Ah-Tah-Thi-Ki Museum

△ 99 A2

✉ Big Cypress Seminole Indian Reservation, 90 minutes W of Fort Lauderdale; exit 14, off I-75

☎ 954/792-0745

🕓 Closed Mon.

💲 $

RECENT YEARS HAVE SEEN A SURGE OF INTEREST IN NATIVE American culture, with museum shows of tribal art and artifacts increasing public awareness of, and respect for, the Indian way of life. Standing on 60 acres of the Big Cypress Seminole Indian Reservation, the Ah-Tah-Thi-Ki Museum is the first comprehensive exhibition of the culture and history of the "unconquered" Seminole Indians in Florida. The 12-million-dollar facility opened in 1997, marking the tribe's 40th anniversary of federal recognition.

Appropriately, the name Ah-Tah-Thi-Ki means "a place to learn, a place to remember," and its five-screen orientation film gives an insight into traditions that few Americans have ever observed.

In the galleries are displays of intricately woven clothes and dioramas of a marriage ceremony and the sacred Green Corn Dance celebration, similar to a harvest festival. Artifacts borrowed from the Smithsonian Institution include baskets woven from local palmetto and sweet grass,

turtleshell rattles, and beaded sashes and bracelets.

You can also meet members of the tribe in the *chickees* (thatched huts) of the living Seminole village, where everyday life in the Everglades of a century ago is demonstrated. Here visitors will see people hollowing out cypress logs to make canoes and making a type of bread from the root of the coontie plant.

A mile-long nature trail runs along a boardwalk through the Big Cypress Swamp. ∎

Fort Lauderdale

FORT LAUDERDALE HAS HAD AN EFFECTIVE AND STYLISH makeover, with a cultural renaissance. Water taxis are the fun and practical form of transport in this "Venice of America," with its 300 miles of canals.

New River runs through the city center and is bordered by the Riverwalk, which links many of the city's cultural attractions. Take a ride on the free Downtown Trolley to familiarize yourself with the main sights (*Tel 954/761-3543*).

Located in the downtown Cultural District, at the points of a geographical triangle, are three museums. One of the best of its kind in Florida is the **Museum of Discovery and Science.** Eight themed areas range from Florida Ecoscapes, with a re-creation of a sinkhole and a walk-through reef, to Gizmo City, where you can program a robot or play virtual volleyball. With an IMAX theater, interactive exhibits, and up-to-the-minute technology, this museum makes learning fun—for adults as well as children.

The modern **Museum of Art** hosts traveling exhibits as well as rotating shows from its three permanent collections: Picasso Ceramics, the Art of the CoBrA (derived from the names of the capitals of the founders' homelands: Denmark, Belgium, and the Netherlands), and works by William J. Glackens.

Halfway between the two is **Old Fort Lauderdale,** a complex of five historic buildings scheduled to open in 2000. You can't miss the restored New River Inn; right on the river, it dates from 1905 and is the new home of the **Fort Lauderdale Historical Society Museum** (*219 S.W. 2nd Ave., Tel 952/463-4431, closed Mon.*), with local history exhibits.

History fans should also visit the riverside **Stranahan House** (*335 S.E. 6th Ave., Tel 954/524-4736, closed Mon.–Tues.*), a restored 1901 family home.

From here, stroll eastward along Las Olas Boulevard, filled with sidewalk cafés, bookstores, specialty shops, and art galleries. ■

Fort Lauderdale
🅰 99 C1
Visitor information
✉ 1850 Eller Dr.,
Suite 303
☎ 954/765-4466

Water taxis
☎ 954/467-6677

Museum of Discovery and Science
✉ 401 S.W. 2nd St.
☎ 954/467-6637
💲 $$–$$$

Museum of Art
✉ 1 E. Las Olas Blvd.
☎ 954/525-5500
🕐 Closed Mon.
💲 $

Cultural attractions such as the Museum of Art are building blocks in Fort Lauderdale's new look.

Boca Raton

Boca Raton

🅰 99 C2

Visitor information

✉ 1800 N. Dixie Hwy.

☎ 561/395-4433

International Museum of Cartoon Art

✉ 201 Plaza Real

☎ 561/391-2200

🕐 Closed Mon.

💲 $

Boca Raton Museum of Art

✉ 801 Palmetto Park Rd.

☎ 561/392-2500

💲 $

Spiderman image at the International Museum of Cartoon Art

ALTHOUGH ARCHITECT ADDISON MIZNER'S PLANS FOR Boca Raton were halted by the Depression, many of his buildings survive in a community more oriented to homes than to hotels. In 1991, the city gained a focal point with the classy shopping village, Mizner Park, home of a unique cartoon museum.

There are few museums where visitors chuckle and even laugh out loud, but good humor is the main feature of this modern gallery housing the **International Museum of Cartoon Art.**

Every aspect of the genre is covered, from hard-hitting editorial comment to gags where the punch line is as important as the artwork. The displays include newspaper strips, magazine cartoons, and comic books. There is even a section where you can draw your own cartoon.

Originally cartoon artwork was thrown away, so Mort Walker, of Beetle Bailey fame, decided to save his own, began collecting the work of fellow mirthmakers, and finally opened his first museum in New England more than 20 years ago. In 1993, it relocated to Boca Raton. With more than 160,000 pieces of artwork, it is the largest collection of cartoon art in the world.

The Hall of Fame highlights the influence of early artists such as Thomas Nast (1840–1902), the creator of the Republicans' elephant, the Democrats' donkey, and Uncle Sam.

In a few years' time, there will be another museum at Mizner Park. **Boca Raton Museum of Art's** plans for a new home will enable more of its collection to be shown. Until then, the main draw in the small museum is the Mayers Collection of late 19th- and early 20th-century art, featuring works by Picasso, Matisse, and Braque, as well as American artists such as Bellows and Prendergast.

Balancing the cultural offerings of the town is the undeveloped beach reached via two parks, **Spanish River Park** and **Red Reef Park.** Both are well-equipped with picnic areas and walks, as well as access to the beach.

Located in Red Reef Park, next to the Intracoastal Waterway, is the **Gumbo Limbo Nature Center** (*Tel 561/338-1473*), a 27-acre nature reserve. Take the boardwalk through the tropical hammock and mangroves, climb the 40-foot-high observation tower for views of the ocean and the town, then watch loggerhead turtles swimming and diving in their tank. The center runs an extensive program of guided walks and offers turtle watches during nesting season. ∎

Delray Beach

RESIDENTS OF DELRAY LEAVE THE HIGH LIFE TO MIAMI and Palm Beach, opting for the low-key atmosphere of this attractive and affluent town. The hub of activity is Atlantic Avenue, the main east–west road leading to the sea. Here is the restored historic district and shops. But there is a surprise inland from the ocean: an enclave of Japanese culture in what was once farmland.

Many Florida yards are ablaze with exotic flowers, but at the **Morikami Museum & Japanese Gardens** (*4000 Morikami Park Rd., Tel 561/495-0233, closed Mon., $*) the motto could be "less is more."

The only museum of its kind in the United States began in 1904 as a memorial garden, dedicated to the Japanese immigrants who founded the Yamato Colony. The story of the community is told in the **Yamato-ken Museum.** To enter this copy of a 19th-century Japanese villa, you must take off your shoes.

Inside, photographs before and after the arrival of the pioneers show how they gave up sandals for lace-up shoes, and kimonos for suits. By the 1920s, only George Sukeji Morikami remained. In 1974, as a memorial to the efforts of his fellow pioneers, Morikami left 200 acres of land to the state. Three years later, the Japanese-style garden, complete with bonsai and antique stone carvings from Japan, opened to the public. To get the best out of the gardens follow the nature trails, but take it slowly. Stop, sit on a bench, and appreciate the subtle harmony of the Japanese style.

Heading east from Morikami Gardens you'll find the **Old School Square Cultural Center,** where several former school buildings now house museums. Among them, the **Cornell Museum of History and Art** (*51 N. Swinton Ave., Tel 561/243-7922, closed Mon.*) has traveling exhibitions; a new children's museum is expected to open after 2000.

Water sport enthusiasts will not be disappointed at **Delray Beach.** The beaches are popular for outdoor recreation; ramps make it easy to launch boats; and divers can explore the wreck of the S.S. *Inchulua* a few hundred yards offshore. ■

Delray Beach
is a popular
destination for
water sport
enthusiasts.

Delray Beach
⚠ 99 C2
Visitor information
✉ 64A S.E. 5th Ave.
☎ 561/278-0424

Palm Beach

Palm Beach
- 🅰 99 D3

Visitor information
- ✉ 45 Cocoanut Row
- ☎ 561/655-3282

Henry Morrison Flagler Museum
- ✉ 1 Whitehall Way
- ☎ 561/655-2833
- 🕐 Closed Mon.
- 💲 $

NOWHERE ELSE IN FLORIDA IS THE FLAGLER EFFECT SO obvious. The railroad magnate attracted the rich and famous to his hotels a century ago, and they are still coming. High real estate prices and the continuing presence of scions of society maintain Palm Beach's exclusivity. Worth Avenue's fabulously expensive shops and boutiques cater to the wealthy, but window shopping is free. Although a Rolls-Royce seems essential for residents of the mansions on Ocean Boulevard, you'll find it easy to get around on foot.

However, you might like to take a city tour for an overview of the area. For information about tours contact Palm Beach Convention & Visitor Bureau (*Tel 561/471-3995*).

An absolute must-see for visitors to Palm Beach is Whitehall, once Henry Flagler's home and now his memorial, the **Henry Morrison Flagler Museum.** The mansion was a four-million-dollar wedding gift from Henry Flagler to his wife.

He was 71 and Mary Lily Kenan only 34 when they married 1901. He needed a hostess; she came from a well-to-do North Carolina family and enjoyed entertaining. But what sounds like a marriage of convenience was really a love match.

Until Flagler's death in 1913, they spent each winter here, hosting afternoon teas, dinners, and grand balls. Entering through the ornate gate (part of the 900-foot-long, wrought-iron fence), guests were welcomed into the **Marble Hall,** spacious enough to hold a regulation basketball court, with room to spare. What looks like a fresco is actually canvas, seamed together and glued in place; the marble flooring was sent over from Italy in numbered sections.

With more than 70 rooms, including 22 bathrooms, Whitehall was designed by architects John Carrère and Thomas Hastings. Furnishings, chosen by the decorators, came from Europe.

Touring the house gives an insight into this railroad magnate, with family portraits in the **Italian Renaissance Library.** The **Music Room** next door was Mrs. Flagler's territory. The **Swiss Billiard Room** was a masculine retreat, like the library, so Flagler insisted that cuspidors (spittoons) be installed.

Standing in the white, gold, and mirrored **Ballroom,** you can imagine the 1903 Bal Poudré, "one of the most sumptuous social affairs ever attempted south of Washington," according to newspaper reports. Note the pineapple motif, a traditional symbol of hospitality, and perhaps a reminder to Flagler of the investment he made in a pineapple plantation that failed. He could afford it: He was worth 100 million dollars at a time when he paid the men on his railroad $1.50 per day (see pp. 106–107).

Whitehall was sold in 1925 and served as a hotel until 1959. Rescued by Henry Flagler's granddaughter, it was renovated and reopened as a museum.

From Whitehall, it is just a few blocks' walk north to the **Hibel Museum of Art** (*150 Royal Poinciana Plaza, Tel 561/833-6870, closed Mon.*). In this delightful museum, changing exhibits from a collection of 2,000 of Edna Hibel's works reflect her range. Born in Boston in 1917, she now lives and works in Palm Beach.

From here, you can walk over to the Gothic Revival **Bethseda-by-the-Sea Episcopal Church** (*141 S. County Rd., Tel 561/655-4554*), which has a cloistered courtyard and a magnificent blue stained-glass window. The Cluett Memorial Gardens outside invite quiet contemplation.

To complete the Palm Beach experience, you must stop by

The Breakers (*1 S. County Rd., Tel 561/655-6611*). It stands on the site chosen by Henry Flagler for his second hotel in Palm Beach. Two earlier wooden structures burned down. This enormous 1936 Italian Renaissance hotel overlooking the Atlantic Ocean is an attraction in its own right. Regular guided tours are led by the local historian; call the hotel for information. ■

What Fifth Avenue is to New York, Worth Avenue is to Palm Beach. Below left and right: Mary and Henry Flagler and Whitehall, their grandiose vacation home

Flagler & the railroad

In Florida, a town, county, college, and roads are all named for Henry Morrison Flagler (1830–1913), who left school with an eighth-grade education but nevertheless made a fortune in oil and railroads. By constructing a railroad from the Georgia border to Key West, Flagler not only opened up the east coast, but also built hotels and helped found cities such as Palm Beach and Miami—foundation stones in the tourism industry in Florida.

The hero of this rags-to-riches story was a New England clergyman's son who left home at the age of 14 to find a job. First, he worked in a general store in Ohio, then went into partnership with John Davison Rockefeller. Together they founded the Standard Oil Company in 1870. Known as the best partner Rockefeller ever had, Flagler employed dubious business methods that triggered the 1890 Sherman Anti-Trust Act.

By then, however, Flagler was well on his way in his second career: tourism. His first experience of Florida was a trip to Jacksonville, not for a vacation, but because his wife was in poor health. After her death, he remarried and in 1884 returned to the south.

Although Flagler enjoyed the little town of St. Augustine, there were two drawbacks: It lacked luxury hotels and the railroad link from Jacksonville could not accommodate his private car. Flagler's entrepreneurial instincts sensed an opportunity, and by 1888, his modern railroad was pushing south from Jacksonville to St. Augustine. Here, he built the Spanish Renaissance Hotel Ponce de León Alcazar, now the Lightner Museum. Determined to upgrade the small town into the new "American Riviera," he also built a hospital, city hall, and churches.

Flagler's forerunner of the package tour meant that vacationers not only traveled south on his railroad but also stayed in his resort hotels. As he drove his tracks along the east coast, he bought and refurbished a hotel on Ormond Beach (near Daytona) and then

developed Palm Beach. When the Royal Poinciana opened in 1894 it was the biggest hotel in the world, with 540 rooms. Yet demand still outstripped supply, so he increased the size to take 1,750 guests. Its sister establishment, The Palm Beach Inn, was so popular that it, too, expanded. (Rebuilt after a fire, it was renamed The Breakers in 1901, see p. 105.) In 1896 came Miami and the Royal Palm Hotel.

Above: Henry Flagler (1830–1913)
Left: The Orange Blossom Special (1940s):
Most visitors to Florida traveled by train
until the era of inexpensive airplane travel.
Far left: Flagler's trains brought guests
right to the door of the Royal Poinciana
Hotel, Palm Beach, in 1896.

In 1901, when Flagler's second wife developed paranoia, the 71-year-old mogul manipulated Florida's lawmakers and, in a mere eight days, divorced her and married 34-year-old Mary Lily Kenan. For her, he built a mansion called Whitehall in Palm Beach (see p. 104-105). Retirement was not part of the vocabulary of this businessman, and at the age of 75 he took up his biggest challenge, extending his Florida East Coast Railroad to Key West. The project took 400,000 men seven years, building 42 bridges and laying 156 miles of track.

On January 22, 1912, a year before he died, Flagler arrived in Key West aboard a train. "The railroad that went to sea" had cost 35 million dollars and 1,000 lives. It was the final component in an empire that encompassed 11 hotels and more than 2 million acres of land, about the size of Rhode Island and Delaware combined.

Sadly Henry Flagler did not live to see the completion of the Casa Marina Hotel in Key West, which survives as Marriott's Casa Marina. ∎

West Palm Beach & beyond

The use of innovative street sculpture, such as these stylized palm trees at West Palm Beach, is a feature of many Florida cities.

DIVIDED FROM PALM BEACH BY THE INTRACOASTAL Waterway, West Palm Beach is most associated with the wide range of sports found here, especially polo, golf, and tennis. By contrast, there is also a cultural explosion, epitomized by the world-class collection of art at the Norton.

Since the founding of the United States, European painting and sculpture had always been considered the apogee of culture, with American art coming in second best. The **Norton Museum of Art,** founded in 1941, helped to change that perception.

The museum trebled in size in 1997, enabling more of its 4,500 works of art to be shown. Among the significant new works acquired from 1996 to 1997 is David Hollowell's vast tribute to the pointillists, called "La Galleria."

There are three primary areas in the museum, covering the art of the United States, Europe, and China.

Popular because of its local connection is Thomas Moran's "Florida Scene" (1878). The English-born illustrator, on assignment for *Scribner's Monthly* magazine, painted Fort George, at the mouth of the St. Johns River. Another notable work is

Georgia O'Keeffe's "Red Flower" (1918–19), the first time the artist filled the canvas with a flower, a style that became her signature. Edward Hopper, known for the mysterious women in his pictures, creates his familiar brooding atmosphere in "August in the City" (1945).

Many paintings have a tale to tell. For example, Stuart Davis's "New York Mural" (1932), painted to get employment at the new Rockefeller Center in New York City, is full of political symbols and social references. The Empire State Building was known as Smith's Folly, and the brown derby was the trademark of Al Smith, the governor of New York who ran for President in 1928. The bananas refer to his campaign song, "Yes! We Have No Bananas." Rockefeller Center was not amused, but Radio City Music Hall commissioned a mural.

West Palm Beach

🗺 99 C3

Visitor information

✉ 1555 Palm Beach Lakes Blvd., Suite 204

☎ 561/471-3995

Norton Museum of Art

✉ 1451 S. Olive Ave.

☎ 561/832-5196

🕐 Closed Mon. May–Dec.

💲 $

Purchased in 1971, "Night Mist" (1945) by Jackson Pollock is a transitional piece painted before the abstract impressionist began splashing paint from the can. Pollock was still using a brush, but squirted color directly from the tube. As Diana McClintock writes in the catalog, Pollock was "on the verge of a breakthrough which forever changed the course of twentieth-century art."

Among the significant European masterpieces, look for Claude Monet's "Gardens at Bordighera" (1884), one of five scenes of the exotic grounds on the Italian Riviera—the inspiration for his gardens in Giverny, France.

Don't miss the Chinese Collection, among the finest Asian displays in the United States.

About half a mile away is the **Ann Norton Sculpture Garden** (*253 Barcelona Rd., Tel 561/832-5328, closed Sun.–Mon.*), named for the second wife of Ralph Norton. This two-story house was her home and studio; known as a sculptor, her outsize works in brick and granite are in the lovely garden.

Some 3 miles to the south is the **South Florida Science Museum** (*4801 Dreher Trail N.,*

Tel 561/832-1988, $$). Especially popular with children, there are interactive displays on light, color, and weather. The tornado display is excellent. Planetarium shows happen most days.

Twenty miles west of town is **Lion Country Safari** (*Southern Blvd. W., Loxahatchee, Tel 561/793-1084*). Opened in 1968, this was the first "cageless zoo" in the United States. With 23 species and a total of 500 animals, you are sure to see lions, zebras, giraffes, and more wandering in some 250 acres. It takes about an hour to follow the 4-mile-long drive; keep car windows shut and watch out for the mischievous chimps who clamber over vehicles.

Around 15 miles south of here is the northern entrance to the **Arthur R. Marshall Loxahatchee National Wildlife Refuge** (*10216 Lee Rd., off US 441, Boynton Beach, Tel 561/734-8303*). Its 147,368 acres are all that remain of the northern Everglades. To understand the five different habitats here, stop at the visitor center, then follow one of the self-guided trails, ranging from under half a mile to 12 miles. Canoes may be rented outside the refuge. ■

"The Agony in the Garden" (1889) by Paul Gauguin, at the Norton Museum of Art

"We were not partial to paintings of any one painter, or paintings of any special type, or any particular period. Our aim was to select pictures which gave us aesthetic satisfaction." —Ralph Norton, on his and his wife's taste in art

Lake Okeechobee is a magnet for bass fishermen. The name means "Big Water."

More places to visit north of Miami

ELLIOTT MUSEUM
This small gallery is dedicated to 19th-century father-and-son inventors, Sterling and Harmon Elliott. Of their 230 patents, the most impressive are for Sterling's Quadricycle (1886), which solved the problem of keeping all four wheels on the road during sharp turns, and Harmon's Addresserette, a revolutionary addressing machine. There is also a huge collection of baseball memorabilia, including a ball signed by Babe Ruth.
✉ 99 C4 ✉ 825 N.E. Ocean Blvd., Hutchinson Island, Stuart ☎ 561/225-1961

GILBERT'S BAR HOUSE OF REFUGE
Back in 1875, when boats provided Florida's main means of transportation, the keeper's job was to search for shipwrecks, pick up survivors and give them shelter in the House of Refuge. This is one of only ten built along Florida's east coast—the lookout tower was added during World War II to survey the seas for German submarines. The refuge was renovated in 1998.
✉ 99 C4 ✉ 301 S.E. MacArthur Blvd., Hutchinson Island, Stuart ☎ 561/225-1875

"THE LAST GALLEON"
Since 1995, divers have found cannonballs, Ming dynasty china, and coins; all, they hope, from a shipwreck. The search is on to find "The Last Galleon"—one of several Spanish ships that foundered on Juno Beach. Visit the small headquarters and see some of the discoveries.
✉ 99 C3 ✉ 759 Parkway St., Jupiter ☎ 561/747-7700 🕐 By appointment only

LAKE OKEECHOBEE
This shallow, 700-square-mile lake is the second biggest freshwater lake inside the United States. It looks calm and friendly, a vast reservoir that provides water for both agricultural irrigation and municipal needs. However, Okeechobee hit the national headlines on September 17, 1928. The day before, a hurricane had swept through Palm Beach at 5 p.m. and continued inland. There was little or no warning for the farming community as the wind, moving at 130 mph, piled up the water until it crashed through the dike like a tidal wave. Between 1,800 and 3,000 locals were drowned and 15,000 families lost their homes. A 110-mile primitive trail encircles the lake.
✉ 99 B3 ☎ 941/763-3959 ∎

A couple of decades ago, Southwest Florida was still sleepy, with few tall buildings and comparatively little development. Now towns like Naples and Fort Myers are booming, putting the fragile environment under pressure.

Southwest Florida

Gulf Coast seashells

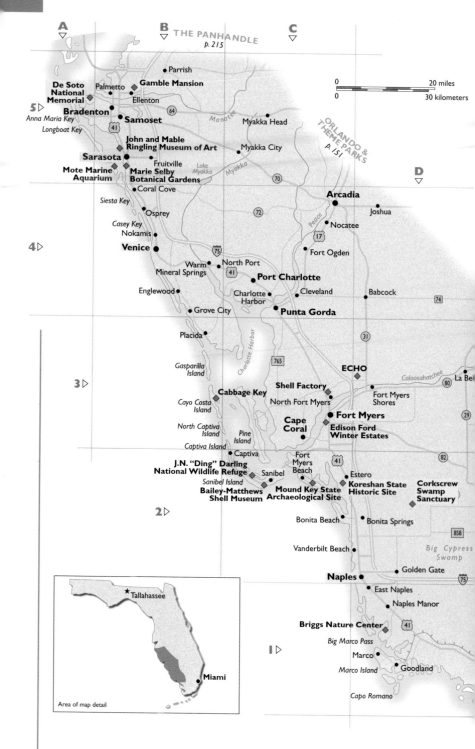

A

THE PANHANDLE
p. 215
B

C

• Parrish

De Soto
National
Memorial
• Palmetto
◆ Gamble Mansion

Bradenton
• Ellenton

64

Anna Maria Key
• Samoset

Longboat Key
41

5▷

◆ John and Mable
Ringling Museum of Art
• Myakka Head

• Myakka City

ORLANDO &
THEME PARKS
p. 151

Sarasota
Lake
Myakka
Myakka

D

Mote Marine
Aquarium
• Fruitville
Marie Selby
Botanical Gardens
• Coral Cove

Arcadia

• Joshua

Siesta Key

72

Peace

• Nocatee

Casey Key
• Osprey

17

Nokamis

75

• Fort Ogden

4▷
Venice

Warm
• North Port
41

Mineral Springs

Port Charlotte

• Cleveland
• Babcock

Englewood •

Charlotte
Harbor
70

74

• Grove City

Punta Gorda

Placida •

31

Charlotte Harbor

765

ECHO
Caloosahatchee
La Be

3▷

Gasparilla
Island

Cabbage Key
Shell Factory
North Fort Myers
Fort Myers
Shores
80

Cayo Costa
Island

Fort Myers

29

North Captiva
Island

Cape
Coral
Edison Ford
Winter Estates

Pine
Island

Captiva Island
• Captiva

82

J.N. "Ding" Darling
National Wildlife Refuge
• Sanibel
41

Fort
Myers
Beach

• Estero

Sanibel Island
Koreshan State
Historic Site

Corkscrew
Swamp
Sanctuary

Bailey-Matthews
Shell Museum
Mound Key State
Archaeological Site

2▷
• Bonita Beach
• Bonita Springs

858

• Vanderbilt Beach

Big Cypress
Swamp

Naples
• Golden Gate

75

• East Naples

• Naples Manor

Briggs Nature Center ◆

41

1▷

Big Marco Pass

• Marco

Marco Island
• Goodland

Capo Romano

0   20 miles
0   30 kilometers

★ Tallahassee

• Miami

Area of map detail

Southwest Florida

THE PACE OF LIFE HAS ALWAYS BEEN SLOW IN SOUTHWEST FLORIDA. Activities were rarely more strenuous than a walk on the beach before breakfast or sipping a cocktail as the sun sank into the Gulf of Mexico. In between there was golf or fishing, little more. As the next pages show, all that has changed. Start in Naples and move north along the coast to Fort Myers, and on to Sarasota.

Naples has long had a reputation for subdued sophistication, thanks to wealthy visitors who value their privacy. Today, the town boasts sidewalk dining and elegant shopping as well as an impressive arts center. It also claims to have the highest number of golf courses per capita in the world. For nature lovers, Naples is a base for excursions into the Everglades as well as smaller conservation areas such as Big Cypress National Preserve and Corkscrew Swamp. Farther north, Fort Myers is synonymous with Thomas Edison, whose winter home and workshop are open to the public. Many of the towering royal palms that he planted at the end of the last century still grace McGregor Boulevard. Some visitors head for two offshore islands, Sanibel and Captiva, linked by causeway to the mainland. Their beaches, covered with shells of all shapes and colors, attract both amateur and professional collectors. The best shells, however, are on the uninhabited islands that can only be reached by boat.

Sarasota, the most obviously urbane city of them all, owes its present charm to a wealthy and dynamic individual: John Ringling of circus fame. He and his wife not only endowed Sarasota with a grand mansion and an equally impressive collection of paintings, they also contributed to the beautification of the city itself. Although the Ringlings' legacy is the jewel in Sarasota's cultural crown, the city has plenty to offer, including a vigorous live theater scene sparked by the drama program at Florida State University. ■

The beaches of Southwest Florida attract shell seekers as well as water sport enthusiasts.

E ▽

nmokalee

NORTH OF MIAMI p. 91

㉙

• Sunniland

ALLIGATOR ALLEY
(EVERGLADES PARKWAY)

F ▽

㉙

BIG CYPRESS
NATIONAL PRESERVE

• Jerome

Ochopee   Monroe   **Oasis
Station   Visitor
Center**

Paolita

TAMIAMI TRAIL

**Shark
Valley**

EVERGLADES & THE KEYS
p. 73

Naples

NAPLES, FAMOUS FOR ITS PHOTOGENIC PIER, ALSO HAS fine, sandy beaches. Old Naples, the downtown area, retains the spirit of a village, while the "Phil," the grand, new Philharmonic Center for the Arts, hosts everything from Broadway shows to the Miami City Ballet. This urban growth is in stark contrast to the plentiful wildlife nearby.

The historic downtown area of **Old Naples** is a pleasant place to stroll, visit interesting shops and galleries, or stop for a light lunch.

Heading east along Fifth Avenue South to Gulf Shore Boulevard, either go about half a mile south to **Naples Pier** (*12th Ave. S.*) or go 1.5 miles to the north for **Lowdermilk Park,** where visitors can picnic, play games, or enjoy the excellent beach.

West of the park is **Caribbean Gardens,** a 52-acre zoological and botanical garden founded in 1919, and featuring many rare plant and animal species. There are guided catamaran tours that negotiate waterways and islands. **Safari Canyon** is an exciting live animal and multimedia presentation.

Adjacent to Caribbean Gardens is the **Naples Nature Center**, the headquarters for the Conservancy of Southwest Florida and a classic example of a private group working to preserve Florida's natural heritage.

In the center's **Museum of Natural History,** its "Florida: Coast to Coast" exhibition explains the importance of water in the state, highlighting the relationship between marine life and the wetlands. Having seen the displays, you should sign up to see the real thing on a naturalist-led walk or boat tour through the mangroves. A special, hi-tech video monitoring system allows you to watch animals in the **Wildlife Rehabilitation Center,** rather like a hospital for injured animals and birds.

South of Naples in Rookery Bay, the **Briggs Nature Center** is a must if you are a birdwatcher. Here, visitors spot residents such as eastern towhees and migrants such as the shiny cowbird. A boardwalk leads to an overlook where a telescope stands ready to focus on herons, ospreys, and, occasionally, eagles. From December through April, there are boat tours with a naturalist, and canoe tours. ∎

Ochopee's claim to fame

The smallest post office in the U.S.

Seemingly in the middle of nowhere, cars pull off US 41 (Tamiami Trail) and stop in front of a small, white hut. The Stars and Stripes waves proudly above this post office, which has room for only two customers and the mail person, behind her counter. Serving a community of just more than a hundred, it survives on sales of postcards (with stamps, of course).

In the 1950s, the post office staff newsletter decided to find America's smallest post office and, although Diehlstadt, Mississippi (100 square feet), and Farnhurst, Delaware (105 square feet), claimed the title, *Postal News* announced that the former toolshed in Ochopee, measuring a mere 60 square feet, was easily the smallest of all. ∎

Big Cypress National Preserve

In Big Cypress National Preserve cypress trees are thought to "breathe" through their "knees," drawing in carbon dioxide and exhaling oxygen.

IN 1922, HENRY FORD DECIDED TO BUY BIG CYPRESS SWAMP and donate it to the state. His plan fell through, but in 1974 the swamp, the ancestral home of the Seminole and the Miccosukee Indians, was given official protection by Congress. Despite the name, the trees here are not the big bald cypress, but the dwarf-pond variety. They cover about a third of the 729,000 acres. The rest is a mixture of mangroves, hammocks (woods), and saw grass that shelters abundant wildlife.

Big Cypress plays the role of buffer between the ever eager developers and the precious Everglades to the south. When Congress set aside the land, occupants were allowed to stay on, so oil prospectors and ranchers continue their work, and some hunting and fishing is allowed.

To get a feel of this wilderness area, take County Rd. 94 from Monroe Station to 40-Mile Bend. It is a rough, dusty route with no habitation along the way. Bolder folk, with skins thick enough to withstand the insects, hike through here on the **Florida National Scenic Trail** (see p. 23). Their reward is sightings of wood storks, white ibises, egrets, and woodpeckers. The fabled Florida panther is rumored to live among the slash pines and hardwood hammocks. ■

Big Cypress National Preserve
🏕 113 E1
✉ Oasis Visitor Center, 45 miles E of Naples on US 41 (Tamiami Trail)
☎ 941/695-4111
💲 $

Corkscrew Swamp Sanctuary

TUCKED AWAY FROM THE BUSY GULF BEACHES, THE world's largest stand of 500-year-old bald cypress trees is at the heart of this 11,000-acre wilderness refuge.

From time to time, Corkscrew is also home to the United States' largest colony of wood storks. A 2.5-mile boardwalk, complete with shelters and benches, wanders over wet prairie and **Lettuce Lake,** through bromeliad-laden pines and bald and pond cypresses.

The bald cypress, a deciduous conifer, drops its needles in winter—hence the name. Valuable to the lumber trade for its tough, rot-resistant wood, this tree has been one of the most exploited of Florida's natural resources. Under threat at the start of the 20th century, these survivors are magnificent, with girths of 25 feet and reaching 130 feet tall.

The white wood stork, the only stork to nest in the United States, is an endangered species. With no feathers on its dark head, it, too, looks bald. It breeds at Corkscrew during the winter, building nests high in the bald cypresses or mangroves, away from the raccoons. After the mating ritual, the female lays three to four eggs. Between them, the parents and chicks devour about 440 pounds of fish, tadpole, and crayfish during mating and rearing. Nine weeks after birth, the fledgling stork has grown enough to leave the nest. In 1996, 1,400 were born at Corkscrew.

Outside the visitor center, a board carries field notes on what is currently in bloom, as well as what wildlife to look for, and where. The sanctuary manager recommends you should arrive between 8 a.m. and noon, and you will need to protect yourself against the mosquitoes. As well as taking a good pair of binoculars, it is important to stop and listen. In the fall, for example, Yellow-throated Kentucky and Hooded warblers add their distinctive, high-pitched songs to the squawks of year-round inhabitants. Don't miss the living machine, the ecologically advanced wastewater treatment system north of the visitor center. ∎

Corkscrew Swamp Sanctuary
- 112 D2
- 375 Sanctuary Rd., Naples (20 miles from downtown Naples)
- 941/348-9151
- $

**Above:
Boardwalks at Corkscrew Swamp Sanctuary allow close and clear views of the wilderness, minimizing the impact of tourism on the environment.
Left: Little blue herons often feed close to the boardwalk.**

Koreshan State Historic Site

In 1894, Dr. Cyrus Teed arrived here on the banks of the Estero River, with more than 200 followers from Chicago. They put their money and energy into creating a "New Jerusalem," an ideal Christian society.

This was a communal fellowship; to earn credits at the society's store, members worked in the saw mill, bakery, and citrus groves.

You can go into a dozen of the buildings that still stand on this 156-acre site. Planetary Court is still impressive, with its wraparound second-story balcony and unusual staircase. Inside, the handsome Eastlake-style bedroom furniture proves that members still liked their creature comforts.

Take time to look at the map outlining Teed's vision of a city measuring 6 square miles, with homes for eight to ten million inhabitants. The large globe provides a three-dimensional statement of his belief in "cellular cosmogony." Teed believed that the planets, stars, and moon existed inside a hollow planet earth. ■

🅰 112 C2　✉ US 41, Estero
☎ 941/992-0311　💲 $

An original building at Koreshan State Historic Site

Hurricanes & tornadoes

"When it comes to hurricanes, Florida is the most active spot in the Northern Hemisphere," according to a spokesman for the National Hurricane Center in Miami, "and Southwest Florida is the most vulnerable."

Even William Shakespeare had heard about the terrifying storms in the New World. In *King Lear,* the demented ruler exhorts the winds to blow and "you cataracts and hurricanoes, spout till you have drench'd our steeples, drown'd the cocks." Cyclones, hurricanes, typhoons: Call them what you will, these areas of low atmospheric pressure are a frightening reminder of the power of nature.

Named for the huracan, or evil spirit in the Taino Indian language, hurricanes are born on the eastern side of the Atlantic Ocean, off the coast of Africa, between June and October. As they grow and move, their wrath frequently targets Florida. The core of what is often compared to a doughnut shape is the calm eye of the storm. Around it, bands of strong winds, rain, and cloud rotate in a storm that travels at more than 75 mph, and can reach speeds in excess of 150 mph, whipping up tidal waves, blowing down buildings and trees, and flooding the land.

Hurricanes are intertwined with the history of the state. On a personal level, they are the timetable by which southern Floridians date events in their lives (in northern Florida the "Great Freezes" serve the same purpose). The Keys were ravaged in 1919, while the center of Florida from Tarpon Springs to St. Augustine was wrecked in 1920. Miami suffered in 1926, but one of the most infamous storms appeared in September 1928, claiming 1,800 to 3,000 lives when the earthen dike surrounding Lake Okeechobee collapsed (see p. 110). As historian Frederick Lewis Allen pointed out in.*Only Yesterday* (1931), the glib real estate agents' promises of "soothing tropical wind" were less attractive when those zephyrs got a running start from the Caribbean.

In 1935 the Labor Day Hurricane hit the Keys with winds clocked at 150 mph. It destroyed 16 miles of roadbed and whipped up tidal waves, which killed more than 400 World War I veterans working to replace the railroad bridges with a road link. Ernest Hemingway, living at Key West at the time, went out on his boat *Pilar* to search for survivors and found only casualties. In a rampaging article entitled "Who killed the Vets?" he wrote, "You see them everywhere, and in the sun all of them were beginning to be too big for their blue jeans and jackets that they could never fill when they were on the bum and hungry."

The Spanish recorded storms according to the saint's day on which the hurricane arrived. In the early 1950s, the weather forecasters issued nicknames in alphabetical order, originally female, to identify each of about a dozen hurricanes that would brew up every year. Hurricane Donna in 1960, Cleo in 1964, and Betsy in 1965 again claimed dozens of lives. More recently, in 1992, Hurricane Andrew devastated a huge area of southern Florida and is considered the biggest natural disaster in United States history, responsible for 30 billion dollars of damage. In 1995, Hurricane Opal swerved unpredictably and hammered the beaches around Pensacola. In 1998 Hurricane George caused flooding, but no lives were lost.

Tornadoes are often considered less terrifying than hurricanes, yet the 20 or so that are expected in Florida each year still cause considerable, if localized, damage. The most ferocious twisters tend to occur during February and March in the Panhandle region. Elsewhere they hurtle along from the southwest to the northeast between April and June, carving a long, narrow path, little more than 400 yards wide, but often 15 miles long. The damage is caused by the counterclockwise, vacuum cleaner effect, which sucks up anything in its path. Weather forecasters issue a tornado watch when storms are predicted for an area; a tornado warning is issued only when a twister has been seen. ∎

Top: From space, the eye of Hurricane Florence (1994) is clearly visible in the center of the spiraling clouds.
Bottom: The funnel of a tornado consists of condensed water droplets and dust.

Fort Myers

Fort Myers

🅰 112 C3

Visitor information

✉ P.O. Box 9332

☎ 941/332-7600

Edison and Ford Winter Estates

✉ 2350 McGregor Blvd.

☎ 941/334-3614

💲 $$

Launch tours

☎ 941/334-7419

MOST VISITORS COME TO TOWN TO TOUR THE HOME OF Thomas Edison. Legend has it that when the inventor offered to illuminate the city streets with his new-fangled electricity, he was told the lights would keep the cows awake. A more lasting legacy includes avenues of palm trees, which explains the nickname the City of Palms.

In recent years, the city has rediscovered two of its greatest assets, the historic district and the Caloosahatchee River. The upgraded Southwest Florida International Airport has made the area easier to get to and so has helped tourism to flourish. There are several attractions, including the **Fort Myers Historical Museum** (*230 Peck St., Tel 941/332-5955*), where you will see exhibits of Calusa and Seminole artifacts as well as a railcar, the *Esperanza*, that you can walk through. The **Calusa Nature Center and Planetarium** (*3450 Ortiz Ave., Tel 941/275-3435*) has boardwalk trails, and snake and alligator demonstrations. The planetarium is always popular with its laser and star shows.

Possibly the biggest attractions here are the **Edison and Ford Winter Estates.** From 1885 until his death in 1931, Thomas Edison spent his winters on the banks of the Caloosahatchee River.

Thomas A. Edison (1847–1931)

No single American has matched the creativity of Thomas Edison. The inventor registered more than 1,000 patents, including 75 in 1882 alone.

Born in Milan, Ohio, he was labeled "addled" by an elementary school teacher, who no doubt heard tales of his experiments, such

Thomas Edison, aged 81, poses beside the first phonograph.

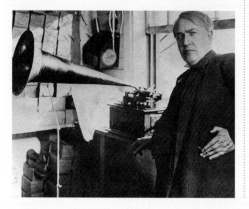

as sitting on chicken eggs to make them hatch. Later, working as a telegraph operator, he rigged up a clock mechanism to send signals automatically, as well as a rat paralyser to kill the office rodents.

Edison not only developed his own ideas, he also improved those of others, including the telephone of Alexander Graham Bell. A shrewd businessman, he perfected a workable light bulb, then a meter to charge customers for the electricity they used. His Edison General Electric Company, founded in 1890, employed more than 7,000 people.

Although the press dubbed him "The Wizard," Edison never pretended that inventing was easy. "Genius is one percent inspiration and ninety-nine percent perspiration" is one of his best known sayings. ■

The 14-acre estate, now bisected by McGregor Boulevard, has a laboratory and museum on one side, and two homes on the other. One house belonged to Edison, the other was bought by his younger friend, Henry Ford, in 1916.

The museum showcases the immensity of Edison's creativity and you can see inventions galore in the four galleries. For example, when he dreamed up the electronic voting machine in 1869, the United States Congress turned it down, prompting the 22-year-old Edison to declare he would "never again invent anything that nobody wanted." The $40,000 he made from inventing the stock market ticker-tape machine in 1871 freed him to become a full-time inventor.

Ideas that developed into standard office equipment range from the "electric pen" (that led to the mimeograph), to the Voicewriter of the 1880s, the grandfather of the modern dictaphone.

"Of all my inventions I like the phonograph best," admitted Edison, who was virtually stone deaf. The line-up here ranges from the tiny GEM version for $7.50 to a grand $6,000 model. A large phonograph is scarred with Edison's teeth marks on the side. Because "sound is just a series of vibrations," he listened to music by biting into the wood, allowing vibrations to pass through his teeth and jaw into the ear.

Standing outside the visitor center, a banyan tree, measuring 400 feet in circumference and covering half an acre, was a gift from another inventive Fort Myers neighbor, tire mogul Harvey Firestone, in 1925.

In 1928, Firestone and Ford financed a laboratory to find a rubber-producing plant that would grow in the United States, breaking the Dutch and British monopoly. Aged 80, Edison was no botanist, but he tested 17,000 plants before deciding that goldenrod was the most efficient source. The antithesis of a modern research lab, the Rubber Laboratory is more like a barn, filled with work counters, sinks, and endless drawers of seed packets.

Tours are offered throughout the day, and you can also take a ride on the Caloosahatchee River in a copy of Edison's electric launch. ∎

Thomas Edison's laboratory, where the inventor's workshop team included a machinist and a glassblower to make bottles, flasks, and test tubes on site

"I would like to live about three hundred years. I think I have ideas enough to keep me busy that long."
—Thomas A. Edison

Around Fort Myers

IN THE AREA SURROUNDING FORT MYERS, YOU WILL FIND the communities of North Fort Myers, Cape Coral, and, to the south, Fort Myers Beach on Estero Island. The marina on Estero Island is the place to find cruises and fishing trips. There are several excursions visitors can take with Fort Myers as a base.

However, North Fort Myers is the home of the **Shell Factory,** a huge storehouse of shells from Florida and around the world. Visitors can wander and look but will probably be tempted to buy something. As well as shells, there are gifts and other goods.

A visit to **ECHO,** a few miles east, is an interesting and unusual outing. "What vegetables will grow in the hot, humid tropics?" "Does mulching make sense in semi-arid areas?" "How can I keep baboons out of the garden?" Finding answers to questions such as these is the mission of the Christian-based Educational Concerns for Hunger Organization, founded in 1981 and dedicated to fighting world hunger.

Instead of displaying the luxuriant tropical foliage and flowers typical of most Florida gardens, this 21-acre farm shows how to grow crops using tin cans, coconut husks, old pipes, and a couple of seed packets.

Take the farm tour and you will be inspired by experiments in this practical outdoor laboratory that prove that plants can be grown almost anywhere: in rocky ground, infertile soil, and wet as well as arid climates.

All it takes is a little creativity and some space; even a rooftop will do. A couple of old tires recycled as plant containers hold herbs grown as a cash crop, as well as vegetables for a household. In a nearby cage are rabbits, which provide both meat and manure.

Larger spaces can provide food for a small community. In the greenhouse, which reproduces the heat and humidity of a tropical rain forest, fish swim in pools surrounded by passion fruit and bananas, pineapples and papayas, beans and root crops. The gourds are a variety whose waxy coating protects them from insects and makes them safe to store. Enough food is produced on one-third of an acre to feed 20 families.

Technology is simple and inexpensive. Buckets and tubing are

Consider relaxing on Fort Myers Beach before exploring the area.

recycled as a "drip system" for irrigation. An old bicycle is converted into a "motor" to pump water up from a cistern. New ideas are constantly being tested by the scientists, the horticulturists, and the trainees, who later take these practical solutions to the developing world. Seeds from a bank of 450 varieties are also sent out to 140 countries worldwide, with valuable feedback logging the successes and analyzing the failures. To inspire American gardeners, there is also an Edible Landscape Nursery.

Described as one of the most important archaeological finds in North America, **Mound Key State Archaeological Site** has no museum, no parking lot, and no food franchise. It is on Mound Key, a tiny island near Fort Myers Beach. The only way to visit and understand the site is to go on a tour with one of two charterboat services. When the Spanish landed in the southern half of the Florida peninsula, they encountered the Calusa, an ancient tribe now extinct. This "brave and skillful

people" demanded tribute from others in the region, which could be food, animal skins, ornamental feathers, or Spanish captives. According to contemporary Spanish reports, the Calusa appear to have had a complex social system as well as elaborate religious rituals.

Maps and memoirs point to Mound Key as Calos, the capital of the Calusa empire. If so, then it could also be the site of San Anton de Carlos, a Jesuit mission where attempts to convert the indigenous people were unsuccessful.

Excavations in the shell mounds the Calusa left behind show that their diet was dominated by fish and seafood. They had sophisticated ways of catching fish: fine nets and tidal traps. Visitors can see the water court, a specially built harbor for Calusa canoes, a 32-foot-high shell mound, as well as shards of pottery lying on the ground. (Collecting any artifacts is strictly forbidden.) Archaeologists have also excavated invaluable carved wooden animals, drawings, and elaborate masks, all preserved in the peat. ■

Tours to Mound Key State Archaeological Site:
Calusa Coast Outfitters
✉ Fort Myers Beach
☎ 941/463-3600
Estero Bay Boat Tours
✉ Bonita Springs
☎ 941/992-2200

Cabbage Key Inn
✉ Pine Island Sound, Channel Marker 60
☎ 941/283-2278

Cabbage Key

At the peak of her fame in 1938, mystery writer Mary Roberts Rinehart (1876–1958) built herself a retreat on this tiny island. Later, her home became the Cabbage Key Inn, with simple lodging and a bar that was a meeting point for commercial fishermen. To make sure they were bankrolled for a beer on their return, they pinned a signed dollar bill to the wall. Now visitors copy the fishermen, papering the walls with thousands of autographed, dated greenbacks.

Accessible only by boat, the islet reverts to solitude once the daytime vacationers leave and recovers the ambience that attracted singer/songwriter Jimmy "Margaritaville" Buffett, who supposedly wrote a hit tune here: "Cheeseburger in Paradise." ■

Yachts at anchor outside Cabbage Key Inn

Sanibel

SANIBEL GIVES ITS NAME TO THE SANIBEL STOOP, THE hunched-over position adopted by shell hunters as they shuffle along the beach. To identify their hauls, they head for the island's shell museum. To see wildlife, they could get up early to visit the "Ding" Darling National Wildlife Refuge, or rent a boat to explore the barrier islands to the north.

If you plan to travel by road to Sanibel, you should be aware that there is a toll to pay on the causeway (currently $3). While sun worshipers and shell hunters flock to the sandy beaches on Sanibel's Gulf shore, bird lovers head for the other side of this 12-mile-long barrier island. Along Pine Island Sound is the 6,000-acre **J.N. "Ding" Darling National Wildlife Refuge,** dedicated in 1978 to "Ding" Darling, who wintered on neighboring Captiva Island. Darling was awarded the Pulitzer Prize in 1923 and again in 1942 for his political cartoons, and also won the plaudits of conservationists for his campaigns to protect wildlife.

Established in 1945, this safe haven provides a home to nearly 300 species of birds, 50 types of reptile, and some 30 mammals. Follow the 5-mile, one-way Wildlife Drive starting from the visitor center and looping through the refuge. From fall to spring look for Yellow-throated warblers and white pelicans; in spring and summer, the black-whiskered vireo. More

commonly seen varieties include red-shouldered hawks, often sitting on a dead tree trunk by the road, and the endangered wood stork. Only the eagle-eyed will be able to pick out the shy mangrove cuckoo.

One of the finest sights in Florida is the shell-pink roseate spoonbills feeding in the morning and evening. Hike out along **Indigo Trail** to see them at Cross Dike, or rent a canoe to paddle into the mangrove swamps. Check with the rangers at the new Center for Education to see which species are "at home" in the refuge.

All ages, from the smallest child to veteran collectors, will spend hours scanning the sands for shells. These delicately colored bits of calcium carbonate are impossible to resist. Since 1995, the **Bailey-Matthews Shell Museum** has satisfied even the most frustrated shell seekers, who can at least see what they may not be able to find. Among the thousands of shells from around the world on display, one of the most coveted of all is the Junonia. This rare variety is four

"Ding" Darling's original "Duck Stamp"

Duck stamp

Jay Norwood Darling, who signed his cartoons "Ding," was a keen hunter and fisherman. Appointed by President Franklin D. Roosevelt to run the U. S. Biological Survey (later the U. S. Fish and Wildlife Service), he introduced a

hunters' license known as the "Duck Stamp" in 1934. This has since raised more than 500 million dollars toward purchasing 4.5 million acres of U.S. wetlands.

Darling designed the first stamp; today, an art competition decides the picture on each year's stamp. ∎

inches long, with regular brown dots along its spiral shape. By contrast, the tree snail shells appear ordinary, until you learn that there are 57 different color forms, from almost pure white to the gaudily striped. Of the 25,000 types, the liguus is becoming scarcer through loss of its hardwood-hammock home, where it lives on smooth-barked trees such as the gumbo limbo.

Other exhibits show the artistic and religious uses of shells. From the Solomon Islands comes a "money ring," like a large bracelet, cut from a giant clam. In Europe the scallop of St. James was worn as a badge by pilgrims, while Korean craftsmen shaped more than 6,000 pieces of abalone shell into the birds, leaves, and fruit that decorate an antique Korean box. ■

Although visitors to Sanibel Island collect shells by the bucket, the supply is replenished by the currents and tides of the Gulf of Mexico.

Shells

With some 3,000 kinds of shells, Florida is a paradise for conchologists and shell collectors, and not for nothing is the southwest coast known as the Shell Coast. Beaches here are encrusted with shells that are swept round the Gulf of Mexico and deposited along the shore.

The art of shell collection, is renowned on and around Sanibel, just off Fort Myers, where competitive enthusiasts go off by themselves to uninhabited islands. They study the tide tables and, eager to be first on the beach, go out before dawn, wearing lamps on their heads like miners. Just as stamp collectors search for rarities, so shell collectors are always on the lookout for hard-to-find helmets, bonnets, and tuns. A specialty of Sanibel is the elongated, delicately spotted Junonia, which vies with the finely banded (striped) tulip for elegance. The prize for "Most Abundant Bivalve" (or mollusk) could go to to the half-inch-long coquina clam. At times, whole swaths of sand seem to be blanketed with their shells, tiny, pastel-colored, and shimmering in the sunshine.

Shells were so abundant in Florida that the Spanish explorers were dazzled by

Pallid janthina

Crown conch

Common fig shell

Shark's eye

Coquina clams

Florida horse conch

them. The explorers who first saw Islamorada, one of the Florida Keys, gave it its name, which means "purple island," because of its profusion of purple janthinas or sea snails.

The delicate angel wings are bright and white and grow in the muddy mangroves. More unusual is the lightning whelk, a univalve that defies tradition by being "left-handed"—spiraling to the left instead of the right. Small children prefer collecting smaller varieties such as the slipper shell, or the equally descriptive Florida cones, which look just like a miniature ice-cream cone. Although they look harmless, these inch-long mollusks harpoon small fish using a special tooth and deadly poison.

Even smaller are marginellas, which come in pretty shades of pink. Also common on the Gulf Coast is the olive, with its smooth, mottled exterior. The sharp points of vases, spindle shells, and spiraling wentletraps are easily broken, so the trick is to find undamaged specimens. Favorite finds are the deep, shiny brown cowries and the classic pilgrim's logo, the scallop. Whether plain white or the garish yellow-orange of the lion's paw scallop, they are gathered by the thousand, ending up in

every bathroom in the land as a reminder of seaside vacations.

Largest, and perhaps most evocative, is the conch. Romantics say you can hear the sound of the surf when you hold it against your ear; in fact, it is only the echo of your own pulsing blood. In 1969 the orange-pink Florida horse conch was chosen as the state shell. Growing up to two feet long, it dwarfs conch cousins such as the Florida fighting conch, often seen on beaches, and the crown conch, with its brown-and-white plaid pattern, which cling to mangroves. Overfishing has depleted the population of the fleshy conch, which has long been a popular ingredient for chowders.

Collectors scorn the squat, ugly shell of the oyster, also prized for its contents— Apalachicola produces one in five of the nation's gourmet oysters. Only archaeologists value the tough carapace of the oyster. When excavated from centuries-old Calusa Indian middens, these shells provide clues to Florida's past. ∎

Junonia

Florida horse conch

Angel wings

Lion's paw scallop

Sarasota

Sarasota

🅰 112 B5

Visitor information

✉ 655 N. Tamiami Trail

☎ 941/957-1877

WITH HIS WIFE, MABLE, SHOWMAN, BUSINESSMAN, AND ART lover John Ringling helped to make Sarasota the sophisticated city it is today. When they donated their winter estate to Florida, the state and its visitors benefited from a magnificent mansion and an art gallery filled with fine works. Sarasota also offers excellent shopping, fine restaurants, and a superb beach.

"… To the State of Florida, I give, devise and bequeath my art museum and residence at Sarasota, Florida… together with all paintings, pictures, works of art, tapestries, antiques, [and] sculptures…"
—John Ringling (1936)

When the Ringlings were in residence at Cà d'Zan, they had the 61-foot tower illuminated at night.

Cà d'Zan, a 31-room Italian palazzo idyllically set on Sarasota Bay, may mean "John's House" in Venetian dialect, but this "house" cost 1.5 million dollars when built between 1924 and 1926. With its lavish detail and superb craftsmanship, it is hard to imagine that this was merely a vacation home, built for fun and parties.

With its 200-foot-long terrace, the west facade on the water is the part that most evokes Venice. Mable Ringling would saunter down the broad, marble steps to her Venetian gondola, and John always had his 125-foot steam yacht, *Zalophus,* standing by to chug across the bay.

Florida's acerbic salt air has done Cà d'Zan few favors: An ongoing restoration program is repairing the fine, decorative terra-cotta tile work made at Crum Lynne in Pennsylvania, and only the guesthouse roof still has the 16th-century tiles brought over from Barcelona.

The heart of the house is the vast living room, overlooked by an elegant gallery. No expense was spared, from its black-and-white

marble floor to its coffered ceiling. The glittering chandelier once graced New York's old Waldorf-Astoria Hotel, and the Aeolian Organ, which is still in working order, can be played manually or electrically, while tapestries neatly hide its 4,000 pipes. Hanging in the reception area near the entrance are portraits of the Ringlings, while more reminders of them are in the French Empire-style master suite on the second floor. In the marble bathroom, an empty barber's chair, complete with a fresh towel, seemingly awaits the master of the house.

The **art museum** is in an Italian Renaissance villa, built to house 30 years of tasteful investment in art. Mable lived just long enough to see its completion in 1929. As this is now also Florida's official state art museum, the original bequest of 625 paintings has been expanded to more than 1,000.

Ringling, who owned the largest private collection of Peter Paul Rubens in the world, commissioned a special gallery to show off his beloved Rubens cartoons. These oil paintings, originally used as templates for tapestries, were commissioned in 1625 by the Archduchess Isabella of Spain. Ringling bought four of the cartoons in the series known as

John & Mable Ringling Museum of Art (the Ringling complex)
✉ 5401 Bay Shore Rd.
☎ 941/359-5700
$ $$ (art museum free on Sat.)

Some of the 91 columns in the art museum's courtyard date back to the 11th century.

Like a Venetian palace, Cà d'Zan overlooks the water.

"The Triumph of the Eucharist." A fifth, "The Triumph of Divine Love," was purchased in 1980. Full of brilliant colors, dramatic movement, and biblical symbolism, they are typical of Rubens's grandiose work.

This is the only gallery with a permanent display—the other 21 have rotating exhibits. Watch for two more paintings by Rubens,

"The Departure of Lot and His Family from Sodom" and the "Portrait of the Archduke Ferdinand," as well as works by Flemish masters Anthony van Dyck and Lucas Cranach the Elder. One of the most impressive Northern European masterpieces is the portrait of Pieter Jacobsz Olycan by Frans Hals. This is a searching

John Ringling

John Ringling (1866–1936) is one of the least recognized of America's "culture barons." He was the business brains of the circus that his brothers set up in 1884. Ringling took time out to visit museums and galleries in Europe, and, in the meantime, his investments in oil wells, railroads, and real estate made him wealthy.

Mable Burton—whom he married in 1905—shared his love of the arts. In 1912 the Ringlings bought a house on Sarasota Bay, and over the years helped to develop the community. A causeway was built to the barrier islands, and the elegant St. Armand's Circle shopping area was developed. To boost the city's flagging economy in 1927, Ringling moved the circus winter headquarters to Sarasota.

The Ringlings wanted a gallery both to showcase their collection and to serve as a memorial to their cultural contribution to Florida. By the time they built the museum in the 1920s, they had amassed a collection of more than 600 paintings, plus tapestries and sculptures. ∎

examination of the craggy Dutch burgher, whose powerful personality leaps off the canvas.

As well as paintings from the baroque period, there are antiquities from Cyprus, and in **Galleries 19 and 20** two complete gilded and paneled rooms. When John Jacob Astor's New York mansion was demolished in the 1920s, Ringling was swift to bid for the Louis XIV-style oak-paneled dining room and the sumptuous Louis XV-style mirrored reception room.

In the **West Galleries,** added in 1966, are works by 20th-century American artists such as Frank Stella and Jack Beal. The villa's **courtyard** doubles as an outdoor exhibit space, with copies of famous Italian statues, fountains, and blooming bougainvillea. Even the columns of the loggias are antiques, some more than 900 years old.

"The Cocoon from which The Greatest Show on Earth Emerges in Its Might and Splendor Each Spring." That is how Sarasota is described in a Ringling Bros. and Barnum & Bailey program on display in what was once the Ringlings' private garage. The **Ringling Museum of the American Circus** opened in 1948 to keep alive "the memory of the man who made Sarasota famous."

The animated miniature circus, a model, shows the layout of a typical circus camp, from the canvas waterproofing department and lumber-seasoning shed to the giraffe house. As well as costumes and posters, the museum has a photo archive. Although visitors admire the craftsmanship of the circus carriages, as well as the Two Jesters Calliope and even Tom Thumb's walking stick, the disappointment is that the museum lacks the fun, noise, and smell of the circus.

The **Asolo Theater** was added to the Ringling complex in 1957. With its 300 seats, the horseshoe-shape 19th-century interior once filled the hall of a castle in Asolo, Italy. Dismantled in 1930 and put into storage, the tiers of boxes, with their gold ornamentation, were eventually reassembled in Florida. No longer open to the general public on a regular basis, the pretty theater is still used for movies and lectures.

Confusingly, the Asolo Center for the Performing Arts and the F.S.U./Asolo Conservatory are across US 41 (the Tamiami Trail) on the campus of Florida State University.

Bellm Cars and Music of Yesteryear is nearly opposite the John and Mable Ringling Museum of Art. This interesting collection has an unusual display of vehicles, ranging from a Rolls-Royce to a DeLorean to a Volkswagen bus. There are thought to be over 2,000 musical instruments here, including hurdy-gurdies and radios. You can end the tour by playing old arcade games.

The Barlow Miniature Circus (1948–1959), part of the Ringling Museum of the American Circus

Bellm Cars and Music of Yesteryear
✉ 5500 N. Tamiami Trail
☎ 941/355-6228
$ $$ (guided tours only for the music collection)

The botanical gardens display orchids for the public to enjoy.

gardening writer Duane Campbell described as "a supernova in the constellation of botanical gardens."

Covering 9 acres, the gardens are divided into 20 distinct areas that are home to 20,000 plants, gathered on 100 scientific expeditions to tropical rain forests around the world. Although the collection ranges from cacti to cycads, the Selby Gardens are best known for their epiphytes, air plants with no roots in the ground. Many grow on trees, yet they are not parasites since the tree provides support, rather than nutrients. One of the most common in Florida is Spanish moss, which does not come from Spain and is not a moss; it is a member of the pineapple family.

There are bromeliads and ferns, but the most exotic of all are the orchids, some 6,000 of them. There are hundreds of varieties in the **Tropical Display House,** with thousands more behind the scenes, waiting until their blooms are ready for their moment in the limelight. Large and showy is the *Cattleya,* the favorite corsage for high school proms. More delicate is the *Paphiopedilum delenatii,* a lady's slipper orchid from Vietnam whose exquisite flower is mainly white, tinged with purple.

Since opening to the public in 1975, the gardens have established an international reputation for research. As well as the **Orchid and Bromeliad Identification Centers,** it hosts international symposia and maintains a store of 73,000 dried plants.

On a local level, the Shoreline Restoration Project demonstrates that environmentally friendly measures can also be attractive. Here, a lagoon filters pollutants from rainwater runoff, while native plants, such as marsh grasses and mangrove trees, prevent beach erosion.

To the south are the **Marie Selby Botanical Gardens.** The wife of an oil magnate, Marie Selby (1885–1971) was a thoroughly modern woman, the first to drive coast-to-coast by car, a competitive sailor, a fine horseback rider, and a passionate gardener. When neighbors built condominiums in the early 1950s, she blocked them out by planting bamboos that shot up to a height of 50 feet. Her legacy, her home and seven acres of landscaped gardens, is now what

Marie Selby Botanical Gardens

✉ 811 S. Palm Ave.
☎ 941/366-5731
$ $$

Across Sarasota Bay, on the northern end of Lido Key at **Mote Marine Aquarium,** you will find the answer to this question: How many people do you think die of shark attacks each year around the world? The answer is between eight and twelve, far less than the number killed each year by elephants, bees, crocodiles, or lightning.

That is just one of the fascinating facts you learn at this combination of aquarium and research center. Founded in 1955, Mote is one of only two privately funded marine research laboratories in the United States. Here, 50 scientists work on projects ranging from fish farming to recycling wastewater. The aquarium has a world-leading Center for Shark Research; as sharks are resistant to cancer, they have become important in cancer research.

Not surprisingly, the fun of seeing barracuda, sharks, dolphins, and manatees is balanced by ecological messages such as the "Marine Debris Biodegradation Time Line," which charts man's effect on the environment.

An expansion program to improve facilities is also giving the public more insight into scientific experiments, such as the lifecycle of loggerhead turtles, which come ashore to nest on Florida beaches (see p. 189). New in 1997 were the two-hour boat tours through Sarasota and Roberts Bays (*Sarasota Bay Explorers Cruises, Tel 941/388-4200*). These are more than just "spot-the-wildlife" cruises; the expert guides answer questions on everything from shells to sand erosion. ∎

Watching the manatees at Mote Marine Aquarium

Mote Marine Aquarium
- ⊠ 1600 Ken Thompson Pkwy.
- ☎ 941/388-2451
- ⑤ $$

Red tide

Jim Brevis sounds just like a cop from a John D. MacDonald thriller, but this particular Floridian is a baddie. In 1996 the waters off Southwest Florida were smothered by a "red tide" that choked millions of fish to death, killed 158 manatees, and affected humans with chronic respiratory problems. It was all Jim's fault. Jim Brevis is the scientists'

nickname for a tiny, single-celled alga, *Gymnodinium breve,* which multiplies inexplicably to produce a brownish-red "bloom" on the surface of the water extending up to several hundred square miles. Although under investigation at Mote Marine Laboratory and other research facilities, no one has yet pinpointed the cause of the red tide. ∎

More places to visit in Southwest Florida

The simplicity of 16th-century Spanish life is re-created at De Soto National Memorial, complete with cooking demonstrations.

DE SOTO NATIONAL MEMORIAL

In 1539, Spanish adventurer Hernando de Soto sailed into Tampa Bay with a fleet of nine ships carrying 700 men, plus horses, dogs, and even pigs. Although this memorial commemorates the official landing site, contemporary diaries describe no more than a large bay and an Indian village, so no one knows the exact spot.

The story of de Soto's arrival and clash with the Indians is told in the small museum at the visitor center. From mid-December to mid-April, interpreters in baggy Spanish costumes re-create life at Camp Utica, the 100-man garrison that de Soto left behind as he set off to explore the New World. A nature trail winds through the dense mangrove swamp, a reminder of what greeted the Spanish four centuries ago.

112 A5   75th St. N.W., Bradenton   941/792-0458 $

GAMBLE MANSION

Judah P. Benjamin was on the run when he stayed here in 1865. The Civil War was lost, and, as the Confederate Secretary of State, he had a $40,000 price on his head. After hiding from Union soldiers in a nearby swamp, he escaped to England, where he became a successful barrister. That is one of the stories rangers tell on tours of what is claimed to be the only surviving antebellum mansion in the state. His Greek Revival home, with its bricks imported from Georgia and Alabama, has two-foot-thick walls and carefully positioned windows and doors to keep the house cool. Rainwater was captured in the gutters, filtered, and stored in a 40,000-gallon cistern, where minnows fed on algae and mosquito larvae.

The sugarcane plantation established by Maj. Robert Gamble in 1844 was always too remote to be a financial success.

112 B5   3708 Patten Ave., Ellenton   941/723-4536   Closed Fri.–Sun. Other days, tours at 9:30 & 10:30 a.m. & 2, 3, & 4 p.m. $ ■

Hernando de Soto

After garnering a fortune in Peru, 39-year-old De Soto sailed for La Florida. On an expedition in search of gold, he marched his men north to what is now Tallahassee, then on through the southern states.

In May 1541, they were the first Europeans to set eyes on the Mississippi River. A year later, de Soto died of fever, but eventually 311 survivors of the expedition reached Mexico. After four years, and traveling more than 4,000 miles, they had found no gold. ■

A romanticized depiction of Hernando de Soto landing in Tampa Bay, 1539

Nowhere else in Florida are two such important cities so close to one another, yet so different. Straddling Tampa Bay, Tampa and St. Petersburg have long engaged in friendly rivalry.

Tampa & St. Petersburg

Baseball bats for spring training

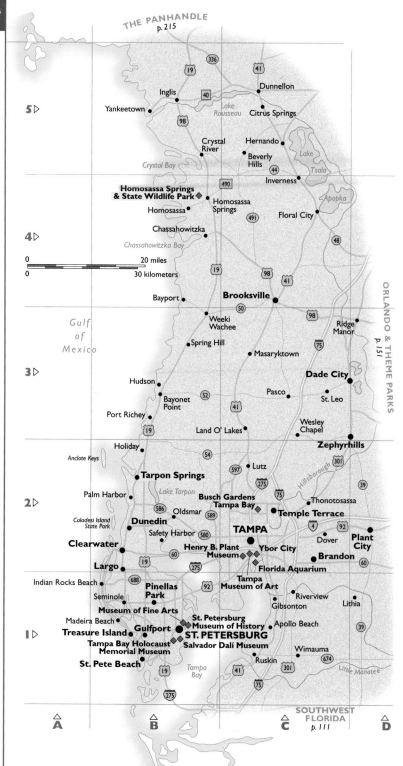

THE PANHANDLE
p. 215

336

19

41

Inglis

Dunnellon

40

5 ▷

Yankeetown

98

Lake Rousseau

Citrus Springs

Crystal River

Hernando

Beverly Hills

44

Lake Tsala

Crystal Bay

490

Inverness

Homosassa Springs & State Wildlife Park ◆

Homosassa

Homosassa Springs

491

Floral City

Apopka

Chassahowitzka

4 ▷

Chassahowitzka Bay

48

| 0 | | 20 miles |
| 0 | | 30 kilometers |

Bayport

Brooksville

50

Gulf of Mexico

Weeki Wachee

98

Ridge Manor

75

Spring Hill

Masaryktown

Dade City

3 ▷

Hudson

52

Pasco

St. Leo

Bayonet Point

41

Port Richey

Land O' Lakes

Wesley Chapel

19

Zephyrhills

Holiday

54

Anclote Keys

597

Lutz

Tarpon Springs

301

39

Palm Harbor

Lake Tarpon

Busch Gardens Tampa Bay ◆

275

Hillsborough

Thonotosassa

2 ▷

586

Oldsmar

589

Temple Terrace

75

Caladesi Island State Park

Dunedin

Safety Harbor

580

TAMPA

4

Dover

92

Plant City

Clearwater

60

Henry B. Plant Museum ◆

Ybor City ◆

Brandon

60

Largo

19

275

Florida Aquarium ◆

Indian Rocks Beach

688

Pinellas Park

92

Tampa Museum of Art

Riverview

Lithia

Seminole

Gibsonton

Museum of Fine Arts

Madeira Beach

St. Petersburg Museum of History ◆

Apollo Beach

39

Treasure Island

Gulfport

ST. PETERSBURG ◆

1 ▷

Tampa Bay Holocaust Memorial Museum

Salvador Dalí Museum ◆

Wimauma

674

St. Pete Beach

19

Tampa Bay

41

Ruskin

301

Little Manatee

275

75

SOUTHWEST FLORIDA
p. 111

ORLANDO & THEME PARKS
p. 151

△ A   △ B   △ C   △ D

Tampa & St. Petersburg

THE CITIES OF TAMPA AND ST. PETERSBURG TEND TO BE LUMPED TOGETHER under the umbrella title of Tampa/St. Pete. Yet, until they were linked by the Gandy Bridge across the bay in 1924, they were totally separate communities. Even today, they still look and feel different. St. Petersburg faces east over the bay, but is best known for its sandy Gulf beaches to the west; Tampa thrives on business, thanks to its deepwater port and railhead. In this section, the emphasis is very much on exploring the growing number of museums in the two cities, with side trips to Busch Gardens and, north along the coast, to the Greek community of Tarpon Springs and to Homosassa Springs to see the few surviving manatees.

The arrival of Henry Plant's railroad in 1885 put Tampa on the map. The entrepreneur's shipping interests ensured that the port boomed, while on the eastern edge of town, cigar factories were the mainstay of Ybor City. With its Hispanic heritage, the Ybor City district adds a colorful dimension to Tampa. During Prohibition, this was where baseball players staying in St. Petersburg for spring training headed for a wild night out. Thanks to recent renovations, Ybor City is once more a lively, if not a wild spot on weekends. The renaissance extends to the downtown area, where glistening skyscrapers house the booming financial services sector in the third largest city in the state.

The marina and pier at St. Petersburg

But this is not an all work and no play city: Each year, locals dress up in outrageous nautical costumes, stick on fake mustaches, and celebrate the region's piratical past. All year long, they can canoe past rare wildlife along the Hillsborough River. One of Florida's most popular attractions, Busch Gardens, is in their backyard. The Florida Aquarium is one of the best in the state. Across the river from the Moorish-looking University of Tampa building (which houses the little museum dedicated to Henry B. Plant) is the small Museum of Art.

St. Petersburg is in heavily populated Pinellas County, with 3,000 residents per square mile. Today, the population covers a wide age range, destroying the old image of St. Pete as a retirement community. The city looks younger than ever thanks to a face-lift that includes palm trees on broad boulevards and newly planted gardens and parks. The catalyst in this dramatic renaissance is culture. The Bayfront Center is the hub for the performing arts. Although the best known landmark is the touristy pier, which attracts two million visitors a year, don't miss the nearby Historical Museum, the Museum of Fine Arts, the thought-provoking Holocaust Memorial Museum, and the world-class Salvador Dalí Museum.

Out of town, eat Greek food in Tarpon Springs' Little Athens and take a boat tour to find out about the history of sponge fishing. Leave time for the manatees of Homosassa Springs: These Floridians were here before the Native Americans and the Europeans. They may need your help to survive. ■

Tallahassee

Miami

Area of map detail

Tampa

TAMPA WAS A BACKWATER UNTIL THE MID-1880S, WHEN transportation and tobacco put it on the map. Henry B. Plant extended his railroad line to connect with his steamship line, and Vicente Martínez Ybor opened his cigar factory in Ybor City. By the turn of the century, the 700-strong village had mushroomed to a town of more than 10,000. Today, the city boasts a small, mainly modern downtown, a revitalized port area, and the restored historic Ybor City to the east of Tampa's business district.

Tampa honors one of the significant names in Florida's history in the **Henry B. Plant Museum.** By 1891, vacationers were able to begin their journeys in New York and arrive at the Tampa Bay Hotel without changing trains. Today this enormous, Moorish-style building is part of the University of Tampa, with one wing serving as a small museum. Beneath the 13 silvery minarets, today's vacationers glimpse the grandeur that was Henry B. Plant's pet project.

The hotel was the hub of a 150-acre resort, where guests played golf, tennis, and croquet, fished, rode horses, and listened to concerts. They swam in the indoor "Natatorium," and all 511 rooms had electricity, telephones, and piped organ music; most also had private bathrooms, all for $5 per night. Funded by 2.5 million dollars of his own fortune, Plant then spent another $500,000 on antiques, such as the Chinese urns and Japanese cabinet, the Venetian glass mirror, and Louis XIV furniture. Only men were allowed in the Writing and Reading Room. The special staircase to the left of the windows led to the basement, where gentlemen could drink and play cards in the company of ladies.

Across the Hillsborough River, the low, modern building (1979) of the **Tampa Museum of Art** has

The lights of downtown Tampa are reflected in the Hillsborough River after dark.

Henry B. Plant

Entrepreneur Henry Bradley Plant of Connecticut (1819–1899) did not finish high school. He rose in the Adams Express Company and married into a wealthy family. Moving to Augusta, Georgia, in 1853, he set up the Southern Express Company, which thrived during the Civil War. In 1862, Plant started buying up bankrupt southern railroads. Soon he owned 1,665 miles of track.

Where his rival, Henry M. Flagler, extended his railroad down the east coast, Plant ran his line from Georgia down to Tampa, connecting with his steamship line to Cuba. In 1898, when Tampa was the jumping-off point for the Spanish-American War, Plant supervised the transportation operation. His railroads brought in soldiers, his hotels housed officers (including one Theodore Roosevelt), and his ships carried both the troops and the wounded. When he died, his estate totaled some ten million dollars. ∎

Tampa Museum of Art

- 600 N. Ashley Dr.
- 813/274-8130
- Hours vary, call ahead
- $

Florida Aquarium

- 701 Channelside Dr.
- 813/273-4000
- $$$

collections from opposite ends of the artistic timescale. Although the Greek and Roman antiquities are regarded as some of the best in the United States, the 2,000 sculptures, models, and drawings by C. Paul Jennewein are more accessible. In 1907, the 17-year-old, German-born sculptor moved to New York. Now his powerful works are everywhere, from Rockefeller Center, New York City, to the Department of Justice Building in Washington, D.C. Look for the model of his most familiar work above the entrance: the animated pediment for the Philadelphia Museum of Art, seen in the movie *Rocky*.

Traveling east across the downtown area, you will find the **Florida Aquarium**. While every city seems to have an aquarium, this practical, concrete building (1995) takes a different approach. The theme is the story of water and its importance to the rich variety of wildlife in Florida. Visitors follow a drop of water on its journey from a spring to the wetlands and streams, and down to bays and beaches. Even the offshore coral reefs are part of the tale.

In "The Wetlands" section, allow time to spot the real wildlife under the canopy of real trees. Roseate spoonbills are easy to see; camouflaged behind a clump of leaves, a great blue heron is more difficult.

The touch tank at the Florida Aquarium

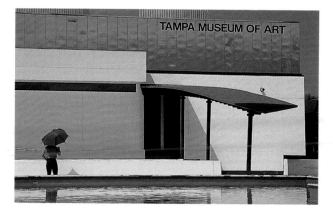

The modern home of the Tampa Museum of Art

Educational elements are presented with a light touch: "The yellow stripes of juvenile alligators allow them to hide in the saw grass; then they grow up and live on golf courses." The environmental message could be stronger: Although the parking lot is a "stormwater management experiment," placards explaining the importance of swales, strands, and stormwater ponds, standing off to one side, are easily missed.

North of the aquarium is **Ybor City.** In 1885, Vicente Martínez Ybor and Ignacio Haya transformed Tampa into the Cigar Capital of the World when they moved their businesses here from Key West. In its heyday, Ybor City had 200 factories employing 12,000 workers.

One of three National Historic Districts in the state, the **Ybor City State Museum** complex (*1818 E. 9th St., Tel 813/247-6323, closed Sun.– Mon., $*) includes cigar workers' homes and the restored Ferlita Bakery. Renovation has revived the area, with Seventh Avenue, known as La Septima, buzzing on weekends.

In north Tampa, **Busch Gardens Tampa Bay** may look like just another theme park, but its origins are unusual. Back in 1959,

Father of Cuban Freedom

"*R*espect for the freedom and ideas of others, of even the most wretched being, is my fanaticism. When I die, or if I am killed, it will be because of that."

—José Martí, Father of Cuban Freedom

A century ago, Ybor City was a hotbed of anti-Spanish sentiment. No wonder Cuban poet and patriot, José Julián Martí (1853–1895) came to solicit funds for the independence movement. Supposedly, his plans for revolution were wrapped, like a cigar, in a tobacco leaf. Martí was shot by Spanish troops in Cuba in 1895, three years before liberation.

In Ybor City, the Parque Amigos de José Martí is on the site of the house where he stayed. His name is still a rallying cry: The United States government-funded radio transmissions to Cuba are known as Radio Martí. ■

the Anheuser-Busch Tampa Brewery decided that its workers deserved a garden with exotic birds, where they could relax, eat lunch, and listen to band concerts.

The brewery has moved to Jacksonville, but the gardens flourish. Today, the 335-acre zoo and theme park is one of the biggest attractions on the Gulf Coast (see p. 157). To get around the complex, visitors can choose between the train, which runs around the perimeter of the park; the **Skyride,** which glides straight across it; or the monorail.

Within the park are more than 340 species of animals, including two dozen that are either endangered or threatened. As well as caring for endangered Mhorr gazelles and golden conuers, zoologists have been studying the way

hippos communicate, both above water and under the surface.

Hippos are among the hundreds of animals roaming freely in the **Serengeti Plain**. Other African animals include lions, hyenas, zebras, and ostriches. Here you can follow the self-guided walking tour or take a monorail, which provides an elevated view of the animals. Best of all is the **Serengeti Safari,** a half-hour tour by truck out into areas inaccessible on foot. It costs extra, but is worth it to have a curator explain the animals' habits, and to hand-feed them.

One of the most popular areas is misty **Myombe Reserve: The Great Ape Domain,** where visitors learn that male gorillas are twice the weight of females, and that nose wrinkles are as individual as a human's fingerprint. ■

Every year, the rides seem to get scarier at Busch Gardens Tampa Bay.

Busch Gardens Tampa Bay
✉ 3000 E. Busch Blvd.
☎ 813/987-5082
www.4adventure.com
💲 $$$$

St. Petersburg

WHEN THE ART CLUB OF ST. PETERSBURG OPENED IN 1919, IT was the first art gallery south of Atlanta, Georgia. Locals then claimed the title Cultural Capital of Florida. It may have sounded impertinent at that time, but the last 30 years have seen a renaissance, thanks to the opening of the concert hall and theater at Bayfront Center, the Museum of Fine Arts, the world-famous Dalí Museum, and the Florida International Museum, showcasing blockbuster exhibitions. Once considered only a retirement haven, the city now boasts a thriving artistic scene.

Combine a walk along the landmark pier with a visit to the **Museum of Fine Arts,** but be sure to allow enough time to do justice to the fine collections on display here. Margaret Acheson Stuart, the museum's founder, would be pleased at the warmth and welcome of this museum, since that is what she set out to achieve.

She was a great fan of 18th- and 19th-century American artists, although the star names of 19th-century European painting are also well represented: landscapes at Giverny and Vétheuil by Claude Monet; a classic Renoir portrait of a woman reading; as well as works by their contemporary, Berthe Morisot.

In her painting, "La Lecture," a young woman reads against a backdrop of lush Floridian foliage. Even more delightful is the tender, yet realistic, bronze head of her seven-year-old daughter.

The American section ranges from early folk art through Thomas Moran's late 19th-century romantic "Florida Landscape (St. Johns River)" and on to Georgia O'Keeffe. Compare her cool, pure "White Abstraction (Madison Avenue)" with the vibrancy of the red and black "Poppy." As well as African, Asian, and South American art and an outdoor sculpture garden, there are furnished reconstructions, such as the complete 1610 Jacobean Room from Staffordshire, England.

Right by the pier is the **St. Petersburg Museum of History.** It is difficult to see where a 3,000-year-old Egyptian mummy fits into the history of St. Petersburg. Donated by a onetime dockmaster who received it in lieu of payment for a bill, this artifact is just one example of the eclectic collection of photographs, travel brochures, documents, and clothing given by members of the community since 1920. Pride of place, however, goes to the working copy of a 1913 seaplane. Hanging from the ceiling in the entrance hall, this commemorates the world's first commercial airline.

"Poppy" (1927) by Georgia O'Keeffe at the Museum of Fine Arts

The world's first commercial airline

In 1913 the journey from St. Petersburg to Tampa took two hours by steamboat, six by train, and often all day by road. A decade after the Wright brothers' first flight, a plane built by Thomas Benoist inaugurated a regular service across Tampa Bay. From January 1, 1914, the St. Petersburg–Tampa Airboat Line operated two round-trips a day for the three-month vacation season, the world's first scheduled air service. By March 31, a total of 1,204 passengers had paid $5 each to fly across the 19 miles of water in just 23 minutes. The plane carried one passenger at a time and flew at 55 mph. In 1922 the 2.5-mile Gandy Bridge across Tampa Bay eliminated the need for such a short shuttle. ■

This 1913 Benoist reproduction hangs in the St. Petersburg Museum of History.

The "Walk Through Time" shows who did what in the St. Petersburg area from the time of the canoe-building Indians to World War II, when the area hosted thousands of servicemen in its hotels. A 19th-century eyewitness account quaintly describes a hurricane as "The Great Gale of 1848." During this storm, a 15-foot tidal surge pushed the Gulf into Tampa Bay.

The Don CeSar, which opened in 1928, gives its name to the registered paint color of Don CeSar Pink.

**Salvador Dalí
Museum**

✉ 1000 3rd St. S.

☎ 727/823-3767

$ $$

"Disintegration
of the Persistence
of Memory"
(1952–54) by
Salvador Dalí, in
the Salvador
Dalí Museum

"United States Art World Dillydallies Over Dalis" was the headline in the *Wall Street Journal* in 1980. The **Salvador Dalí Museum,** the world's biggest private collection of the Spaniard's work, needed a worthy and permanent home, and St. Petersburg came up with both the money and the site on Bayboro Harbor.

The collection belonged to Mr. and Mrs. A. Reynolds Morse, who, as a young engaged couple, visited a Dalí exhibition in Cleveland, Ohio, in 1942. For their first wedding anniversary, they bought "Daddy Longlegs of the Evening—Hope!" and over the next four decades their collection grew to include 94 oils, more than 100 watercolors and drawings, and some 1,300 graphics. Now, in a converted marine storage warehouse, visitors have the rare opportunity of studying a single, well-known artist in depth.

Salvador Dalí (1904–1989) was born in Catalonia in northeastern Spain. The museum divides his career into five periods: early

works, transitional period, surrealism, classical period, and the masterworks. Although the early works (1914–1927) show his classical ability to draw and paint, there are already hints of his well-known eccentricity. In "Self-Portrait (Figueres)," his broad-brimmed hat and half-turned head give him a secretive look. By the age of 25, Dalí was experimenting with surrealism and developing his trademark symbolism and allegory, political references and sexual allusions. The famous melting watches familiar in the 1931 "Persistence of Memory" (Museum of Modern Art, New York) reappear 20 years later in this collection's "Disintegration of the Persistence of Memory." This sequel represents his anxiety about the dangers of the nuclear age. The final challenge of understanding Dalí comes in the last gallery, with the vast canvases labeled "Masterworks." The museum has 6 of the 18 he painted, including his signature work, "Hallucinogenic Toreador."

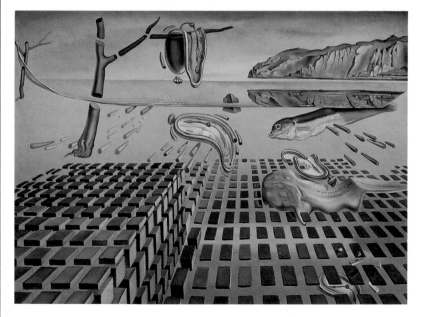

Originally in Madeira Beach, the thought-provoking **Tampa Bay Holocaust Memorial Museum** moved to downtown St. Petersburg early in 1998. One of the largest of its kind in the United States, this examination of prejudice includes tributes to Oskar Schindler (the subject of the 1993 Oscar-winning movie *Schindler's List*) and Swedish diplomat Raoul Wallenberg, who helped Jewish people escape from the Nazis.

It is almost impossible to take in the enormity of the Holocaust. Standing as a silent witness is **Boxcar No. 11306955,** brought to Florida from Poland. Designed to carry eight horses, it transported up to 100 people at a time to the concentration camps. The memories of those who survived can be heard on the audio handsets.

When Adolf Hitler came to power in Germany in 1933, Jewish people were systematically deprived of their legal rights, their jobs, their citizenship, and eventually their lives. From Kristallnacht in November 1938, when 1,000 synagogues and 7,000 Jewish business were attacked, the catalog of horrors continued while the rest of the world stood by. The exhibition reminds visitors that even the United States turned away a German boat full of refugees that approached the Florida coast in 1939.

The story told here, however, covers more than Hitler's mania. This is the "history of hate," tracing anti-Semitism from the early Middle Ages through the eight centuries before the "Final Solution" of the Third Reich.

In 1492, for example, when King Ferdinand and Queen Isabella of Spain sent Christopher Columbus off on his epic voyage, they also expelled all of Spain's Jewish population.

There are photographs, art, statistics, and artifacts—all emphasizing that these atrocities were committed against ordinary people, just because they were Jewish.

The final message is one of hope—that by telling the story of the Holocaust, it will never be repeated. ∎

This exhibit, Boxcar No. 11306955, is a poignant reminder of the Holocaust.

Tampa Bay Holocaust Memorial Museum & Educational Center

✉ 55 5th St. S.
☎ 727/821-8261
$ $

Baseball's spring training

A favorite American ritual is baseball's spring training in Florida, the slow windup to the new season, when players, management, and fans revive their hopes that "this will be our year." What was once merely a way to get fit ahead of the season has developed into a major vacationer attraction, as some two million shivering Northerners combine a winter vacation in the sun with watching their boys get ready. In mid-February, up to 100 players report to each of the baseball complexes, eager to make the 25-man roster announced in early April.

Teams have hopped around the Sunshine State over the decades. The earliest recorded arrival was in 1888, but the real tradition started in 1918 with the arrival of the Pirates and Athletics (Jacksonville), the Braves (Miami), and the Phillies (St. Petersburg). The Detroit Tigers have been loyal to Lakeland since 1934—the longest partnership in spring training. In 1998, 20 of the 30 Major League ball clubs worked out in Florida, with the remaining teams going to Arizona.

Below: Babe Ruth (1895–1948) is the greatest name in baseball history.
Right: At practice behind a fence

Even hardened sportswriters become lyrical during what journalist Thomas Boswell called "baseball's annual indolence," but they still prefer a good story, and players have obliged off the diamond as well as on it. On April 4, 1919, Babe Ruth hammered his longest-ever home run, a record-making 587 feet, at Tampa's Plant Field. When not slamming the ball, the Babe went hunting, once bagging a massive 100-year-old alligator, nicknamed Big Boy.

Some stories, however, were swept under the carpet. Despite Jackie Robinson's breaking the color bar in the Major Leagues (in Daytona), racial segregation persisted for years. As David Halberstam recalls in his baseball

classic, *October 1964*, a wealthy supporter of the St. Louis Cardinals bought the Skyway motel in St. Petersburg, then leased it to the club. That way, "the entire team and their families could stay together....in an otherwise segregated Florida, locals and vacationers alike could see the rarest of sights: white and black children swimming in the motel pool together, and white and black players, with their wives, at desegregated cookouts."

For the superstitious, Pinellas County seems to be a lucky location. Over the years, the 11 Major League clubs that have trained there have won 23 American League pennants, 14 National League pennants, and 24 World Series titles.

As crowds for exhibition games have grown, so has the competition to host the star-studded teams. Towns build stadiums to entice clubs to spend time—and dollars—in their city. In 1998, the St. Louis Cardinals, after nearly 60 seasons in St. Petersburg, moved across the state to Jupiter on the Atlantic Coast. The Atlanta Braves have set up home at the Wide World of Sports Complex in Orlando, while Legends Field in Tampa is really a second home to the New York Yankees: The dimensions are identical to those of Yankee Stadium.

During the lazy afternoons and soft evenings, ball clubs prepare for the new season by playing one another in exhibition games. The results are logged in the Grapefruit League. Analyze the scores and you soon realize that the outcome bears little relation to the season itself. The Toronto Blue Jays, were 13–18 in 1992 and an even worse 11–19 in 1993—yet the Canadian club went on to win back-to-back World Series in both years. ■

Homosassa Springs
State Wildlife Park

**Homosassa
Springs State
Wildlife Park**

⧉ 136 B4

✉ 9225 W. Fishbowl
Dr. (US 19)

☎ 727/628-2311

💲 $

MANATEES CAN BE SPOTTED ALONG BOTH COASTS OF
Florida from fall to spring, at viewing points such as the Big Bend
Manatee Viewing Center near Bradenton and Manatee Park in Fort
Myers. The only place to be sure to see them in a natural setting
all year long, however, is at Homosassa Springs State Wildlife Park.

The park is at the headwaters of the
Homosassa River, where the bub-
bling springs form a large lagoon,
used as a rehabilitation center for
injured or ill manatees. The float-

ing, underwater observatory has
huge picture windows, which
provide a nose-to-nose view of
these extraordinary prehistoric-
looking creatures. Be sure to call
ahead for times of the ranger's talks
about the habits of, and dangers to,
these animals, which are released
back into the wild after recovery.

This was once a private park,
where owners installed the present
floating underwater laboratory
back in 1964. Built like a ship, the
lab was launched down a ramp
covered in ecologically-friendly
bananas instead of grease. The
observatory allows visitors to view
the **Spring of 1,000 Fish,** where
manatees and many species of fish
enjoy the constant temperatures. ∎

Above: Visitors to
Homosassa
**Springs on a boat
trip through the
springs**
Opposite: A 1996
**survey estimated
Florida's manatee
population at
2,639, the highest
since records
began. The
mammals
are, however,
still on the
endangered list.**

Manatees

From above, a manatee looks
like a fat torpedo, with a paddle
for a tail, two tiny flippers, a squat
nose, and doleful eyes. Yet this
homely mammal (also known as
the "sea cow") can grow to 13 feet
long and 3,500 pounds in weight,
and is surprisingly endearing.

Closely related to the elephant,
it is slow, shy, harmless, and without any means of self-defense.
Females bear a solitary calf every
three to five years. Manatees live in
fresh and brackish water, devouring
up to 200 pounds of vegetation
every day. Their primary enemy is
man and his accoutrements: fishing

hooks and lines, crab traps, trawling
nets, and water pollution. Worst
of all are the slashing propellers
of leisure boats: When the manatees come to the surface for air,
they are frequently hit and injured
by the blades.

In 1973, once the manatee had
been placed on the Federal List of
Endangered Species, a public awareness campaign began, and thanks to
education programs and speed
restrictions, numbers are stabilizing.
Although in the summer they travel
as far as Louisiana in the west and
Virginia to the north, they always
return to Florida. ∎

Tarpon Springs

THE SELF-PROCLAIMED SPONGE CAPITAL OF THE WORLD trades on its Greek heritage, and the waterfront is lined with souvenir and sponge shops. The story here is fascinating: Sponge-collecting was an early Florida industry, as these marine animals flourished along the Gulf Coast. Growing in shallow water, they were easily hooked with a pole from a boat, but John Cocoris, a Greek immigrant, revolutionized the trade.

Tarpon Springs
136 B2
Visitor information
11 E. Orange St.
727/937-6109

St. Nicholas Greek Orthodox Cathedral
36 N. Pinellas Ave.
727/937-3540

Finding plentiful beds in the deeper water offshore, Cocoris used the Mediterranean method of diving for sponges. Word soon reached Greek sponge fishermen, and by the 1930s there were 200 boats in the Anclote River marina. With a population of more than 2,500, the Greek community decided to build a cathedral. To raise the $200,000 needed to put up a copy of St. Sophia in Constantinople, the fishermen donated their best sponges, which were auctioned off at top prices. In 1943 the Patriarch of all Orthodoxy in Constantinople dedicated **St. Nicholas Greek Orthodox Cathedral.** This magnificent cathedral is visited by thousands to view its iconography, and at Epiphany it is the center of a lively midday Blessing of the Waters (see p. 263).

An unexplained blight in the 1930s here killed off 90 percent of the sponges. Not until the 1960s did the industry recover, and now locals are trying to revive the traditional auction at the **Sponge Docks.**

Greeks and their descendants still make up about one-third of the Tarpon Springs community. The telephone book lists names such as Billiris, Pappas, Tsourakis, and Poulos, while restaurants such as Dino's on Athens Street have traditional music and dancing. The institution of the Greek coffeehouse survives, and, close to Dino's, the Dodecanese Café follows Greek custom: It's for men only. ∎

This store on Dodecanese Boulevard displays Tarpon Springs' famous product.

Sponges

When you scrub yourself with a sponge, you are using the skeleton of a marine animal. You would not, however, want to use one straight from the seabed. When brought to the surface, sponges are slimy, squishy, and black. Once out of water, they dry out, but still need repetitive beating, scraping, and rinsing to separate the decayed animal matter from the skeleton. Machines are not used, so this demands two to three days of sheer muscle power. As for the argument about the difference between a Gulf of Mexico and a Mediterranean sponge, one local insists that the "Mediterranean variety has less body, so you are buying more holes." ∎

In the heart of Florida's citrus country, Orlando is now synonymous with fun, thanks to its world-famous theme parks. The magnet may be Walt Disney's loveable creations, but there's more to Orlando than Mickey and Goofy.

Orlando & the theme parks

Mel's Diner, Universal Studios Escape

Orlando & the theme parks

THE ARRIVAL OF WALT DISNEY AND HIS EMPIRE HAS TRANSFORMED ORANGE groves into a sprawl of shopping centers, hotels, and tourist attractions. Orlando, and adjoining towns such as Kissimmee, are still growing as more and more entertainment complexes cash in on the Disney success. However, as Orlando matures into a proper city, so cultural attractions, such as museums and art galleries, have developed.

Most of the major attractions are within a short drive of one another. One exception is Cypress Gardens, the area's original theme park. Nearby is the total tranquility of Bok Tower Gardens, while farther to the west in Lakeland is a little known legacy of architect Frank Lloyd Wright.

It is easy to assume that theme parks are all about having a good time, eating popcorn, and screaming on thrill rides. In fact, the best parks have considerable educational merit, with plenty to absorb for young and old alike. The "behind the scenes" tours are especially recommended, unless you fear that the magic spell will be broken by learning the tricks of the trade. On the following pages, the focus is on those attractions with a story to tell as well as the nerve-jangling thrill rides (see pp. 156–57).

To get the best value for what is an expensive day out, a visit to a theme park needs the strategic planning of a military campaign. Start with when you plan to go. The winter months are the busiest and lines are longest during the school vacations. There are lulls in early December, late January, and between Labor Day and Thanksgiving. In summer, central Florida is hot and sticky, which is tiring for that growing group of vacationers: grandparents with young

Once a rural county seat, Orlando is one of the fastest growing cities in the state.

grandchildren. Parks are open from 10 to 12 hours a day, longer during school vacations. At Christmas, New Year's, Easter, and the Fourth of July, there are extra shows and entertainment. So, if you have the energy, you may want to go at these times, when the buzz is best.

You should consider the benefits of a package, with flights, accommodation, and tickets included. At Walt Disney World Resort in Florida, for example, guests at Disney hotels have the advantage of access to the parks before the rest of the public. In addition, hotel staff can help you to get the most out of your visit. On-site hotels save commuting and parking time as well as stress and aggravation. Some regular visitors boast that they can enjoy a vacation there without using a car at all.

Visiting a theme park demands stamina. It is important to consider whether you need to purchase a single day ticket or take advantage of the price reduction on a pass for a longer period. Some people are happy to have three concentrated days of action; others prefer to break up a visit with R&R days at a water park. The main problem is always choice, with too much for an individual or a family to see in a week, let alone a day. When planning each day, start with a map and highlight the shows that begin at fixed times. Arrive when the gates open, and head straight for the far side of the park, well away from the main entrance. Remember: Less is more. ∎

Area of map detail

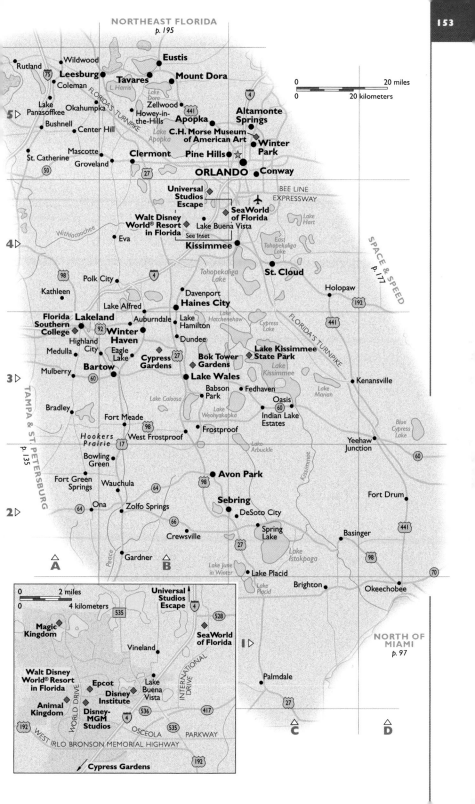

Orlando drive

Around the world, Orlando is synonymous with the name of Disney, but there is more to the city than theme parks and thrill rides. Follow this route to find museums, art galleries, and a charming lakeside community. Allow one hour, or more if you want to stop along the way.

Start in downtown Orlando, at **Church Street Station** (*129 W. Church St*). From this popular restaurant, shopping, and entertainment complex, proceed east on Church Street, turning left on Rosalind Avenue. Here you will find **Lake Eola** ❶ (*Central Blvd. and Rosalind Ave.*). This is where, in 1965, Walt Disney revealed that he was the buyer of 27,500 acres of farm and swampland.

Continue on Rosalind Avenue, which becomes Magnolia Avenue, and then turn right on Orange Avenue—do not go on to I-4. Drive along Orange Avenue, past the shops, which give it the nickname "Antique Row." Turn right on Princeton Street, which leads through Loch Haven Park, whose trio of museums makes it the cultural center of Orlando.

The first of these is the **Orlando Science Center** ❷ (*777 E. Princeton St., Tel 407/514-2000*). Here you can play a harp with no visible strings (they're laser beams), discover why you would weigh less on Mercury, and spot the queen bee in a real hive. This state-of-the-art museum opened in 1997. From the silver observatory dome, anyone can stargaze through the telescope on Friday and Saturday evenings. A perfect antidote for the relentless pace of theme parks.

Continue on Princeton Street to Mills Avenue and turn left. Museum number two is on the corner of Rollins Avenue. The **Orlando Museum of Art** ❸ (*2416 Mills Ave., Tel 407/896-4231*) has a growing collection of 19th- and 20th-century American art ranging from Thomas Hart Benton and John Singer Sargent to Georgia O'Keeffe and Frank Stella. Also on show are pre-Columbian and African art and artifacts.

Behind the art museum is the **Orange County Historical Museum** ❹ (*812 E. Rollins Ave., Tel 407/897-6350*). In the year 2000, a move to the old Orange County Courthouse building near Church Street Station will provide much-needed space. Learn the story of the citrus industry and study the extensive collec-

tion of old photographs, which shows Orlando "B.D." (Before Disney).

Continue on Mills Avenue, also signposted Orlando Avenue and US 17/92. Turn right on Fairbanks Avenue, which leads into Winter Park and becomes Osceola Avenue. The house and gallery at No. 633 is the **Albin Polasek Museum and Sculpture Garden** ❺ (*Tel 407/674-6294*), commemorating the Czech-American sculptor. The free tour is the best way to appreciate the works of this classical realist, who spent the last 15 years of his life here. From monumental statues of heroes to portrayals of his wife, his creativity never stopped. At the age of 80 and despite a stroke, he was still working. He died in 1965.

Return on Osceola Avenue to Park Avenue. Turn right and drive past the upmarket galleries and boutiques of Winter Park. On the left is a gem of a museum, the **Charles Hosmer Morse Museum of American Art** ❻ (*445 Park Ave. N., Tel 407/645-5311*). Don't leave town without seeing this huge collection of stained glass by Louis Comfort Tiffany. A century ago, he created a chapel interior for the 1893 exposition in Chicago. In 1999, the Chapel Tiffany was reassembled here in its entirety. Also on show are works by René Lalique and Edward Burne-Jones. tour ends here. ∎

🅰 See area map p. 153
▶ Church Street Station
🔁 About 6 miles
🕐 1 hour
▶ Charles Hosmer Morse Museum of American Art

NOT TO BE MISSED
• Orlando Science Center
• Orlando Museum of Art
• Orange County Historical Museum

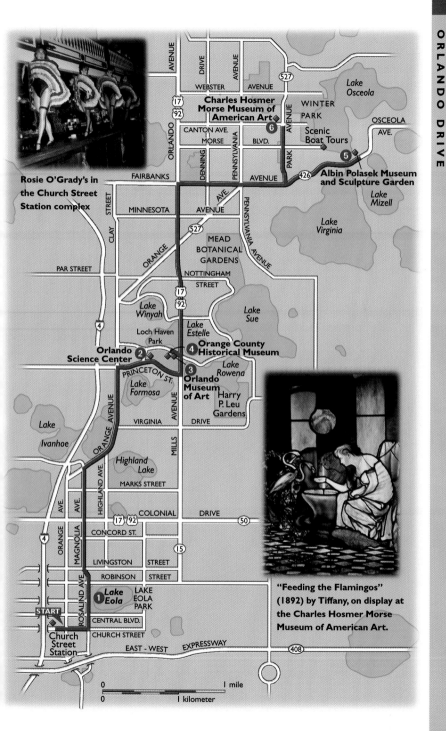

Rosie O'Grady's in the Church Street Station complex

Charles Hosmer Morse Museum of American Art

Scenic Boat Tours

Albin Polasek Museum and Sculpture Garden

MEAD BOTANICAL GARDENS

Orlando Science Center

Orange County Historical Museum

Orlando Museum of Art

Harry P. Leu Gardens

START

Church Street Station

"Feeding the Flamingos" (1892) by Tiffany, on display at the Charles Hosmer Morse Museum of American Art.

0   1 mile
0   1 kilometer

Florida's thrill-a-minute rides

Central Florida is the thrill center of the world. Nowhere else has as great a concentration of rides that churn stomachs, blast the senses, and send adrenaline levels off the charts. Moreover, fierce competition ensures that new attractions open almost every year in the major theme parks. The following are some of the latest tests for visitors' nerves.

Walt Disney World Resort in Florida

(See also pp. 158–65)
Not to be outdone by the expanding Universal Studios Escape, Disney also introduced new rides in 1999. The Rock 'n' Roller Coaster at Disney-MGM Studios hurtles through the dark, twisting and turning to a pounding rock soundtrack, and looping upside down to increase the thrill factor. Disney has also updated the Tower of Terror, the landmark in the park and an established favorite. A third drop that is faster than gravity increases the screams as the errant elevator rises and falls in the spooky 200-foot-high Hollywood Tower Hotel.

Over in the Asia sector of Disney's Animal Kingdom Theme Park, water is the force for fun on the Kali River Rapids. This is a classic white-water ride, with T-shirt and shorts essential. The storyline has passengers looking for illegal loggers in the forest. As burning trees and logs threaten to topple onto your circular raft, you escape dramatically down a waterfall.

At Epcot, even a thrill has an educational element. Test Track, however, is no simulation; quite simply, it shows how General Motors vehicles are tested before production. Braking, cornering, skidding, and more lead up to a trial of acceleration and speed. Sixty-five mph may not sound fast, but on the banked track, which loops in and outdoors, this is more than exhilarating. Your test vehicle is controlled by computers whose processing power is greater than those used in the space shuttle!

SeaWorld of Florida

(See also pp. 166–67)
"Wetter than standing in a shower" is the claim for Journey to Atlantis, a ride that combines the speed of a roller coaster with the drenching of a water ride. The plot revolves around a battle between the Sirens and Hermes, with special effects, a Greek fishing village, temples, and the lost city of Atlantis. There are two 60-foot drops. On the first, you plunge into the main harbor; on the second, in the dark, you drop into the Sirens' lair.

Universal Studios Escape

(See also pp. 168–71)
In 1999 the original movie-based theme park, already known for popular rides such as JAWS and Back to the Future, expanded. In the new park, Islands of Adventure, each of the areas has its own theme; on Marvel Super Hero Island, for example, one of the rides is The Adventures of Spider-Man. This is a battle to recapture the Statue of Liberty in New York; luckily, Spider-Man is on your side. Universal Studios claims new dimensions of fun and fear on this ride, thanks to 3-D images created by dozens of projectors. Meanwhile, over on the Lost Continent

Island, a terrifying head-on crash between the Dueling Dragons double roller coasters is avoided at the last possible second by pushing riders through a camelback, double-helix, and compound inversion.

Busch Gardens Tampa Bay
(See also p. 141)
The fifth roller coaster in the park, Gwazi, is Florida's first dueling wooden roller coaster. Opened in 1999, the two-minute ride is

Top: A colorful ride in Tampa
Above left: Journey to Atlantis at SeaWorld of Florida
Above: Dueling Dragons at Universal Studios Islands of Adventure

themed on a legend about a lion with a tiger's head. The two coasters, Gwazi lion and Gwazi tiger, travel at speeds over 50 mph. When they hurtle past one another six times, the combined fly-by effect is a terrifying 100 mph. ■

Walt Disney World
Resort in Florida

Walt Disney World (Magic Kingdom, Disney-MGM Studios, Epcot, Disney's Animal Kingdom)

🅜 153 B4

✉ 20 miles SW of Orlando at Lake Buena Vista

☎ 407/824-4321
www.disney.go.com/DisneyWorld

💲 $$$$.
One-day tickets cover admission to one park only. Longer stay visitors will find multi-day combination tickets such as 4-, 5-, 7-, & 9-day All-In-One Hopper passes offer considerable savings and provide admission to all four Disney theme parks, three water parks, Pleasure Island nightclubs, Disney's Wild World of Sport Complex (excluding separately priced events), and unlimited use of the Walt Disney World transportation system.

DISNEY'S DAZZLING FLORIDA SHOWCASE, WALT DISNEY World offers four separate theme park experiences plus three adventure water parks, world-class sports facilities, nightclub and entertainment complexes, shopping, dining, and 26 hotels scattered around a site that is twice the size of Manhattan.

The first step in Disney's Orlando empire was Magic Kingdom Park, opened in 1971, and based on the successful fairy-tale formula of the Disneyland park in California. It was followed by the futuristic Epcot complex in 1982; the film and television center, Disney-MGM Studios, in 1989; and the wildlife attraction, Disney's Animal Kingdom Theme Park, in 1998. Fierce competition from rivals has kept the Disney "imagineers" busy inventing and adding up-to-the-minute rides, attractions, and dozens of imaginative shows that form an important part of the park experience.

MAGIC KINGDOM PARK

The classic Disney park packed with favorite Disney characters and some great rides, this is the one that nobody wants to miss. The 100-acre park is divided into seven themed lands radiating from the turrets and towers of Cinderella Castle. City Hall, at the entrance to the park, is the main information center and the place to make reservations for the character restaurants. Then visitors head up cute Victorian-style **Main Street, U.S.A.,** the first themed district and the location for the daily character parade, to Cinderella Castle and access to the other lands

Circling the park in a clockwise direction, your first stop is **Adventureland.** Here, tropical architecture and adventure outfit-

ters' stores set the scene for an exploration of the Swiss Family Treehouse, a huge model banyan with leafy "rooms." A comic skipper takes the helm for the scenic Jungle Cruise, which survives a (fake) hippo attack en route to a (real) elephant bathing pool; while the rambunctious Pirates of the Caribbean boat ride provides plenty of buccaneering action and loud cannon fire. On a gentler note, the Enchanted Tiki Room presents a flock of animated feathered friends chirping along to a mixed bag of popular melodies.

In **Frontierland** step back into the Wild West with the *Country Bear Jamboree;* tackle the Splash Mountain log flume; or jump aboard the Big Thunder Mountain Railroad, which packs passengers onto a cute lil' ole train for a wild roller-coaster ride down the mountain. Nearby motorized rafts make the crossing to the unexciting Tom Sawyer Island.

Liberty Square is altogether more sedate with its attractive colonial buildings and spreading live oak known as the Liberty Tree. On a mildly educational level, **The Hall of Presidents** invites guests to encounter robotic versions of former U.S. Presidents giving short lectures. Considerably higher up the entertainment scale, the hilarious Haunted Mansion ride piles on the kitsch thrills at every turn.

Around the back of Cinderella Castle, **Fantasyland** is designed to

appeal to smaller children. The scaled-down rides and shows, such as Cinderella's Golden Carousel, feature storybook characters. Ariel's Grotto from *The Little Mermaid* has waterspouts where kids can play and cool down.

Adjacent to Fantasyland, **Mickey's Toontown Fair** is another top attraction for little people. It is home to Mickey and Minnie Mouse, where Mickey's country house comes complete with wardrobes full of big, black boots and little red jackets and Pluto's kennel resides in the garden. It is a good place to take time out of the stroller in the Donald's Boat play area, or catch a not-too-thrilling roller-coaster ride on The Barnstormer at Goofy's Wiseacre Farm.

The most famous sight at Walt Disney World is Cinderella Castle in the Magic Kingdom.

If thrill rides are at the top of your Magic Kingdom Park agenda, beat the inevitable lines and start the day at Space Mountain in **Tomorrowland.** This terrific roller-coaster ride in the dark is arguably the park's best attraction, and there are more mind-bending thrills in store at the neighboring

A re-creation of Munich's Hofbrau Haus is part of Germany's representation at World Showcase.

ExtraTERRORestrial Alien Encounter. Buzz Lightyear's Space Ranger Spin is a hugely popular interactive ride with guests manning laser guns to battle the evil Emperor Zurg; or climb aboard the Astro Orbiter for a bird's eye view of the park. Other attractions include a comic time travel adventure with The Timekeeper, and the cloyingly nostalgic Walt Disney's Carousel of Progress.

EPCOT

Epcot was Walt Disney's pet project. He envisioned a working scientific community, the Experimental Prototype Community of Tomorrow, which would showcase new technologies while developing environmental concepts and problem-solving philosophies to improve the way

future generations would live. Though Walt Disney's original plans died with him in 1966, Epcot incorporates several of his ideas and offers a semi-educational theme park experience promoting knowledge of science, technology, and the world around us.

Epcot's massive site is divided into two "lands": Future World and World Showcase. Future World handles the science stuff in pavilions dedicated to the land, the seas, communication, imagination, energy, technology, and motion. World Showcase focuses on the culture of 11 nations through miniature "villages" reflecting the architecture, food, crafts, and customs of each country. Most of the park's rides are found in Future World, which is also strong on interactive displays; while World Showcase is

the chief entertainment zone with a round of shows and street entertainers performing throughout the day.

The entrance to Epcot is overshadowed by the landmark giant silver geosphere, **Spaceship Earth,** which looms over Guest Relations where reservations can be made for restaurants in World Showcase. This is **Future World,** the best place to start exploring the park. Spaceship Earth contains an entertaining ride through the history of communications. Just ahead, the central plaza is flanked by the two **Innoventions** pavilions where hi-tech companies, such as IBM, Motorola, and Apple, demonstrate new products.

Working clockwise around the outer pavilions, **Universe of Energy** presents a humorous

investigation into energy sources hosted by comedian Ellen DeGeneres and a cast of imposing animatronic dinosaurs. The human body comes under the microscope at **Wonders of Life** with a high-speed race around the bloodstream at the Body Wars thrill ride, and the amusing *Cranium Command* show that flips the lid on the peculiar workings of a 12-year-old boy's brain. The next pavilion is closed as this guide goes to press; a new attraction is in the planning stages. There is lots of fun to be had at **Test Track,** where guests discover how new cars are tested and then take to the track themselves (see p. 156).

In the second section of pavilions, **Journey Into Imagination** offers a cutesy fantasy ride, popular with grandparents but less so with the young, who would much rather

The enormous, silver, geodesic dome of Spaceship Earth is the focal point of Future World.

The Tower of Terror at Disney-MGM Studios

"I hope we never lose sight of one fact...that this was all started by a mouse."
—Walt Disney on Mickey Mouse

and Mounties, and the **United Kingdom's** pubs and thatched cottages, the **Millennium Village** offers an exciting lineup of events and festivities. There will also be an all-new "IllumiNations" nighttime spectacular with fireworks, lasers, and dramatic special effects.

Continuing around the lagoon, there are sidewalk artists and a miniature Eiffel Tower in **France;** an attractive Moorish souk and belly-dancing displays in **Morocco;** and elegant gardens and koi fish ponds framing **Japan's** pagodas. The centerpiece of World Showcase is the **American Adventure,** which presents a patriotic romp through United States history, narrated by animatronic figures from Benjamin Franklin to Mark Twain.

Next door, **Italy** is represented by a charmingly re-created pint-size Venice, while neighboring **Germany** settles for a jolly *biergarten.* A half-size copy of Beijing's Temple of Heaven dominates the **China** exhibit, and there is a stunning CircleVision 360-degree movie presentation. **Norway** offers a thrill ride aboard the Viking longboat *Maelstrom,* and **Mexico** has a boat ride through history, plus mariachi players and sombrero sellers gathered in front of a Mayan pyramid.

get sniffled by a huge dog in the terrific *Honey, I Shrunk the Audience* 3-D movie. At the **Land** pavilion, take a boat ride though fascinating futuristic greenhouses where horticulturists tinker with the food crops of the future, and catch an engaging eco-conscious movie starring characters from *The Lion King* in the Circle of Life Theater. Lastly, **The Living Seas** is a favorite stop. This spectacular six-million-gallon marine exhibit is inhabited by 5,000-plus tropical reef fish, sharks, dolphins, turtles, and Florida manatees.

World Showcase's 11 villages are laid out in a 1.3-mile-long arc around World Showcase Lagoon. From October 1999 to January 1, 2001, World Showcase also hosts Walt Disney World's millennium celebrations. Positioned between **Canada's** totem poles

DISNEY-MGM STUDIOS
The birthplace of the movies transported to Florida, Disney-MGM Studios re-creates an idealized corner of vintage Hollywood complete with pastel-painted art deco architecture, perambulating movie star look-alikes, and a variety of movie-oriented shows and rides.

Traditionally shorter on rides than Universal Studios Florida, Disney is hoping to redress the balance with the Rock 'n' Roller Coaster thrill ride (opened in summer 1999), and the frequently updated shows and exhibitions that showcase the best new Disney productions as well as reviving old favorites.

The Disney-MGM Studios experience is divided into three main themes: thrill rides, behind-the-scenes attractions, and shows. The two latest thrill rides are located side by side at the end of **Sunset Boulevard.** Here, the Twilight Zone Tower of Terror (see p. 156) features a plummeting elevator. Next door is the Rock 'n' Roller Coaster (see p. 156). The park's other thriller is Star Tours, a stomach-churning intergalactic voyage into the world of George Lucas's *Star Wars.*

For movie buffs keen to take a look behind the scenes, stroll down **Mickey Avenue.** The Magic of Disney Animation tours the art department where real animators crouch over drawing boards, and video monitors explain the evolution of an animated movie from the initial development of the storyline through to the final retouches in the Ink and Paint departments.

At "The Making of…," documentary-style films illustrate how recent Disney productions were made, spliced with on-set interviews with the cast and crew. **Backstage Pass** offers an opportunity to see a live television production. The Backlot Tour is a good place to take the weight off your feet as the tram ride trundles through wardrobe, props, and special effects departments before passengers are involved in an explosive mini drama staged in Catastrophe Canyon.

Hollywood Boulevard is a home-away-from-home to a full-scale re-creation of Mann's Chinese Theater. Star footprints and handprints adorn the courtyard, and, inside the theater the Great

Movie Ride presents a very popular but sedate celebration of classic scenes from Hollywood movies with the star parts re-created by animatronic figures.

There is plenty of choice when it comes to shows. In the **Echo Lake** district, the action-packed *Indiana Jones Epic Stunt Spectacular,* loosely

Disney Enterprises Inc.

based on *Raiders of the Lost Ark,* piles on the earthquakes, explosions, and fight scenes. In **New York Street,** little kids (and big kids) will find plenty of giggles at *Jim Henson's Muppet Vision 4-D,* while elsewhere in the park *Voyage of the Little Mermaid* corners the cute vote, and Disney's musical prowess is represented by *Beauty and the Beast Live on Stage* and *The Hunchback of Notre Dame.* The park closes after the spectacular nighttime *Fantasmic!* show.

Street sets at Disney-MGM Studios

DISNEY'S ANIMAL KINGDOM THEME PARK

Walt Disney World's latest park focuses its attention on the animal kingdom with a vast 500-acre site showcasing more than 200 species in exotic surroundings. The park's spring 1998 opening was followed a

Disney Enterprises Inc.

Countdown to Extinction, the most popular ride at Disney's Animal Kingdom

year later by the unveiling of the new Asia rain-forest section, making a total of six themed districts. Dedicated animal watchers will find an early start pays off here since, despite every effort to make animals visible to guests throughout the day, they keep their own timetable and are generally more active in the early morning.

Guests enter the park through **The Oasis,** a leafy tropical garden with splashing waterfalls, small animals, and eye-catching flowers designed to slow the pace to a gentle stroll. A bridge leads across to **Safari Village,** the hub of the park and home to the Tree of Life, a 140-foot-tall icon for Disney's Animal Kingdom adorned with 325 carved animals, mythical creatures, and supposedly a few Disney creations carved into its trunk and branches. Meandering trails give a close-up view of the tree, and a movie theater tucked away in the roots presents *It's Tough to be a Bug,* a 3-D view from the insect world.

The first of the park's main themed areas is **Africa.** Another bridge crossing lands guests in Harambe Village, starting point for

Kilimanjaro Safaris, Africa's top attraction. As safari vehicles journey into a well-stocked game reserve, there are opportunities to see and photograph lions, rhinos, hippos, giraffes, crocodiles, wildebeests, and more (segregated by clever landscaping where necessary), until the safari is interrupted by poachers and the vehicles set off in hot pursuit. Still in Africa, gorillas, birds, and weird naked mole rats feature on the Pangani Forest Exploration Trail, and the Wildlife Express to Conservation Station promises animal encounters of a close-up variety.

The steamy rain forests of **Asia** form the backdrop to Kali River Rapids, guaranteed to cool down all on board (see p. 156), and trained birds put on an amazing show at Flights of Wonder. On the Maharajah Jungle Trek, hikers venture though jungle scenery past ancient fortified villages and ruins inhabited by tigers, gibbons, and other exotic Asian animals.

Dinoland U.S.A. offers a complete break from reality. The Oldengate Bridge, a 40-foot *Brachiosaurus* skeleton, marks the entrance to this wacky world of fossils and bones. The top attraction here is Countdown to Extinction, a time travel thrill ride generously punctuated by hurtling meteorites and angry dinosaurs. Gentler diversions include the Cretaceous Trail, lined with plant and animal species that have survived since the dinosaur era, and the Fossil Preparation Lab, where the largest and most complete *Tyrannosaurus rex* skeleton ever found is in the process of being reassembled. Take a break at the *Journey into Jungle Book* stage show and kids can be unleashed on The Boneyard play area.

The final district, **Camp Minnie-Mickey,** is geared toward younger guests with character greetings areas and shows. The best of these is the excellent *Festival of The Lion King,* a high-energy singing, dancing, carnival-style event with specialty acts including acrobats, fire-jugglers, and stilt-walkers.

OTHER WALT DISNEY WORLD ATTRACTIONS

Disney's three water parks offer a fun break from the sight-seeing trail. Take the day out, or just a couple of hours, to sample the imaginatively themed surroundings and adventure activities (admission is included in All-In-One Hopper passes).

Blizzard Beach brings a ski resort to the sun with a dozen adventure zones featuring waterslides, raft rides, tube runs, and lazy Cross Country Creek circling the slopes of Mount Gushmore. The centerpiece at shipwreck-themed **Typhoon Lagoon** is a 2.5-acre wave pool, and there are flumes, waterslides, and the saltwater Shark Reef exhibit where snorkelers can swim with real tropical fish. **River Country** is the oldest and smallest water park, but its rustic-style swimming hole surrounded by giant boulders, rope swings, and

water chutes is great for children. River Country is located in the **Fort Wilderness Resort and Campground,** where guests will find all sorts of outdoor activities from bike and canoe rentals to horseback riding and basketball.

On the shores of Lake Buena Vista, **Downtown Disney** is the Walt Disney World's 66-acre shopping, dining, and entertainment complex. There are three areas, starting with **Marketplace,** a collection of boutiques, cafés, souvenir shops, and World of Disney, the world's largest Disney superstore. The **West Side** entertainment district boasts a 24-screen cinema, the avant-garde brilliance of Cirque du Soleil's stage show, interactive family entertainment at DisneyQuest, and outposts of House of Blues and Gloria Estefan's Bongos Cuban Café for live music and dining, as well as unusual retail stores.

Pleasure Island is Disney's nightclub zone, where a New Year's Eve Street Party is staged at midnight 365 days a year, and guests can dance, dine, and shop until 2 a.m. The clubs include the Rock 'n' Roll Beach Club (hits from the 1960s to the present day); Mannequins Dance Palace (contemporary); BET SoundStage Club (rhythm and blues); and the Wildhorse Saloon (country). ∎

Kilimanjaro Safaris take visitors on the trail of game poachers in Disney's Animal Kingdom.

Disney Enterprises Inc.

SeaWorld of Florida

**SeaWorld
of Florida**

⚠ 153 B4

✉ 7007 Sea World Dr.,
Orlando

☎ 407/351-3600
www.seaworld.com

$ $$$$ (children
under 3 free). Also
great value 4-park
Orlando Flexitickets,
which cover
admission to
SeaWorld, both
Universal Studios
Escape parks, and
the Wet 'n' Wild
water park; 5-park
Flexitickets
include Busch
Gardens, Tampa.

A MARINE THEME PARK THAT DOUBLES AS AN ANIMAL rescue, conservation, and research facility, SeaWorld is a lot of fun as well as being gently educational. The world's most popular sea life park casts its net wide and gathers an all-star cast of performing killer whales, dolphins, sea lions, and otters to accompany excellent aquarium displays and informative presentations on other finned and winged inhabitants of the park.

Orlando's only marine attraction gets busy, but its built-in advantage over conventional parks is the show-driven format with few rides and therefore few lines. The best way to visit the park is to pick up a map at the ticket plaza and plot an itinerary around the shows. Reservations for fascinating glimpses behind the scenes can be made at the adjacent guided tours desk.

One of the park's top attractions is the **Whale & Dolphin Stadium** in the colorful **Key West** themed area. Atlantic bottle-nosed dolphins and false killer

Close encounters with marine life are part of the fun at SeaWorld.

whales provide an action-packed and graceful show, and can also be seen in the two-acre **Dolphin Cove Lagoon.** Rescued turtles look quite at home sunning themselves on the rocks of **Turtle Point,** and guests can pet the inhabitants of **Stingray Lagoon.**

Moving clockwise around the park, **Manatees: The Last Generation?** introduces Florida's loveable but endangered giant sea cows. There are perhaps fewer than 2,000 Florida manatees left in the wild, and SeaWorld makes every effort to rehabilitate and return these rescued manatees.

From an uncertain future to a hair-raising past, the next stop is Journey to Atlantis, the park's only thrill ride (see pp. 156–57). On a gentler note, drop in on the **Penguin Encounter,** which provides both a chance to cool down and cute entertainment as jaunty penguins and their alcid cousins (puffins and mures) waddle about on a re-created ice floe and dive into chilly waters behind the viewing windows.

The atmosphere is definitely West Coast at the **Pacific Point Preserve,** where California sea lions, harbor seals, and South American fur seals lounge around a rocky wave pool. Their hardwork-ing neighbors in the **Sea Lion & Otter Stadium** present one of the best shows in the park involving a hearty dose of slapstick comedy and an endless supply of fishy rewards for the star performers.

There are few jokes but lots of toothsome grins at **Terrors of the Deep.** Dim lights and sugges-tively spooky music accompany a stroll past coral reef aquariums inhabited by lurking moray eels, barracuda, and other predatory

denizens of the deep before a moving walkway takes you through the 660,000-gallon shark tank enclosed in a perspex tube.

Back in the sunny light of day, children might like a quick visit to the **Clydesdale Hamlet** to see the huge Scottish Clydesdale draft horses, while beer lovers can "product sample" at the Anheuser-Busch Hospitality Center.

Past the Flamingo Lagoon and around the central lake, where aquabatic water adventure shows are staged, **Shamu Stadium** is home to the world-famous killer whale and the park's most popular show, a splashtacular event guaranteed to soak everybody in the front 14 rows (and quite a few besides). Behind the stadium, **Shamu's Happy Harbor** is an adventure playground for kids with all sorts

of climbing nets, sliding tubes, a sandpit, and radio-controlled trucks and boats.

The **Wild Arctic** presentation does not sit particularly well with SeaWorld's efforts to provide reasonably natural habitat enclosures for animals largely born in captivity. The somewhat underwhelming simulated helicopter ride to an Arctic base station transports guests to what feels like a darkened subterranean lair where polar bears and walruses sit around with expressions of stultifying boredom, and ghostly gray beluga whales swim endlessly around in circles. The wisdom of relocating species such as these to Central Florida is questionable.

The final stop is **Bayside Stadium,** with seating for the water adventure spectaculars. ∎

The attractions at SeaWorld range from dolphins performing choreographed routines to aquariums with fish and mammals from around the world.

Universal Studios Escape

Universal Studios Escape

🔼 153 B4

✉ 1000 Universal Studios Plaza, Orlando

☎ 407/363-8000
www.universalstudios.com

💲 $$$$ (children under 3 free)

OPENED IN 1970, UNIVERSAL STUDIOS SOON OUTSTRIPPED Disney-MGM Studios for the coveted title of the world's number one combined movie studio and theme park. Disney's arch-rival in Orlando is now set to double in size for the millennium with the opening of the Universal Studios Islands of Adventure theme park in 1999. The two theme parks will be the linchpin of the Universal Studios Escape facility equipped with hotels, entertainment, sports, and shopping complexes.

UNIVERSAL STUDIOS FLORIDA

Universal's original Florida attraction lives up to its "Ride The Movies" slogan with an exciting combination of cutting edge thrill rides, shows, and attractions drawn from the big and small screens. If there is only time for one movie-style attraction on the Orlando theme park itinerary, this is it, but be prepared for lots of walking as the site, which is divided into districts with themed architecture such as Hollywood and San Francisco, is well spread out. Information is available from Guest Services in the Front Lot area, just inside the gates.

To the right of the entrance, the **Hollywood** district is a colorful Californian pastiche of art deco buildings and palm trees harboring

two excellent shows. Don't miss the *Terminator 2:3-D* show, the most elaborate and technologically advanced virtual adventure ever created for a theme park, and the most expensive film frame-for-frame at 24 million dollars for 12 minutes. Specially shot by the original *Terminator* cast and creative team, it is a genuine thriller featuring film footage, live action stunts, and amazing special effects. Next door, it is the story behind special effects that occupies the *Gory, Gruesome, & Grotesque Horror Make-Up Show*.

Moving counterclockwise around the park's central lagoon (the focal point for waterskiing displays and the nightly fireworks), you'll find the **Woody Woodpecker's Kidzone,** opened in the summer of 1999, with plenty to

offer families with small children. Kids can cool off playing in the waterspouts, fool around in Fievel's Playland, and ride the thoughtfully scaled-down Woody Woodpecker's Nuthouse Coaster. The loveable purple dinosaur from TV steals the show at *A Day in the Park with Barney;* junior eco-warriors can hop aboard moving bicycle seats for a cute fantasy ride to rescue the Green Planet in E.T. Adventure; and the entertaining *Animal Actors Show* stars an array of talented birds and beasts. Just around the corner, one of the park's top attractions is the rip-roaring Back to the Future…The Ride, which takes a 21-million-jigowatt time travel spin in Doc Brown's gull-winged DeLorean.

At the far end of the lagoon, the sprawling **San Francisco/Amity** district incorporates a diverse

Convincing effects such as noise, wind, and spray re-create the terror of the 1996 movie, *Twister*.

The rotating globe at the entrance to Universal Studios Escape, flanked by the nighttime laser display

collection of rides and shows. *The Wild, Wild, Wild West Stunt Show* is a good place to take a break and watch the cowboy capers. JAWS is a few-surprises boating encounter with the toothsome one, while Earthquake—The Big One promises a subway journey from hell as passengers experience a simulated quake measuring 8.3 on the Richter scale with tons of tumbling masonry falling around their ears and 65,000 gallons of water swirling through the subway station. It makes the swinging, Motown-singing monsters in *Beetlejuice's Graveyard Revue* look like the participants in a teddy bear's tea party!

New York is the natural home for "Kongfrontation!"—a precarious aerial tramway ride across a darkened Manhattan under siege from an angry four-story-high, six-ton ape. There are more thrills in store at Twister…Ride It Out, where onlookers brave a five-story tornado complete with savage winds and lashing rain passing within 20 feet of their position.

Finally, there is a mixed bag in store at **Production Central,** starting with *Hercules and Xena: Wizards of the Screen,* featuring the TV characters in live action stunts, special effects, and behind-the-scenes action. *Alfred Hitchcock: The Art of Making Movies* is a riveting homage to the master of suspense. The FUNtastic World of Hanna-Barbera offers a family-friendly simulator ride in the company of Yogi Bear, the Flintstones, and others. For fans of the Nickelodeon kids' TV channel, there are back-stage tours of the soundstages, game testing labs, and show tapings at **Nickelodeon Studios.**

UNIVERSAL STUDIOS ISLANDS OF ADVENTURE

Universal's ambitious new theme park takes its inspiration from a host of popular comic book heroes and cartoon characters, classical mythology and mystical legends. The world's most technologically advanced theme park boasts a range of spectacular rides designed to carry Universal into the 21st century way ahead of its rivals.

Access to the park is through the Port of Entry, indicated by the landmark Pharos Lighthouse. Five individually themed "islands" are set around a giant lagoon representing the oceans of the world.

From the Port of Entry it is a short step straight into the bold, primary-colored world of **Marvel Super Hero Island,** and a stunning selection of world-class thrill rides. The Amazing Adventures of Spider-Man (see pp. 156–57) instantly engages guests: Be prepared for a high-speed 3-D chase and stomach-lurching 400-foot "sensory drop." There are more opportunities to lose breakfast by plummeting down the 200-foot towers of Doctor Doom's Fearfall, or hop aboard the Incredible Hulk Coaster (which glows an eerie green at night) to experience G-force similar to that experienced by the pilot of an F16 fighter jet, weightlessness, and seven inversions.

Toon Lagoon is home to the Sunday comics from Beetle Bailey and Hagar the Horrible to Betty Boop, who hang out in Comic Strip Lane. The rides are water-oriented with passengers aboard the distinctly splashy Dudley Do-Right's Ripsaw Falls, helping the Canadian Mountie to rescue his girl and ending up 15 feet below the water level in the first flume to venture below the surface. Popeye & Pluto's Bilge-Rat Barges are 12-man rafts heading for a white-water experience. Little kids can also get truly drenched in Me Ship, Me Olive, an interactive play area.

For a close encounter of the dinosaur kind, make tracks for **Jurassic Park.** Based on Spielberg's movie blockbuster, this lush, tropical area harbors the gently educational Jurassic Park Discovery Center, and Jurassic Park River Adventure, a boat ride past extraordinarily realistic five-story-high dinosaurs with a scary plunge off a waterfall at the end. The Triceratops Encounter offers a chance to pet a "living" dinosaur, actually one of the most realistic animatronic creatures ever made. For a bird's eye view of Jurassic Park, hitch a ride on one of the Pteranodon Flyers atop the Camp Jurassic play area.

Myths and legends form the backdrop to the **Lost Continent.** *Poseidon's Fury: Escape From The Lost City* pitches visitors into a battle between the Greek gods of water (Poseidon) and fire (Zeus) with staggering special effects. *The Eighth Voyage of Sinbad* features a dramatic stunt show involving

shipwrecks, water explosions, and some 50 flaming pyrotechnic effects. Yet the Lost Continent's outstanding offering is probably "Dueling Dragons" (see pp. 156–57).

After all the excitement, take time to relax in the wacky

surroundings of **Seuss Landing.** The whimsical world of Theodor Geisel, better known as Dr. Seuss, comes alive in this escapist fantasy-land where the designers took extra care to keep straight lines to a minimum and horticulturists are busy trying to grow spiral-shaped trees true to the original storybook illustrations. Six-passenger "couches" carry visitors through The Cat In The Hat ride with its jokey animatronic characters and special effects. The One Fish Two Fish Red Fish Blue Fish ride allows kids to guide their Seussian-style fish transport through a series of water-spouts, streams, and squirt posts that douse riders who fail to follow the special rhyme.

Other adventures include the Caro-Seuss-el, with its cast of favorite Seuss characters, and **If I Ran The Zoo,** an engaging play area with "toe tickle" stations where little kids can tickle the toes of a laughing Seussian creature. ∎

Young visitors enjoy meeting Barney, the big purple dinosaur.

Lake Wales

Lake Wales

🅜 153 B3

Visitor information

✉ 340 W. Central Ave.

☎ 941/676-3445

Bok Tower Gardens

✉ 1151 Tower Blvd.

☎ 941/676-9412

💲 $

Lake Wales

HALF AN HOUR'S DRIVE FROM WALT DISNEY WORLD AND 60 miles southwest of Orlando, Lake Wales is a small town on a small lake. The community is proud of its old-fashioned main street, and of being the winter home of the Black Hills Passion Play. In the surrounding countryside are orange groves and, rising up to a towering 250 feet about sea level, the ridge that runs down the middle of Florida.

Although there are numerous gardens in Florida, nowhere has the spiritual quality of the hilltop **Bok Tower Gardens.** A sacred place for the Indians and the highest point on the whole peninsula, its views stretch for miles across the orange groves and houses. At the heart of the 157 acres is a 200-foot-high tower with a 57-bell carillon. Wherever you are, you can hear the music, whether recorded or played live by the carillonneur.

When Bok bought the first tract of land here in 1922, it was a sandy hill covered by native pine trees. Today, in the shady garden designed by Frederick Law Olmsted, Jr., and William Lyman Phillips, plants bloom year long. Visit in March and April, when banks of nun's orchids wave in the breeze, their white blossoms like the wimples of a nun's habit. Pay your respects to Edward Bok, whose simple grave is across the reflecting pool, in front of the tower. ■

Highly decorated with sculptures and tiles, Bok Tower is built of pink and gray Georgia marble and Florida coquina rock.

Edward Bok

Edward Bok achieved the American dream. Born in the Netherlands in 1863, he moved to the United States when he was six years old. From a lowly office boy, he worked his way up to be editor of the *Ladies Home Journal.* By selling the magazine for only 10 cents, he undercut more serious and expensive rivals and gained a circulation of more than one million copies.

But Bok was more than just a publishing mogul; he fought for better childcare and sex education, and endowed numerous public awards, including $100,000 for the American Peace Award. These projects, and the garden itself, were ways of thanking his adopted country. ■

Cypress Gardens

AFTER A CAREER AS A PUBLICIST, DICK POPE DECIDED TO open an exotic garden to the public. A perfectionist who was never afraid to get his hands dirty, his crowd-pullers were photography and publicity.

Cypress Gardens is well-known for innovative routines in water-skiing, including daredevil extreme skiing and ballet on skis. Over 50 years ago, the cast of the show consisted of four children, aged between 8 and 13. During World War II, Dick Pope was away in the army, leaving his wife, Julie, in charge. The day after the *Orlando Sentinel* ran a photograph of the gardens, which by chance showed water-skiers in the background, three GIs turned up wanting to see "the show." When Julie's kids and their friends came home from school, the first-ever show commenced. Dick Jr., aged only 11 at the time, went on to become the world's first great water-ski champion and the first person ever to ski barefoot, in 1947.

From the original 37 acres, the park has expanded to more than 200 acres, filled with 8,000 varieties of subtropical and tropical flowers and plants. The most relaxing way to see them is on the guided **Botanical Boat Cruise** (tours start near the main entrance), gliding through the canals past huge, bald cypress trees—related to Sequoias and among the earth's oldest living plant life. Continuing through the canals, the boatman points out the flowers and wildlife; then, right on cue, you pass a Southern belle sitting prettily on a bench, waiting to be photographed.

For a bird's-eye view of the park and surrounding countryside, go up in the viewing tower, which rises 16 stories and slowly revolves. From here you can spot Bok Tower some 10 miles away (see p. 172).

Apart from the botanical interest, there are regular shows: big band concerts, ice-skating, hang gliding, and the world-famous water-skiing performances. One of the most popular year-round displays is in the **Butterfly Conservatory.** Among the thousand fluttering pairs of wings, a flash of iridescent sapphire could be the Blue Morpho from the Amazon, but there are more than 30 other varieties. ■

Cypress Gardens

◮ 153 B3

✉ Fla. 540, off US 27, Winter Haven

☎ 941/324-2111
www.cypressgardens. com

💲 $$$$

Cypress Gardens has hosted regular water-ski shows for over 50 years.

Orange Picking Time in Florida

Orange picking 1941: Before Disney, central Florida was best known for its citrus industry.

Florida's citrus treasure

Study a map of Florida and you'll find a dozen towns with Orange in their names, let alone Satsuma, Mandarin, and Lemon Grove. Florida produces one-third of the world's grapefruit, while only Brazil produces more oranges. Over 300 million boxes of citrus fruits are harvested annually, mainly from the 100-mile-long spine in central Florida, from Leesburg to Sebring.

After the role of citrus in preventing scurvy was recognized 500 years ago, Spanish sailors were ordered to carry orange seeds to plant in the New World. Thanks to Ponce de León's men, wild oranges thrived around St. Augustine in the 16th century, but it took a Yankee to grow them commercially. When the Spanish left St. Augustine in 1763, Jesse Fish bought 10,000

acres at a knockdown price and started mass production. Grapefruit were introduced to Florida by a French count, Odet Philippe, who planted the first significant groves near Safety Harbor on Old Tampa Bay in 1823.

The story of citrus in Florida is one of boom and bust. In 1835 a crippling freeze wiped out almost all the orange trees in northern Florida. Only Douglas Dummett's grove near Indian River survived, and Indian River has been synonymous with extra-sweet, extra-juicy fruit ever since. After the Civil War, the industry boomed, reaching a record harvest of one million boxes. Then came "the freeze of the century" in the winter of 1894–95. On December 29, train whistles blew a warning in Orange County as the temperature plummeted to 24°F. Overnight a grove worth $45,000

Oranges come in all shapes and sizes: a drive-in restaurant in Orlando

became worthless. A second frost five weeks later finished off nearly all the remaining citrus trees in northern Florida.

> …trees popped like pistol shots as trees burst their bark! It sounded like the 4th of July.
> —A little girl's diary, Orange County, February 7, 1895, the night the temperature dropped to 17°F.

Growers planted farther south, but normal production levels were not reached until 1910.

In 1935 a new Citrus Commission gave the industry a focus. As quality and distribution were improved, sales increased. Today, the industry employs 100,000 workers and generates eight billion dollars a year from the 12,000 growers, who own more than 100 million trees, covering nearly a million acres. At Lake Alfred, scientists at the Citrus Research and Education Center not only strive to perfect the popular varieties of fruit, but keep a constant vigil for the destructive "Medfly," the Mediterranean fruit fly.

An important development was the invention, just after World War II, of a way of concentrating, then freezing, orange juice. Since then, a glass of OJ, with its 50 milligrams of vitamin C, has been a part of breakfasts around the world. Today, 90 percent of all Florida's oranges are immediately made into juice, a total of 1.5 billion gallons each year. No wonder it was declared the official state beverage in 1967. The waste peel, seeds, and pulp are all used: Useful oils and scents are retrieved, but most is reprocessed for cattle fodder.

To see a grove and how the packing process works, take a self-guided tour at Palm Beach Groves (*7149 Lawrence Rd., Lantana, FL 33462, Tel 407/965-6699. Closed May–Oct., call ahead*). ■

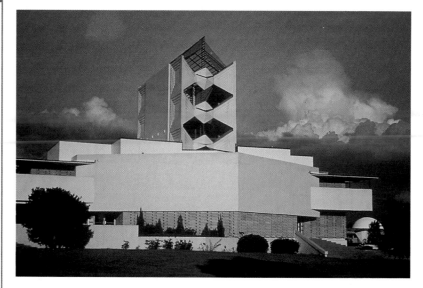

Lakeland

LAKELAND IS NOT WELL KNOWN IN FLORIDA, LET ALONE outside it, yet this town is a place of pilgrimage for fans of architecture. Here, the largest one-site collection of Frank Lloyd Wright buildings stands on the Florida Southern College campus.

In 1938, Wright was 67 when he was lured to the small Methodist institution of **Florida Southern College** by the promise of carte blanche from the president, Dr. Ludd Spivey, who dreamed of building the modern American campus. Wright designed 18 structures, of which 12 were built between 1938 and 1958. They still look strikingly contemporary.

Students helped construct the **Annie Pfeiffer Chapel,** the first building on campus, whose tower is irreverently known as the "bicycle rack in the sky." Look for the small blocks of yellow and blue glass, put in place by hand, through which light enters and breaks up the stream of concrete. The last building was the **Polk County Science Building,** whose trilevel flat roofs and long, horizontal lines typify Wright's style. Linking the structures is the **Esplanade,** a 1.5-mile system of covered walkways.

"Was Frank Lloyd Wright short?" is a common question from those perplexed by the college's low roofline. For Wright, design was sometimes more important than practicality. When Dr. Spivey complained that his office ceiling leaked, dripping water on to his papers, Wright replied: "Move your desk." Few alterations have been made. In the sweeping curve of the **E.T. Roux Library**'s reading room, a dropped book sounded "like a bomb going off," so carpet was laid.

Yet the whole remains true to Wright's vision of "organic architecture," representing "...the laws of harmony and rhythm." ■

Lakeland
Ⓐ 153 A3
Visitor information
✉ 35 Lake Morton Dr.
☎ 941/688-8551

Florida Southern College
✉ 111 Lake Hollingsworth Dr.
☎ 941/680-4110
Ⓢ Free. Self-guided walking tour pamphlet available from Frank Lloyd Wright Visitor Center on FSC campus

Nowhere are there greater contrasts in Florida. Juxtaposed with the original denizens of the coastal marshlands are the metallic monoliths representing man's lust for speed and the conquest of space.

Space & speed

At Daytona, the race is on.

Space & speed

ALONG THIS PART OF THE FLORIDA COAST, THE WIDE, FLAT ATLANTIC beaches and water sports are the main draw. Some towns, such as Daytona Beach, are dedicated to out-and-out fun; others, like Cocoa and New Smyrna Beach, are quieter, with an old-fashioned atmosphere. Most people spend their time fishing or sailing on the rolling ocean, or along the calm ribbon of water wedged between the mainland and the barrier islands. For the sightseer, the coast has three major magnets: the rockets of Kennedy Space Center; the automobiles of Daytona International Speedway; and the often less appreciated wildlife that survives, and even thrives, on and around Merritt Island.

Motorcycle enthusiasts flock to Daytona to experience the thrill of the track.

The Kennedy Space Center dominates the long, thin strip that is Brevard County. The livelihood of the inhabitants is inextricably linked to the U.S. space program, which has grown dramatically since its first faltering steps after World War II. Although the major feature of this section is KSC, the popular shorthand for the Kennedy Space Center, farther north is Daytona Beach, where the automobile broke speed records on the hard-packed sand.

Other attractions well worth visiting include an observatory and a garden that has just been revived after years of neglect. Cape Canaveral is where the starter fired the gun for the Space Race.

When an unmanned U.S. satellite was eventually launched successfully from Cape Canaveral in January 1958, it was the size of a Florida grapefruit. For a decade, the Soviets were always one step ahead as both countries battled to put their man on the moon first. In September 1968, Zond 4, an unmanned capsule, was the first spaceship to loop around the moon. On July 20, 1969, as the world watched live on television, the spiderlike lunar module landed safely, and Neil Armstrong announced "That's one small step for man, one giant leap for mankind."

Daytona Beach is in Volusia County, where the wide, flat beaches have sand hard enough for cars to not only drive but also to

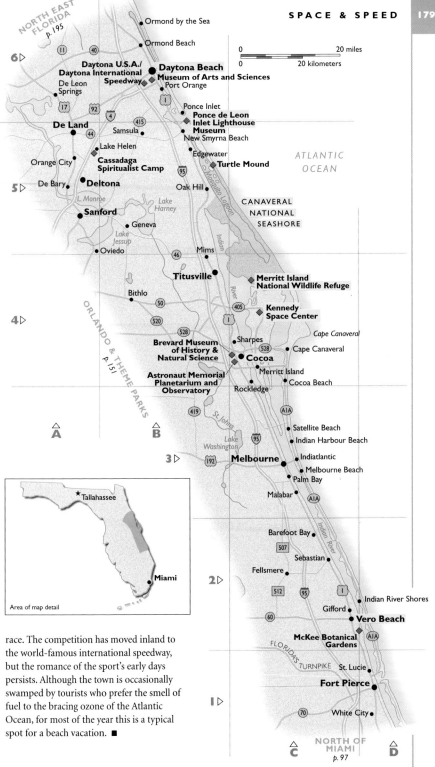

p. 195

NORTH EAST
FLORIDA

Ormond by the Sea
Ormond Beach

0   20 miles
0   20 kilometers

6 ▷

Daytona U.S.A./
Daytona International
Speedway
De Leon
Springs

Daytona Beach
Museum of Arts and Sciences
Port Orange

De Land

Ponce Inlet
Ponce de Leon
Inlet Lighthouse
Museum
New Smyrna Beach

Samsula

Lake Helen

Cassadaga
Spiritualist Camp

Edgewater
Turtle Mound

Orange City

5 ▷

De Bary   **Deltona**

Oak Hill

ATLANTIC
OCEAN

L. Monroe   Lake
Harney

Sanford

Geneva

Lake
Jessup

Oviedo

CANAVERAL
NATIONAL
SEASHORE

Mims

Titusville

Bithlo

Merritt Island
National Wildlife Refuge

4 ▷

ORLANDO & THEME PARKS
p. 151

Kennedy
Space Center

Cape Canaveral

Sharpes
Brevard Museum
of History &
Natural Science
Cocoa

Cape Canaveral

Astronaut Memorial
Planetarium and
Observatory

Merritt Island
Cocoa Beach
Rockledge

△ A   △ B

St. Johns

Satellite Beach
Indian Harbour Beach

Lake
Washington

3 ▷   **Melbourne**

Indiatlantic
Melbourne Beach
Palm Bay

Malabar

Tallahassee

Barefoot Bay

Sebastian

Fellsmere

Miami

2 ▷

Indian River Shores

Gifford
Vero Beach

Area of map detail

McKee Botanical
Gardens

FLORIDA'S
TURNPIKE   St. Lucie

race. The competition has moved inland to
the world-famous international speedway,
but the romance of the sport's early days
persists. Although the town is occasionally
swamped by tourists who prefer the smell of
fuel to the bracing ozone of the Atlantic
Ocean, for most of the year this is a typical
spot for a beach vacation. ■

Fort Pierce

1 ▷

White City

△ C   NORTH OF
MIAMI
p. 97   △ D

Vero Beach

Vero Beach
🄰 179 C2
Visitor information
✉ 1216 21st St.
☎ 561/567-3491

McKee Botanical Gardens
✉ 350 US 1,
S of Vero Beach
☎ 561/794-0601
💲 $$

A 60-year-old postcard of McKee gardens

VERO BEACH IS ONE OF FLORIDA'S LESSER KNOWN RESORT towns, and locals are happy for it to remain so. Mainly residential, this affluent community is proud of its theater, arts center, a restored exotic garden that is an important part of Florida's horticultural heritage, and superb beaches.

Take 17th Street Bridge or Barber Bridge across the Intracoastal Waterway to Orchid Island, where the Riverside Park cultural complex stands in a huge waterside park. Here you will find the **Riverside Theater** (*3250 Riverside Pk. Dr., Tel 561/231-6990*), which stages several shows a year, and the **Center for the Arts** (*3001*

WATER LILIES IN BEAUTIFUL FLORIDA—F91
MCKEE JUNGLE GARDENS, VERO BEACH

Riverside Pk. Dr., Tel 561/231-0707). This museum has an eclectic collection of mainly 20th-century works, galleries for temporary exhibitions, and the largest museum art school in Florida.

Just south of town the **McKee Botanical Gardens** reopened in late 1999 after a major restoration. Back in the 1930s, these were a major attraction, a Ripley's Believe It or Not! of botany.

So why is McKee not better known today? The story dates back to the 1920s, when Cleveland industrialist Arthur McKee and citrus farmer Waldo Sexton saved a slice of coastal hammock from being turned into yet another orange grove. They introduced exotic plants from South America, and in 1932 hired landscape designer William Lyman Phillips.

Phillips' instructions were to transform 80 acres into a "World's Fair of Nature," a jungle garden that would be a public attraction. Botanist David Fairchild supplied exotic plants and seeds, while McKee designed the world's first mechanically run, air-conditioned greenhouse for his beloved orchids, which featured in NATIONAL GEOGRAPHIC in 1958.

What you see today is the renovated **Hall of Giants,** the **Spanish Kitchen,** and the core of Phillips' design. Footpaths lead past native and exotic plants, including species ranging from the Old Man in the Jungle, a 350-year-old live oak, to the rare Malaysian black sugar palm. ■

Cocoa

ON YET ANOTHER BARRIER ISLAND, COCOA BEACH HAS more to offer than a broad beach, oceanfront hotels, and the local landmark, Ron Jon's Surf Shop. Across the causeway on the mainland, the restored Cocoa Village is a charming, old-fashioned enclave.

Soak up the atmosphere as you wander through the brick paved historic downtown with its popular shops and restaurants. A short drive from here are two attractions that deserve to be better known.

About 6 miles northwest of town, the **Brevard Museum** may be small, but it holds important archaeological clues to Florida's ancient past. In 1984, as a

Weapons, food, and jewelry in the graves prove that the tribe believed in an afterlife.

A visit to the **Astronaut Memorial Planetarium and Observatory,** a few minutes by car from the Brevard Museum, is a must. Where else can you look through a 24-inch telescope at skies that are clear on 300 nights every year? An expert is on hand to

Cocoa

🗺 179 C4

Visitor information

✉ 400 Fortenberry Rd., Merritt Island

☎ 407/459-2200

Brevard Museum of History & Natural Science

✉ 2201 Michigan Ave.

☎ 407/632-1830

🕐 Closed Mon.

💲 $

The sleepy town of Cocoa

bulldozer was clearing a swamp by Windover Pond, to the south of Titusville, the driver struck what he thought were rocks. In fact, they were human skulls. Archaeologists moved in, uncovering a 7,000-year-old burial ground. With complete skeletons and even brain tissue, experts can run DNA tests to reveal new insights into an ancient people.

The museum's display portrays the life of the Indians, while the re-creation of a grave shows how bodies were placed in the fetal position, covered with a burlaplike material and anchored into the swamp with sharpened sticks.

explain what you are seeing, perhaps a straightforward planet, or "Globular cluster M53"; looking like a fuzzy ball of light to the untutored eye, this is actually several hundred thousand stars traveling together like a swarm.

Downstairs in the planetarium, you can sit back and see the sky as the astronauts do, thanks to the simultaneous playing of two different projection systems. There are also laser shows with music and exhibits on the development of manned space programs, as well as the scientific principles relating to space exploration. ∎

Brevard Community College Astronaut Memorial Planetarium and Observatory

✉ 1519 Clearlake Rd.

☎ 407/634-3732

🕐 Call for hours, program schedules, & telescope viewing

💲 $

Kennedy Space Center

AS EXCITING AS A THEME PARK, AND AS EDUCATIONAL AS A museum, the John F. Kennedy Space Center is one of Florida's finest attractions. This is the place to learn about the past, present, and future of the American space program. At the end of the day, enthusiasts will be ready to sign up for a mission, while even die-hard opponents of the world's most expensive scientific research project must acknowledge the scale of man's achievement.

Kennedy Space Center Visitor Complex

🅰 179 C4
✉ NASA Pkwy. (Fla. 405)
☎ 407/452-2121
www.kennedyspace center.com
🆂 Visitor complex free; bus tour $$

Dominating the landscape for miles around is the Vehicle Assembly Building (V.A.B.), one element of a massive complex about one-fifth the size of Rhode Island. Just offshore on Merritt Island, NASA shares its hi-tech home with rare and endangered wildlife. On the 220 square miles of sand, swamp, and waterways, manatees and bald eagles coexist peacefully with the launch pads for giant rockets. A little farther to the east is another island, Cape Canaveral, used both by the United States military and to launch commercial payloads (see pp. 187).

Allow at least one full day to explore the **Kennedy Space Center Visitor Complex,** which covers 70 acres, including an outdoor gallery of rockets, a copy of the space shuttle orbiter, and IMAX theaters. Special bus tours leave regularly from the visitor complex to drive past the launch pads, the V.A.B., the Shuttle Landing Facility, and the runway where returning orbiters land. These working areas are not open to the public. Since 1998, the buses also stop at the Apollo/Saturn V Center, the Launch Complex (L.C.) Observation Gantry, and the International Space Station Center.

On a second route, the tour bus covers the early days of the space program by visiting the Air Force Space Museum on Cape Canaveral. An early start is advisable to avoid long lines, although listening to Houston mission control over loudspeakers is an entertaining diversion. Aboard the Kennedy Space Center tour bus, the recorded commentary is by James Lovell, Commander of Apollo 11.

VEHICLE ASSEMBLY BUILDING

The V.A.B. is the first building the bus passes on the tour. Its claim to being the third largest building in the world is based on volume rather than height (it is 535 feet tall). Each stripe of the American flag painted on the outside is ten feet wide; the blue field behind the stars is larger than a basketball court. Designed to accommodate four Saturn V rockets, the V.A.B. could swallow up two Empire State Buildings. When it was adapted later for the shuttle program, its entrances had to be widened at

Launch information

Both NASA and the Air Force have regular rocket launches throughout the year. For information, call 407/867-4636. For vehicle passes allowing access to the Kennedy Space Center during a launch, call 407/867-6000. Otherwise, the best viewing sites are along US 1 and the Indian River in downtown Titusville, or one of the nearby beaches. ■

The space shuttle *Endeavour* leaves the launch pad at Kennedy Space Center.

Top: The U.S. Astronaut Hall of Fame Gallery of space memorabilia
Above: Simulating a space shuttle landing

the bottom, since the shuttle has stubby landing wings. These doors are so large that three people need about 45 minutes to open them.

Inside, shuttles are prepared for launch. Step-by-step the vehicle is "stacked" (or assembled) on a mobile launcher platform. First come the twin solid rocket boosters, then the orange external tank. The shuttle orbiter is hoisted high, then gently lowered into place and attached to the tank. Once all is ready, the two crawler transporters —giant tractors on caterpillar treads, each half the size of a soccer field—lumber along to the launch pad. With a top speed of one mph, the short journey takes seven hours. In 30 years, the machines have covered 1,000 miles, powered by engines that get a mere 35 feet to the gallon with a shuttle on board.

L.C. 39
OBSERVATION GANTRY

The bus tour stops near two launch pads, 39A and 39B, allowing time to see film and videos that bring the monolithic structures to life. These are the lunar lift-off sites; all but one of the moon missions blasted off from here. Below each pad is a flame trench; nearby is a water tower. Twenty seconds before take-off, 300,000 gallons of water are released onto the pad. The liquid helps to reduce the awesome power of the sound waves, preventing them from bouncing back off the ground and damaging the rocket.

While walking down the stairs, take a moment to look at one of the shuttle's main engines. Although it looks ordinary, it generates 375,000 pounds of thrust and is fueled with 500,000 gallons of cryogenic propellant. Its job, to take the shuttle out of earth's gravity field, lasts for only 8.5 minutes.

APOLLO/
SATURN V CENTER

This stop is the most impressive and exciting part of the entire tour.

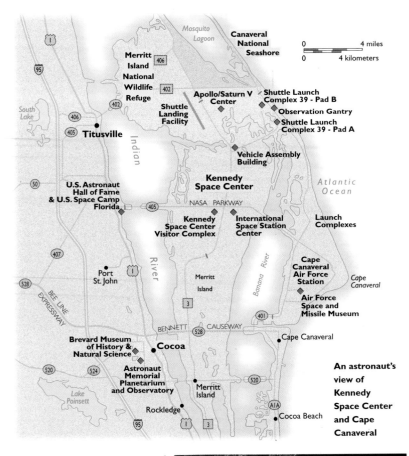

Mosquito Lagoon

Canaveral National Seashore

Merritt Island National Wildlife Refuge

0 ——— 4 miles
0 ——— 4 kilometers

Apollo/Saturn V Center

Shuttle Launch Complex 39 - Pad B

Observation Gantry

Shuttle Launch Complex 39 - Pad A

Shuttle Landing Facility

Titusville

Vehicle Assembly Building

Indian

Kennedy Space Center

NASA PARKWAY

Atlantic Ocean

U.S. Astronaut Hall of Fame & U.S. Space Camp Florida

Kennedy Space Center Visitor Complex

International Space Station Center

Launch Complexes

River

Port St. John

Merritt Island

Cape Canaveral Air Force Station

Cape Canaveral

Banana River

Air Force Space and Missile Museum

BEE LINE EXPRESSWAY

BENNETT CAUSEWAY

Cape Canaveral

Brevard Museum of History & Natural Science

Cocoa

Astronaut Memorial Planetarium and Observatory

Merritt Island

Lake Poinsett

Rockledge

Cocoa Beach

An astronaut's view of Kennedy Space Center and Cape Canaveral

In the Firing Room Theater, a multimedia show traces the development of the rocket that took American astronauts to the moon. It is a heroic tale.

In 1967 a fire in the capsule of Apollo 1 killed three astronauts during tests. The whole project went back to the drawing board. A new rocket was designed and built: the Saturn V. At 36 stories high, it had the explosive power of an atomic bomb; for safety, all staff had to be 3 miles away at lift-off. The fuel in the tank was so cold that ice formed on the outside; astronauts could hear the metal skin expanding and

Space shuttle
orbiter
Columbia at
Launch Pad 39A,
ready for take off

**U.S. Astronaut Hall
of Fame**

✉ 6225 Vectorspace
Blvd. (Fla. 405),
Titusville

☎ 407/269-6100

💲 $$

U.S. Astronaut Hall of Fame

While the Kennedy Space Center gives an overview of the American space program, the Hall of Fame focuses on the astronauts. As well as memorabilia, computer displays, and films, there is a time line that places space milestones against events of American life in the 1960s.

The Apollo program was the latest in technology, but the computer known as the "fourth crew member" only had the "smarts of the average pocket calculator" of today. On display is a mission checklist covered by the scribbled calculations of Fred Haise, a sobering souvenir of the near disaster Apollo 13 in 1970.

For would-be spacemen and women, there are hi-tech simulators in "Astronaut Adventure" that will allow visitors to experience a shuttle landing. Adjacent is United States Space Camp Florida, where campers build and launch a rocket, simulate zero gravity on a special climbing frame, experience a G-force trainer, and perform experiments in a copy of Skylab. ■

Next door, in the hangarlike room, is one of the Saturn V rockets from the Apollo missions. The sheer scale of this rocket leaves everyone open-mouthed. One of only three remaining and the largest ever made, it is twice the size of a space shuttle and longer than a soccer field. Now fondly called the old man's rocket because of its smooth ride, the Saturn was an astonishing 19 times more powerful than the Titan rocket that had propelled the Gemini crews only two years earlier.

INTERNATIONAL SPACE STATION CENTER

When you step into this building, you cross the threshold to the future. An elevated walkway provides a view of technicians at work, dressed in the blue "bunny suits" that are sterilized as carefully as if they were employed in a hospital operating room. Their job is to test and check the components of the modules that will be taken into space, ready to be fitted together to build the space station. When finished, in 2002, the station will be as large as two soccer fields and visible from earth. On board will be seven laboratories for experiments in growing plants and measuring combustion in microgravity.

CAPE CANAVERAL AIR FORCE SPACE & MISSILE MUSEUM

Not far from Kennedy Space Center is Cape Canaveral Air Station, used for military launches and commercial payloads. The exhibits here are interesting but decidedly old-fashioned. They trace the progression of rocketry over the centuries, while outside, like old soldiers on parade, weapons of destruction such as the Polaris or Pershing missiles are placed alongside the Atlas and Redstone rockets, which were later adapted for space exploration. ■

Cape Canaveral Air Force Space & Missile Museum
✉ 191 Museum Circle, Patrick A.F.B., Cape Canaveral
☎ 407/853-3245

contracting. The first launch depended on the perfect functioning of more than two million separate systems—which could not be tested together until the actual day. On December 21, 1968, the Apollo 8 crew, William Anders, Frank Borman, and James Lovell, were the guinea pigs for man's first mission to the moon. As you watch a film of the historic events on a huge screen, tension mounts. From "ignition" to "lift-off" feels more like minutes than seconds. Finally, the umbilical cord falls away and the rocket slowly surges skyward. There is an audible sigh from the audience.

Merritt Island
National Wildlife
Refuge

🅐 179 C4

✉ Kennedy Space
Center, Fla. 402,
Titusville

☎ 407/861-0667

🕐 Visitor center closed
Sun. April–Oct.
Refuge closed dusk
to dawn & during
shuttle launches

💲 $

**Merritt Island
National Wildlife
Refuge is a
paradise for
birdwatchers.**

Merritt Island National Wildlife Refuge

ALTHOUGH YOU CAN SEE THE VEHICLE ASSEMBLY Building at Kennedy Space Center (see pp. 182–84) as you drive into the refuge on Fla. 402, the noise and tremors of a launch do not seem to bother the wildlife. This 25-mile-long barrier island is not only a transition zone between the temperate and subtropical climates, it is on the major north–south flyway. Of all the national wildlife refuges around the country, only two have a greater variety, and only those in Hawaii protect more endangered species.

Here, bird life ranges from the permanent residents, such as the endangered wood storks, only seen in the southeastern United States, to migratory warblers. These transients, weighing only one ounce, ride the cold fronts at night, but can spend weeks here, depending on the weather. Add in the blue-winged teal, American wigeon, Yellow-rumped warbler, and raptors such as the bald eagle, and this is a bird-watcher's paradise.

Follow the self-guided, 6-mile **Black Point Wildlife Drive** or walk one of the three trails. In winter, take a guided tour or join a birding class to learn how to spot the different species. In the heart of the refuge are orange groves, descendants of the trees planted by Douglas Dummett in 1830 (see p. 174). ∎

Canaveral
National Seashore

THIS CONSERVATION AREA PROTECTS MORE THAN 57,000 acres. The 24 miles of shoreline comprise the longest stretch of unspoiled beach on Florida's east coast. There are two access points: Fla. 406/402 from Titusville enters the South District, with a large array of wildlife; and US 41A reaches the North District, with more history, via New Smyrna Beach.

Canaveral National Seashore

🅐 179 C5
☎ 407/267-3036
🅢 $

There are more than a hundred Indian mounds, including **Turtle Mound** and **Castle Windy,** a midden, or hill of discarded shells, left by the Timucuan. They lived in this area from 800 to 1400. From the lookout, the view northward is pure 20th century. Gaze to the south, however, and you look over the hammock to the lagoon and sea, as the Timucuan would have done.

Visitors stop at one of two parking areas along the coast and take the boardwalks to the beach, which offers something for everyone, from surfers to families to nature lovers.

This is a great area for turtle-watching. Visitors are led by rangers between May to August (you will need to reserve a place well in advance) and may see loggerhead and leatherback turtles.

Other activities here include ranger-led canoeing trips and talks on fish and wildlife. ■

Sea turtles

Once hunted for their meat, sea turtles are now a protected species in Florida. From May to October, beaches double as nesting grounds for the threatened loggerhead, as well as the endangered leatherback and green turtles.

Although turtles can live for 60 to 90 years, they are at their most vulnerable early in life. The females lay their eggs between April and August. Digging a hole in the sand with their flippers, they lay about 100 round, white, leathery eggs. After covering them with sand, they return to the water.

Volunteers often guard the nests. Sixty days later, tiny turtles emerge at night, making a frantic dash for the ocean. The survivors fatten up in the Sargassum Sea, a seaweed-rich area of the Atlantic Ocean. The leatherback, the largest

of the turtles, can grow up to 6 feet in length and up to 1,300 pounds

Educational Turtle Watch programs run between May and October. Contact local national or state park services, museum, or environmental program for details. ■

The green sea turtle can grow to 300 pounds and 3 feet in length.

Birthplace of speed

*…the car was out of sight…obscured by
a swirling sand. We did see a big blue ball
of flame that hung in mid-air for a second…That ear-shattering blast and the
eerie ball of flame when Campbell cut the
throttle are the only memories I have….*
—Bill Tuthill, witness to Sir Malcolm
Campbell's 1935 world speed record

In 1935, Britain's Sir Malcolm Campbell, the
most glamorous driver of his day, hurtled
along Daytona Beach and Ormond Beach at
276.82 mph to set a new world land-speed
record. This "Birthplace of Speed" is not a
racing circuit, but a 26-mile stretch of hard-
packed sand, 500 feet wide.

In the winter of 1902, two rival automobile
manufacturers vacationed here. Ransom Olds
boasted that his Oldsmobile was faster than
Alexander Winton's Winton. A year later, they
returned to settle the dispute. Winton's car,
the Bullet, was like a box on wheels, with the
driving seat on top of the chassis. The Pirate,
driven by Olds, looked like a trotting sulky
with a torpedo-shape engine. On March 26,
1903, they raced all day on the sands, reaching
57 mph. The result was a dead heat.

The following winter, they returned with
professional drivers. Driven by Barna "Barney"
Oldfield, America's leading driver, the Winton
screamed across the sand at 68.19 mph, the first
automobile to break the mile-a-minute barrier.
The speed wars had begun. On January 26,
1907, Frederick H. Marriott reached 150 mph
in Wogglebug, his Stanley Steamer, and drivers
from all over the world came to what was, from
1927 to 1935, the official Automobile Speed
Proving Ground for record attempts. Speed
attempts were made early in the year, when the
tides were particularly high and low, leaving the
beach smooth and wide. The 10-mile strip
allowed drivers to get up to speed before
triggering the steel timing wire that measured
the official mile between posts four and five.

Britain's Sir Henry Segrave, the first man to hold the world land- and water-speed records simultaneously, registered 203.79 mph in a Sunbeam in 1927. The following year Sir Malcolm Campbell, the "dashing Englishman," set several records in his Bluebird cars. Crowds watched from the dunes, including schoolchildren who were given the day off.

Visitors to the DAYTONA U.S.A. exhibit can see Campbell's Bluebird V, the 30-foot, cigar-shape car powered by a V-12, which set the world record of 276.82 mph. The record will never be beaten at Daytona; in 1935 the time trials moved to Utah.

Campbell's record run was watched by "Big Bill" France. Legend has it that when his automobile broke down in Daytona, he decided to stay. The Northerner not only raced his dad's Model T Ford, but also organized races on a 3.2-mile oval circuit that was part

Curious spectators crowd around Sir Malcolm Campbell (above) and his Bluebird car in 1934 before yet another attempt to break the world land-speed record. Rival men and rival machines meet on the firm Atlantic beach where the legend of speed was born at the start of the 20th century: Ransom Olds (left) at the wheel of his Pirate in 1903 and Alexander Winton (right) in Bullet in 1904.

beach and part road. Drivers headed north along the sand, then turned onto the blacktop of Atlantic Avenue, hurtling south on what is now Fla. A1A. The sliding turns were dangerous, but "that was really racing."

Drivers practiced around Daytona, then met up at Charlie's High Hat Club for the race draw. In 1947, France and Bill Tuthill founded a circuit that still flourishes right across the United States. In 1959, France achieved his dream of opening a genuine track. The concrete bowl of the Daytona International Speedway still hosts one of four N.A.S.C.A.R. (National Association for Stock Car Auto Racing) major events on the N.A.S.C.A.R. calendar, the Daytona 500-mile Endurance Race. Meanwhile, the tradition of driving the beach survives: Private cars can cruise the shore for a $5 fee...limited to 10 mph. ∎

Cars hurtle out of the banked bend of Daytona's International Speedway circuit.

Daytona Beach

THIS SEASIDE TOWN HAS A WALL OF TALL HOTELS AND condominiums overlooking the sands. The traditional attractions include a pier, bandstand, and open-air amphitheater, but the major draws are the speedway and museum devoted to automobile racing. The unexpected attraction is the Museum of Arts and Sciences, with its collections of Cuban and American art.

Daytona Beach
179 B6
Visitor information
126 E. Orange Ave.
904/255-0415

DAYTONA U.S.A./Daytona International Speedway
1801 W. International Speedway Blvd.
904/947-6800, 904/254-2700 (speedway information)
$$

Museum of Arts & Sciences
1040 Museum Blvd.
904/255-0285
$$

The Daytona 500 Endurance Race opens the N.A.S.C.A.R. season. One of stock car racing's four major events, it fills the 110,500-seat **Daytona International Speedway** each February for the 200-lap race. But the stadium's appeal spreads to sports where speed matters. Fans flock in winter to the "World Center of Racing" for the winter Speed Weeks, to watch sports cars, motorcycles, and even go-carts. "Big Bill" France, the entrepreneur and race organizer, transformed 450 acres of swamp into a cauldron of noise and excitement, spiced with the ever-present threat of danger. Since 1996, pilgrims visiting the shrine can also tour DAYTONA U.S.A.

Right next to the circuit, the enormous hangar echoes with noise. With videos of cars whizzing around the track, films of race crashes, loudspeakers broadcasting

commentaries, record-setting cars on display, and even a chance to get your hands dirty changing a tire, enthusiasts can see, hear, feel, and almost taste the sport; all that's missing is the smell of high-octane fuel.

The first section traces the role of Daytona Beach in the history of speed (see pp. 190–91), and on to the start of N.A.S.C.A.R. racing in 1948. Tribute is paid to drivers, such as all-time N.A.S.C.A.R. great Richard Petty, who won a record seventh Daytona 500 in 1981.

To appreciate the strength and finesse required to change a set of wheels, fans can grab an impact wrench and try the 16-Second Pit Stop challenge. For an extra fee, a guided tram ride completes a tour of the speedway, including the dizzy view of the 31-degree banking at the east and west ends, which rises four stories high.

A short drive from the noise and excitement of the speedway is the **Museum of Arts and Sciences.** Set in the middle of a nature reserve, this low, contemporary building houses the usual skeletons and exhibits of local flora and fauna, as well as African and Asian art. What makes it special are two important collections, featuring Cuban and American art.

As the capital of Spain's "Key to the New World," Havana was a European city in the tropics, whose artists looked to Madrid and Paris rather than the United States. The **Cuban Museum** covers two centuries, built around paintings taken from Cuba's National Museum by the dictatorial president, Fulgencio Batista, when he fled to exile in Daytona in 1959. For the expatriate Cubans of today, these galleries are a key to their heritage.

Families spend hours here, with parents explaining the social significance of a painting such as "Cuban Sweets" (1941) by Daniel Serra-Badué and waxing nostalgic in front of "On the Way to Mass." This early 20th-century portrait shows a mature, confident woman who could as easily be a *doña* in Spain as in Cuba. By contrast, Lorenzo Romero Arziaga's "Cup of Coffee" (ca 1940), painted in hot, tropical colors, romanticizes peasant life. José Martí, revered as the Father of Cuban Independence, appears in an 1880 portrait with his parents, as well as a 20th-century bronze head.

The **Dow Gallery of American Art** tugs at the same emotional roots as its Cuban neighbor. A stroll through the galleries, with paintings, sculptures, and engravings, plus furniture, glass, and silver, reveals the evolution of a distinct American style.

Start with 18th-century portraits such as Nicholas Pike and Eunice Smith Pike by Samuel King, then progress to the Hudson River school and Asher B. Durand's "The Nutgatherers" (1850). Frank Henry Shapleigh was one of many artists drawn to Florida. His enormous panorama of St. Augustine in 1886, showing the Castillo de San Marcos and the old town, is as informative to historians as it is to art lovers. ∎

Artifacts on display at the Museum of Arts and Sciences include a Ch'ing Dynasty carved wood Buddha (above) and furnishings (below) in the Dow Gallery of American Art.

More places to visit in the land of space & speed

CASSADAGA SPIRITUALIST CAMP

"Camp mediums available today," reads the sign in the bookstore at Cassadaga Spiritualist Camp. Pick up the telephone and talk to one of the on-call mediums, healers, spiritual counselors, and teachers who live in the cluster of houses 10 miles southeast of De Land.

The Ponce de Leon lighthouse may be labeled a museum, but the light still flashes its warning signal.

Cassadaga may sound like a New Age movement, but it is actually more than 100 years old. The village was established by George P. Colby, a New Yorker, dubbed "The Seer of Spiritualism." Told to found a Spiritualist community by Seneca, his spirit guide, he took a steamboat to Florida in 1875 and hiked out into the wilderness. A trance medium, Colby used his gifts to help the police find missing persons and locals find buried treasure. Two decades later, he donated 35 acres to the Southern Cassadaga Spiritualist Camp Meeting Association. (There are no camping facilities: Camp meeting was a term for a religious assembly.) Today, on one side of County Rd. 4139 is the official camp, with the bookstore-cum-information center; on the other side of the road nonmember practitioners live, offering tarot readings and courses in miracles.
🗺 179 A5   ✉ 1112 Stevens St., Cassadaga
☎ 904/228-2880

PONCE DE LEON INLET LIGHTHOUSE MUSEUM

There are taller and older lighthouses along the Florida coast, but this complex is the largest lighthouse village on its original site. From the top, you can see the Vehicle Assembly Building at the Kennedy Space Center, 45 miles away to the south.

When the 175-foot brick tower was completed in 1887, the latest First-Order fixed Fresnel lens from Paris was installed. Fueled by kerosene, the beam could be seen 20 miles away. You see how three families lived here, all helping the keepers to maintain the light. They dusted the separate prisms with a feather brush, wiped them with a linen cloth, and finally polished them with a buffer. Up and down the 203 stairs they went, not just when the watch changed, but also to take up buckets full of heated kerosene to refuel the lamp.

Also on site, the **Museum of the Sea** traces the development of navigation, from the magnetic compass used by the ancient Greeks and Chinese to modern-day satellite-tracking equipment.
🗺 179 B6   ✉ 4931 S. Peninsula Dr., Ponce Inlet   ☎ 904/761-1821   💲 $ ■

Although Jacksonville is one of America's fastest growing cities, there is also a real sense of the past, thanks to more than 400 years of history. Inland, the fertile countryside is a paradise for horses.

Northeast Florida

Historic flags

Northeast Florida

THE NICKNAME OF THE FIRST COAST IS supposed to say it all: This is where Europeans first established a community on North American shores. But, fascinating though St. Augustine is, there is much more to see in this region.

Start with Jacksonville, a tourist destination over a century ago, when Northerners traveled up the St. Johns River to look at exotic plant and wildlife. Today, it is a fast-growing city with two notable museums. To the northeast of the city is Fort George Island, where the remnants of early plantation life have been preserved at Kingsley Plantation. Farther north is Amelia Island, well known for its vacation resorts, golf courses, and beaches, as well as the delightful town of Fernandina Beach. Several pages in this section are devoted to St. Augustine. Schoolchildren on field trips come here to learn the early history of Florida; couples consider it a romantic destination. Plan on staying at least two days if you want to explore the Spanish Colonial heritage, including the *castillo* (fort) and the magnificent buildings put up by railroad magnate Henry Flager a century ago.

Inland is Gainesville, an attractive town that is home to the University of Florida and makes a useful base for exploring some of the state's more unsung sites. Nature lovers should spend time at Paynes Prairie State Preserve. It is as peaceful now as it was over 200 years ago, when the Quaker naturalist William Bartram described the great Alachua savanna in his diary: "a level green plain— herds of sprightly deer, squadrons of the beautiful fleet Siminole horse, flocks of turkeys."

In this region, there are memorials to two American wordsmiths. Marjorie Kinnan Rawlings wrote *The Yearling* in 1938, and her home is open to the public. Stephen Foster's songs are part of the American music tradition. Although he never visited the state, he merits a museum for penning what is now Florida's state song.

The state was an enthusiastic Confederate supporter, but only two Civil War battles were fought on Florida soil: at Tallahassee; and at Olustee, where re-creations of the conflict attract large crowds each February.

If there is one part of the state that takes many by surprise it is Ocala and surrounding Marion County. This is Thoroughbred Country, where rolling grasslands edged with white fences are home to some of the nation's finest racing, jumping, and showing horses. ∎

GEORGIA

Eddy

5 ▷

6

441

41 **Stephen Foster State Folk Cultural Center**

75 **White Springs**

Olustee Battlefield State Historic Site

10

4 ▷ **Wellborn**

90 **Lake City**

Ocean Pond

Olustee

247

100

THE PANHANDLE
p. 215

Ichetucknee Springs State Park
47

Providence 238

Worthington Springs

3 ▷ • **Fort White**

27

High Springs • 441 **Alachua**

Devil's Millhopper
75

Florida Museum of Natural History
University of Florida
24

121

Tallahassee ★

Miami

Area of map detail

I ▷

△
A

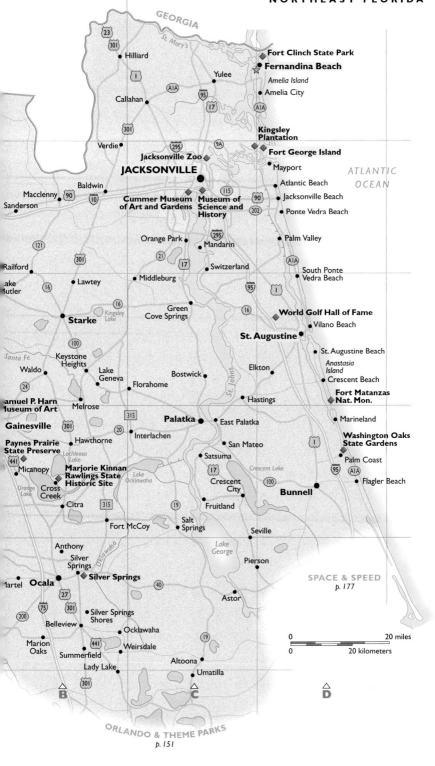

GEORGIA

St. Mary's

23
301
Hilliard

Fort Clinch State Park
Fernandina Beach
Yulee
Amelia Island
A1A
95
Amelia City
Callahan
17
A1A

301

Kingsley
Plantation

Verdie
295
9A
Fort George Island

Jacksonville Zoo
Mayport

JACKSONVILLE
Atlantic Beach

Baldwin
115
ATLANTIC
OCEAN

Macclenny 90
10
90
Jacksonville Beach

Sanderson
Cummer Museum Museum of
of Art and Gardens Science and
History
202
Ponte Vedra Beach

295
Palm Valley
121
Orange Park
Mandarin

301
21
Palm Valley

Railford
17
Switzerland
A1A

Lake
Butler
16
Lawtey
Middleburg
South Ponte
Vedra Beach

16
16
95
1

Kingsley
Lake
Green
Cove Springs
16
World Golf Hall of Fame

Starke
Vilano Beach

100
St. Augustine

Keystone
Heights
St. Augustine Beach

Santa Fe
Waldo
Lake
Geneva
Bostwick
Elkton
Anastasia
Island
Crescent Beach

24
Florahome
Fort Matanzas
Nat. Mon.

Samuel P. Harn
Museum of Art
Melrose
Hastings

Gainesville
301
315
Palatka
East Palatka
Marineland

20
Interlachen
Washington Oaks
State Gardens

Paynes Prairie
State Preserve
Hawthorne
Lochloosa
Lake
San Mateo
1
Palm Coast

441
Micanopy
Marjorie Kinnan
Rawlings State
Historic Site
Satsuma
95
A1A
Flagler Beach

Orange
Lake
Cross
Creek
Lake
Ocklawaha
Crescent Lake
Crescent
City
100
Bunnell

Citra
315
19
Fruitland

Fort McCoy
Salt
Springs
Seville

Anthony
Lake
George

Silver
Springs
Pierson

Martel
Ocala
Silver Springs
40
SPACE & SPEED
p. 177

27
Astor

200
75
301
Silver Springs
Shores

Belleview
Ocklawaha
0   20 miles

Marion
Oaks
441
Weirsdale
0   20 kilometers

Summerfield
Altoona

Lady Lake
Umatilla

301

B
C
D

ORLANDO & THEME PARKS
p. 151

Jacksonville

Jacksonville
🗺 197 C4
Visitor information
✉ 201 E. Adams St.
☎ 904/798-9111

**Museum of
Science & History**
✉ 1025 Museum Circle
☎ 904/396-7061
💲 $

**Jacksonville
Zoological Gardens**
✉ 8605 Zoo Rd.
☎ 904/757-4462
💲 $$$

**In the Cummer
Museum of Art**

JACKSONVILLE IS, ARGUABLY, WHERE MODERN FLORIDA began. After the Civil War, Union officers returned with their families to vacation in "The Winter City in Summerland." By 1875, steam packets from New York were delivering 50,000 sun-starved vacationers who spent more than six million dollars in town.

Among those who made the journey were author Harriet Beecher Stowe, composer Frederick Delius, painter Winslow Homer, and writer Stephen Crane. Thanks to a 1967 vote, Jacksonville is now the largest city, geographically, in the United States, at 840 square miles. Straddling the broad St. Johns River, it is enjoying a renaissance due to banking, insurance, and financial services, supported by first-class medical facilities and museums.

To the north of the city is **Jacksonville Zoological Gardens,** where a multimillion-dollar renovation is taking place. The zoo is involved in conservation programs and is home to a renowned collection of waterfowl as well as over 200 species of animals.

In the heart of the city, the riverfront has been developed, with riverwalks on both sides. On the north bank are the **Time-Union Center for the Performing Arts** and **Jacksonville Landing,** a new development of shops, entertainments, and restaurants.

Across the water is a cluster of museums. Biggest and best is the **Museum of Science and History.** In tune with Florida's newfound enthusiasm for its past, this museum opened a permanent history exhibit in 1998, the "Currents of Time." The story begins 12,000 years ago and traces the rich diversity of the northeastern corner of the state. Despite the lively music, sound effects, and film footage, this is history told in an adult fashion, through letters, tableaux, photographs, and maps. Highlights include the *confesionario* written in 1612 by a missionary, Father Francisco Pareja, to help convert the Indians. Set out in Spanish and phonetic Timucuan, this is the oldest surviving text anywhere in a North American Indian language.

Long overdue recognition is given to ethnic minorities. The displays begin with a lively look at day-to-day life among the Timucuan Indians on the St. Johns

River. Take time to appreciate the contribution of the black community: After the Civil War, a strong black middle class developed here. One example is James Weldon Johnson, remembered as the author of "Lift Every Voice and Sing," the anthem of the Civil Rights Movement. The first African American to be admitted to the Florida Bar, Johnson became the United States consul to Puerto Rico in 1906.

A second permanent exhibit covers natural history. "Atlantic Tails" concentrates on manatees, whales, and dolphins, while the display on the St. Johns River emphasizes the importance of wetlands and marshes, the effect of man's pollution, and the need to protect the Florida aquifer.

Cummer Museum of Art & Gardens stands on the opposite bank of the river. Its well-kept gardens, one in the Italian, the other in the English tradition,

were laid out earlier this century by Mrs. Ninah May Holden Cummer. So keen was she to ensure that Jacksonville had a quality art museum, she not only made a bequest of her collection but also her own home.

Her house was replaced by an unprepossessing 1961 building, where her European and 19th-century American paintings are the core of what staff like to call "a good study collection," with its strong examples of Flemish and Italian Renaissance works. One of the most popular paintings, purchased in 1996, is the bosky idyll portraying "Ponce de León in Florida" by American romantic Thomas Moran (1837–1926).

But it was porcelain that put the Cummer on the must-see list in 1965, when the Wark family donated their priceless collection of early Meissen. Rare and comprehensive, this is the finest collection in the United States. ■

The dynamic city of Jacksonville has reinvented its riverfront, with new restaurants, shops, and walkways.

"We entered and viewed the country thereabout, which is the fairest, fruitfullest, and pleasantest of all the world …"
—French explorer Jean Ribault, sailing up the St. Johns River, May 1, 1562

Cummer Museum of Art & Gardens
✉ 829 Riverside Ave.
☎ 904/356-6857
💲 $ (Free Tues. 4–9 p.m.)

The Palace Saloon on Centre Street is the most famous watering hole in town.

A walk around Fernandina Beach

On the northwest corner of 13-mile-long Amelia Island is Fernandina Beach, whose golden era as a deepwater port and vacation resort ended a century ago when Flagler's railroad bypassed the town. Follow this walk through the charming, old-fashioned streets to discover its colorful past, peppered with names from Florida's history.

Start at **Fernandina Beach Marine Harbor and Shrimp Boat Docks ❶** on Front Street. Locals boast that Fernandina is the birthplace of the modern offshore shrimping industry. Walk east on Centre Street to the **Florida Railroad Depot ❷** (*102 Centre St., Tel 904/261-3248*), now the Chamber of Commerce. Linking the harbor to Florida's first trans-peninsular railroad was the dream of David Levy Yulee, the town's founder, the father of Florida statehood, and the first Jewish person to serve as a United States senator.

Continue east to the corner of Second Street. Dating from 1878 and decorated with elaborate murals and carved caryatids, the **Palace Saloon ❸** (*117 Centre St., Tel 904/261-6320, presently being restored following a fire*) was the ritziest bar in town. As Prohibition came in, it was also the last to close its doors, raking in more than $60,000 on the final day of legal drinking. Proceed to the corner of Fifth Street and Centre Street and to the **Nassau County Courthouse ❹**. Nothing in town can be built taller than the bell tower of this Italianate Georgian Revival building. From 1892 to 1998, this was the legal hub of the county.

Walk along Centre Street to Sixth Street and turn left. Past the First Presbyterian Church is the **Silk Stocking District ❺**. These spacious houses are still private family homes. Turn right on Alachua Street to continue to Eighth Street.

Designed by Robert Sands Schuyler, the New York architect, **St. Peter's Episcopal Church ❻** (*801 Atlantic Ave., Tel 904/261-4293*) was built in the early 1880s by out-of-work shipwrights. On the south side, a stained-glass window commemorates nurse Mary Martha Reid, who was granted a lifetime pension for her work in the Civil War.

Cross Centre Street and walk to Ash Street. On the corner is **Trinity United Methodist Church** (1892), built by and for the African-American congregation that included a local doctor, pharmacist, and newspaper editor.

Go right on Ash Street to **Kate's Tree ❼**. When the town decided this live oak tree should be pulled down to improve traffic flow, Kate Bailey, wife of local bigwig Effingham Bailey, disagreed. About a century ago, sitting on her veranda with a shotgun across her knees, she

Visitors enjoy Fernandina Beach's antique shops and busy harbor.

faced down the workmen. The tree still stands; so does her home, **Bailey House** (*28 S. 7th St., Tel 904/321-0103*), now a bed-and-breakfast inn. Proceed on Ash Street, past the **Tabby House,** another design by Schuyler. Turn right on Third Street. Dating from 1857 is one of the state's oldest purpose-built hotels, the **Florida House Inn ⓾** (*20–22 3rd St., Tel 904/261-3300*). Guests have included President Grant and José Martí, father of Cuban independence, who plotted the 1895 revolution here (see p. 140). The hotel, like the town, is now enjoying a renaissance. ■

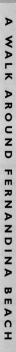

▲ See area map pp. 196–97
► Fernandina Harbor
⬌ 1 mile
🕓 40 minutes
► Florida House Inn

NOT TO BE MISSED
• Palace Saloon
• Silk Stocking District
• St. Peter's Episcopal Church
• Kate's Tree
• Florida House Inn

Fort George Island

Fort George Island
🗺 197 C4–D4

Kingsley Plantation
✉ 11676 Palmetto Ave., Fla. A1A, Jacksonville (on Fort George Island)
☎ 904/251-3537
🕐 Check in advance for special ranger-led tours
💲 $

Fort Clinch State Park, Amelia Island
🗺 197 C5–D5
✉ 2601 Atlantic Ave., Fernandina Beach
☎ 904/277-7274
💲 $

TIMUCUAN INDIANS SETTLED ON FORT GEORGE ISLAND thousands of years ago—long before Florida was invaded by the French and the Spanish. Little trace remains of former settlements, however, and nature is reclaiming the land.

KINGSLEY PLANTATION

Zephaniah Kingsley was an enigma. In the early 19th century, the Quaker plantation owner and slave trader flaunted convention by living with his black Senegalese slave, Anna Madgigine Jai, by whom he had four children. "…She has always been respected as my wife and as such I acknowledge her," he once said of her.

In 1811 she was freed from slavery, along with their children, and six years later Kingsley bought the plantation on Fort George Island to raise corn, sugarcane, and Sea Island cotton. Today, the plain 1798 farmhouse, built by original owner John McQueen, is the oldest of its kind in the state, while the semicircle of 23 ruined slave cabins, built of tabby, a resilient mixture of shells, lime-stone, and water, is equally rare.

By following the self-guided tour, as well as chatting to rangers, a picture grows of how plantations were organized. The "task" system was used here, enabling slaves to cultivate their own plots once their tasks for the day were over.

Although Kingsley owned slaves, he advocated fair treatment of free blacks in a controversial book he published in 1829, *A Treatise on the Patriarchal, or Cooperative System of Slavery As It Exists in Some Governments*. He further enraged his fellow plantation owners by taking two more wives, and recognizing their children as his heirs.

Not surprisingly, Kingsley left Florida in 1835, moving to Haiti, where the first independent black republic in the New World offered greater racial tolerance. ∎

Fort Clinch State Park, Amelia Island

This 19th-century fort seemed obsolete in the 20th century, but in World War II, reservists watched for a possible invasion atop the 28-foot-high brick walls. On the first weekend of the month, rangers in uniform carry out sentry duty and cook meals as if this were 1864. They complain about the Civil War dragging on, the weather, and the bad pay. One weekend they are Confederates, the next Unionists, but the complaints are the same. ∎

Fort Clinch

St. Augustine & beyond

ST. AUGUSTINE HAS ENJOYED TWO PERIODS OF eminence. The first was the town's 235-year reign as the capital of Florida, after the Spanish landed in 1565. This makes it the oldest continuously occupied European settlement in North America. The second was as the "Riviera of the Americas" a century ago, after Henry M. Flagler built a railroad and grand hotels in the seaside town.

St. Augustine

🗺 197 D3

Visitor information

✉ 10 Castillo Dr.

🗺 829/825-1000

Both periods are reflected in St. Augustine, which retains its charm thanks to pedestrianized streets and a fine position overlooking Matanzas Bay. In the **Downtown Historic District,** the atmosphere of yesteryear is re-created with horse-drawn carriages, jingling past houses built two centuries ago and Victorian houses with broad verandas. Many of these are now bed-and-breakfast inns.

St. Augustine has more sights than most towns. Start at the Oldest House, also known as the **Gonzáles Alvarez House** (*14 St. Francis St., Tel 904/824-2872, $*). Built circa 1723, this is now a museum devoted to the city's social history, from its Spanish Colonial days through the brief British occupation.

Elsewhere in the small historic center you will find a host of buildings labeled "oldest": Some are real, others are re-creations. **The Authentic Oldest Drugstore** (*31 Orange St., Tel 904/824-2269*) does have a genuine pharmacy counter; the **Oldest Store Museum** (*4 Artillery Lane, Tel 904/829-9729*) is a reconstruction of a turn-of-the-century general store. Further north from the Castillo de San Marcos (see pp. 204–205) is the first ever **Ripley's Believe It or Not! Museum** (*19 San Marco Ave., Tel 904/824-1606*), opened in 1950. A short walk away is the touristy **Fountain of Youth** (*11 Magnolia Ave., Tel 904/829-3168*), selling the legend that this spring was Ponce de León's fabled

St. George Street, in the heart of old St. Augustine

Castillo de San Marcos National Monument

✉ 1 S. Castillo Dr.
☎ 904/829-6506
💲 $

The Castillo de San Marcos was central to the defense of St Augustine.

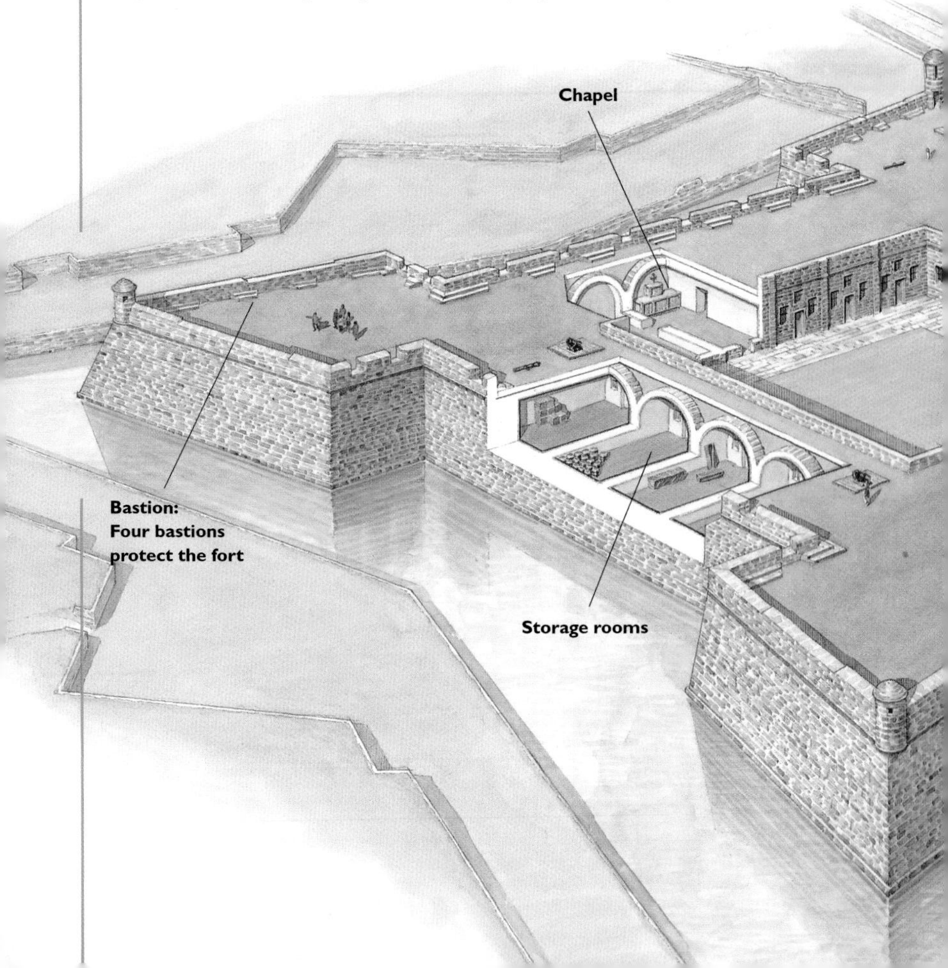

source of everlasting life. Take a short walk through the old town (see pp. 206–207) and out across the Bridge of Lions to enjoy the sunset illuminating Matanzas Bay.

CASTILLO DE SAN MARCOS NATIONAL MONUMENT

This star-shaped fortress has guarded St. Augustine for more than 300 years. It cost so much to build that the King of Spain complained that the walls must have been constructed of silver. In fact, the 12-foot-thick defenses, put up between 1672 and 1695, were made from a tough shell limestone called coquina.

In 1740, British general James Oglethorpe dubbed it the "sponge fort," when his cannon found the walls impenetrable. Never taken in battle, this is the oldest masonry-built stronghold in the United States, standing on the site of the earlier wooden structures that had defended Spanish colonists since 1565. The northern limit of the Spanish-controlled New World, it gave protection against Britain's aggressive colonies in Georgia, as well as pirates.

With its single, heavily guarded entrance, San Marcos was an outstanding example of military design. Spanish engineer Ignacio Diaz simply embellished a basic square by adding a diamond-shaped bastion at each corner. In this way, attackers were vulnerable

Chapel

Bastion:
Four bastions
protect the fort

Storage rooms

to crossfire. The powder magazines were well buried; connected to the bay, the moat would rise and fall with the tides.

Although improvements and alterations have been made over the centuries, the fort looks much as it did in the 18th century. Like many forts, it was also used as a jail. As well as prisoners from the Seminole wars, Geronimo's three wives, a dozen chiefs, and 500 Apache soldiers were held here in 1886.

The best way to understand the construction of the building, as well as what life was like for those who lived here, is to take one of the daily tours. The rangers who lead them explain everything from gun placements to the

sanitary system. From Memorial Day to Labor Day, the two cannon are fired on weekends. Throughout the year there are special themed events, with volunteers in historical costumes.

(Continued on p. 208)

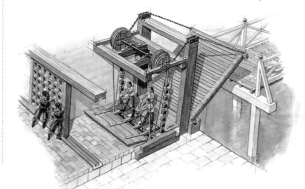

Guard rooms

The detailed diagram above shows how the drawbridge was raised and lowered.

The ravelin shielded the entrance of the fort from enemy attack.

Moat

A costumed procession reenacts historical events at Castillo de San Marcos.

A walk around old St. Augustine

St. Augustine is an early example of town planning in North America, with the *castillo* (fort) at the north end and a grid system of streets extending south to the Plaza de la Constitución.

Start at the visitor information center opposite the castillo. Walk along San Marcos Avenue toward the City Gate. On the right is the **Public Burying Ground ❶**. Although some called it the Huguenot Cemetery, this was the graveyard for any Protestants, not only the French immigrants. Cross the street to the old gate. One of the original entrances to the town, the **City Gate ❷** was started in 1718. The wall was made of earth, palm logs, and coquina stone, with cactus and the sharp-pointed Spanish bayonet plants.

Cross over Orange Street to the start of St. George Street, the main street of old St. Augustine. Originally a dirt road, it was later covered with slices of palm trees, then brick,

and finally today's concrete and tabby. Stroll past the **Oldest Wooden Schoolhouse ❸**, built in the late 18th century, to Nos. 20–24, the **Spanish Quarter Village ❹** (*33 St. George St., Tel 904/825-5033*). Do plan to spend extra time in this museum, a complex of buildings and gardens where costumed interpreters explain how life was lived in old St. Augustine. Two cultures are represented here. First is the workaday world of the Spanish settlement in the 1740s, with its carpenter's workshop and tavern. In the soldiers' houses, you can learn how food was protected from rats and watch a blacksmith make nails, hooks, and other hardware in his forge—the Home Depot of the day.

The other, the **Peso de Burgo-Pellicer House,** is dedicated to farmworkers from Minorca. In 1777 some 600 settlers left plantations at New Smyrna and walked 75 miles to St. Augustine to plead with the governor for their freedom. Three houses remain of their community here.

Proceed along St. George Street to No. 41, **St. Photios National Shrine ❺** (*Tel 904/829-8205*). Flags of the United States and Greece recall the Greeks who came with the Minorcans to New Smyrna and settled here. Cross Hypolita Street and continue to No. 143, the **De Peña–Peck House ❻** (*Tel 904/829-5064*). The two names reflect two owners. The first floor was built in the 1740s by the Royal Treasurer of the Spanish colony, who was miffed that his house was north of the plaza, rather than on the south side with the top government brass. It was enlarged almost a century later by a British doctor, Seth Peck. Stroll toward the plaza. At the side of the cathedral, turn left into the garden. Note the memorial to Father Camps, the priest who led the Minorcans on the long trek from New Smyrna. Locals have worshiped at the **Basilica Cathedral of St. Augustine ❼** (*Tel 904/824-2806*) since 1565, but this building is part 1797, part late 19th-century reconstruction. The classic missionary church facade is at odds with the tower, part of Henry Flagler's beautification program. Cross the street to **Plaza de la Constitución ❽,** a public marketplace since 1598; this was the site of one of Martin Luther King, Jr.'s rallies for civil rights in 1964. Fittingly, the walk ends in this plaza, where a statue of Juan Ponce de León stands, raised arm pointing toward the sea. ■

🏔 See area map pp. 196–97
➤ Visitor information center
⬤ Under 1 mile
🕐 45 minutes (unless you stop along the route)
➤ Plaza de la Constitución

NOT TO BE MISSED
- City Gate
- Spanish Quarter Village
- Basilica Cathedral of St. Augustine

The Oldest Wooden Schoolhouse, in old St. Augustine

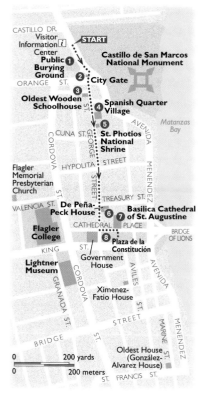

(Continued from p. 205)

FLAGLER'S INFLUENCE

St. Augustine's grandiose 19th-century developments feature two Flagler hotels, both now recycled for contemporary needs. Start at **Flagler College.** A college since 1968, this towered and turreted Spanish Renaissance complex was the first and most luxurious of Flagler's Florida hotels.

Five hundred collegiates use those same hotel bedrooms as a hall of residence, and eat on hand-carved Austrian chairs in the elaborately decorated dining room. They gather beneath the rotunda of the former lobby and perhaps look up occasionally to admire George W. Maynard's themed paintings representing the four elements, as well as adventure, discovery, conquest, and civilization. With its red-tile roof and wrought-iron balconies, the hotel fulfilled Flagler's dream of creating a Spanish look.

Another Flagler project, just across the square from the college, is the **Lightner Museum,** in what was the Alcazar Hotel (1889). Otto C. Lightner, publisher of *Hobbies* magazine, bought the building and reopened it in 1948 to display his collection of 19th-century Americana. After his death the museum closed, but thanks to local volunteers, it was relaunched in 1974 and the building was carefully restored.

In 1997 the **Ballroom Gallery** reopened, filled with antiques and art to recall the days when ladies in long gowns graced the hotel. A collection of Louis Comfort Tiffany glass, as well as dazzling examples of cut-glass from the brilliant period (1876–1906) round out the intriguing museum. For many, the highlight is the daily "concert" in the Music Room, where the mechanical musical instruments are played.

FARTHER AFIELD

With its long-nosed putters and computer-generated video clips, the **World Golf Hall of Fame** museum is dedicated to one of Florida's favorite sports. Eight miles northwest of St. Augustine, off I-95, much of the rare golfing memorabilia came from Pinehurst, North Carolina, including *The Goff,* a rare book published in 1743.

But it is the hands-on element that intrigues visitors, who can test their skills on the copy of a 100-year-old putting green, using wooden shafted putters and gutta percha balls. They can also have their photos taken on the full-scale reproduction of the stone-arched Swilcan Burn Bridge, a feature of the 18th Fairway at the Royal & Ancient Golf Club at St. Andrew's in Scotland.

The 71 members of the Pinehurst World Golf Hall of Fame, as well as the L.P.G.A. Hall of Fame, have been incorporated into the new setting. Johnny Miller (U.S.A.), Nick Faldo (U.K.), and Seve Ballesteros (Spain) were the first inductees elected when the new hall opened in 1998.

On Fla. A1A, some 14 miles south of St. Augustine, is **Fort Matanzas National Monument** (*Tel 904/471-0116*), part of the old city defenses. Built in 1742 to prevent enemies sailing up the Matanzas River to blockade the Spanish colony, the fort never saw military action. Today this is a quiet spot for a picnic, even if the name is a reminder of the Spanish slaughter (*matanza*) of 300 French colonists nearby in 1565. Five miles farther south on Fla. A1A are the **Washington Oaks State Gardens** (*Tel 904/446-6780*). Around the Young House with its interpretive center are formal gardens filled with exotic plants; by the shore are unspoiled coastal scrub and wilderness, rich in wildlife. ■

Flagler College

- ✉ 74 King St.
- ☎ 904/829-6481
- 🕐 Guided tours on the hour May–Aug.

Lightner Museum

- ✉ 75 King St.
- ☎ 904/824-2874
- 💲 $

World Golf Village

- ✉ International Golf Pkwy., St. Augustine (8 miles NW of St. Augustine)
- ☎ 904/940-4000
- 💲 $$

Flagler College, where today students study and live in one of Florida's first five-star resort hotels

Gainesville & beyond

Gainesville
🅼 197 B2
Visitor information
✉ 30 E. University Ave.
☎ 352/374-5231

Florida Museum of Natural History
✉ S.W. 34th St. & Hull Rd., University of Florida Campus, Gainesville
☎ 352/846-2967

Devil's Millhopper State Geological Site
🅼 196 A3
✉ 4732 Millhopper Rd. (Fla. 232)
☎ 352/955-2008
🕐 Guided walk, Sat. 10 a.m.
💲 $

Paynes Prairie State Preserve
🅼 197 B2
✉ Micanopy, Fla. 2 (on US 441)
☎ 352/466-3397
💲 $

LEAFY BOULEVARDS AND A SMALL TOWN ATMOSPHERE make Gainesville (population under 100,000) so pleasant, it was rated as "the best place to live in America" by *Money* magazine in 1995. It is also the home of the University of Florida, the oldest university in the state. The Union Street Historic Downtown District, in the heart of the town, has echoes of yesteryear. The boutiques, restaurants, and cafés that have opened in the restored houses look out on brick sidewalks dotted with old-fashioned lampposts.

On the southwest side of the sprawling campus are two new museums. The **Samuel P. Harn Museum of Art** (*S.W. 34th St., Tel 352/392-9862*) is housed in a striking postmodern building. The extensive collection includes 20th century American art and Asian and African tribal arts and crafts. In addition, the museum hosts several traveling exhibitions each year.

Next door is the **Florida Museum of Natural History.** In 1998 the State Museum of Natural History moved some of its 19 million specimens to a specially designed home. This is a work in progress, to be completed after 2000.

The **Central Gallery** reflects the research of the university and the breadth of the collection. There is a re-creation of Columbus's ship, the *Niña*, a dinosaur skull, and, dominating all, the 17-foot skeleton of a mammoth dating back 18,000 years.

In addition to a hall dedicated to changing exhibits, there are four permanent interpretive galleries. "Northwest Florida" portrays the biological diversity of the Panhandle, complete with a limestone cavern, coastal dunes, and marshes. In the "South Florida Hall," the focus is on the present-day Miccosukee and Seminole tribes, as well as the Calusa, one of the original Native American tribes. Florida's rich array of fossils has a hall to itself. The fourth gallery,

Windows into Natural History, opens in 2001.

About 10 miles north of Gainesville, the 20,000-year-old **Devil's Millhopper** is the oldest sinkhole in the state. There are sinkholes all over Florida. As water dissolves the limestone bedrock, a network of cavities forms, which can turn into underground rivers. From time to time, the limestone caves in, causing a depression or sinkhole at ground level. Houses have disappeared, even a lab at the University of Gainesville. Although as many as 4,000 sinkholes occur annually, few of them are dangerous or deep.

At the Devil's Millhopper, some 232 steps zigzag 120 feet down the face, past the layers of sediment that make this an ideal study site for geologists and school parties; from the modern geology at the rim, you go back millions of years, to the era when ocean covered most of the peninsula. As you walk down past clumps of ferns, the air gets cooler and smells damp and jungly. A 63-acre state park surrounds the sinkhole.

Almost equidistant to the south of Gainesville, the 21,000-acre **Paynes Prairie State Preserve** looks unremarkable at first, but this wet prairie landscape is rated among the most significant natural and historical areas in Florida. A short walk from the parking lot to the visitor center ensures seclusion; a climb up the 40-foot observation tower opens up a grand vista. Buzzards soar overhead while hares and alligators, bison and wild horses still thrive in peace. After ten years of drought, heavy spring rains in 1998 revived the plant life of this wet prairie. Apart from ranger-led visits, visitors can hike, cycle, fish, and go boating or horseback riding.

Twenty miles southeast of Gainesville is the **Marjorie Kinnan Rawlings State Historic Site** at Cross Creek. Marjorie Kinnan Rawlings's classic novel, *The Yearling*, has evoked the Florida of yesteryear ever since its publication in 1938. Rawlings (1896–1953) had moved to Cross Creek in 1928 to write the great American novel.

Her house stands on 68 acres, but visitors expecting a humble, cracker-style cabin are surprised to find comfortable furniture, art deco candlesticks from Paris, and Wedgwood china. As the ranger explains, "This is not *The Yearling* experience." Instead, the single-story home is a memorial to Rawlings. All looks much as it did when the Pulitzer Prize winner lived here; even the rangers who lead tours wear dowdy cotton housedresses, ankle socks, and sensible shoes to complete the effect.

Only small groups are taken through at one time, so you may have to wait. In the sitting room, an antique Royal typewriter has a page from *The Yearling*, as if the writer has just left the room. Sixty years melt away as you enter her bedroom, with her books, jewelry, and suitcase stamped with her initials.

Although eight of her nine books were about Florida, much is made of her cookbook. She prepared dishes ranging from alligator tail to hollandaise sauce proclaiming, "You can be as critical as you like of my literary capabilities, but indifference to my table puts me in a rage." The 1983 movie *Cross Creek* revived interest in her characters/neighbors, ranging from white landowners to poor black sharecroppers. However, those who know her story well maintain it was not altogether accurate. ■

Marjorie Kinnan Rawlings S.H.S.

🅰 197 B2

✉ Cross Creek, Fla. 325 (off US 441)

☎ 352/466-3672

🕐 House tours Thurs.–Sun. 10, 11 a.m., and hourly 1–4 p.m.

💲 $

The kitchen at Marjorie Kinnan Rawlings's house, where she prepared many of the recipes featured in her cookbook.

Horse capital of the world

Back in 1956, the concept of a Kentucky Derby winner coming from the Sunshine State was as improbable as a man landing on the moon. Then Needles, ridden by Dave Erb, shocked the experts at Churchill Downs to win America's top horse race.

Since then, Floridian winners of the Derby have included Carry Back (1961), Foolish Pleasure (1975), the outstanding Triple Crown winner Affirmed (1978), Unbridled (1990), and the star of 1997, Silver Charm. Although Silver Charm also won the Preakness, the colt just missed out on the Triple Crown. The Ocala thoroughbred confirmed his greatness, however, when he traveled more than 8,000 miles to win the four-million-dollar Dubai World Cup in March 1998.

Claims that Marion County is now the "Horse Capital of the World" sound even more convincing when locals add in 6 Preakness Stakes winners, 16 Breeders' Cup Day winners, 5 Horses of the Year, and 52 horses that have won more than one million dollars in prize money.

The greatest of these was Affirmed. Born in 1975, the shiny chestnut colt with a distinctive white blaze was bred at Louis and Patrice Wolfson's Harbor View Farm, near Ocala. In 1977, the rivalry between Affirmed and Kentucky-bred Alydar put horse racing onto the front page. With Affirmed winning seven of his nine starts, he was named champion two year old. The following year, in 11 starts, his eight wins and two seconds included the Triple Crown as well as the Hollywood and Santa Anita Derbies. Successes continued, and he ended his career with 22 wins, 5 seconds, and 1 third, in a total of 29 starts. As Patrice Wolfson said in 1998, "Over the years, we've had a lot of really nice horses…but you don't find many great horses. Affirmed—he's a once-in-a-lifetime horse."

Ocala is at the heart of Marion County, where the trim white fences, freshly painted barns, and rolling meadows look more like Kentucky than the traditional image of Florida. It was back in 1917 that breeder Carl Rose recognized that horses enjoyed northern Florida's climate. In the 1930s, he opened his farm, Rosemere, where his stallions, mares, and foals also benefited from the limestone soil, which provides lush pasture, rich with bone-strengthening minerals, calcium, and phosphorus. No wonder Marion County now has 700 horse farms, including 450 devoted to

Thoroughbreds train and winter in Northeast Florida, where the climate and rich pasture are beneficial.

breeding thoroughbreds foaled in Florida. All around are tack merchants, equine artists, blacksmiths, feed retailers, dentists, and transportation companies providing the necessary back-up for an industry worth four billion dollars and providing 30,000 jobs. In Ocala itself is the University of Florida Horse Research Center, while the university's veterinary school is at Gainesville.

Just as Northerners escape the winter cold by vacationing in Florida, so more and more horses are spending a few weeks in the sun: Some go to Payson Park, north of Miami; others to Ocala itself.

Marion County is too small and peaceful to have a racetrack. Florida's main tracks are at Tampa Bay Downs, and at Hialeah Park, Gulfstream Park, and Calder Race Course, all in Greater Miami. As well as thoroughbreds, Marion County's horse farms also breed massive shire draft horses, elegant Arabians, tiny Dartmoor ponies, delicate Paso Finos, and cute miniatures. The quarter horse, Rugged Lark, a product of Bo-Bett Farm, has been a star for over a decade. Named Superhorse at the 1985 and 1987 World Championships, this intelligent stallion, whose bridleless performances to music thrill audiences all over the United States, was Equine Ambassador to the 1996 Atlanta Olympic Games.

Throughout the winter months, Marion County hosts a series of events, such as the Horse Shows in the Sun series (February to mid-March), the Ocala Breeders' Sales Race Day (March), and the Sunshine State Games Equestrian Classic (April). The Florida Thoroughbred Breeders' Association arranges two-hour visits to horse farms by appointment (*Tel 352/629-2160*). ∎

Each year costumed Confederate and Union troops reenact the skirmish at Olustee.

More places to visit in Northeast Florida

OLUSTEE BATTLEFIELD STATE HISTORIC SITE

"It was a fair, square stand-up fight in pinewoods…." Participants such as Unionist colonel Joseph Hawley kept a diary after the four-hour battle of February 20, 1864, but even after reading extracts, it is hard today to envisage what happened 130 years ago. Olustee, site of the biggest Civil War battle on Florida soil, is little more than a clearing, with an interpretative center in a cabin and memorials to the Confederate troops and "…their devotion to the cause of liberty and state sovereignty."

The 5,100 Union soldiers were defeated by 5,200 Confederates, and Northern hopes of bringing Florida back into the Union were crushed. One-third of the Union troops were black, including the 54th Massachusetts Colored Infantry, the heroes of the 1988 movie *Glory*. Here, they held off the opposition while their compatriots began the retreat to Jacksonville.

Apart from the annual reenactment each February, there is little to see on site.
🅰 196 A4 ✉ US 90, Olustee
☎ 904/758-0400

STEPHEN FOSTER STATE FOLK CULTURAL CENTER

"Way Down upon the Pee Dee River" did not sound right, so Stephen Foster (1826–1864) checked an atlas and substituted Florida's Suwannee River for South Carolina's Pee Dee River…and the rest is showbiz history.

The prolific songwriter ("Oh! Susanna," "Beautiful Dreamer," "My Old Kentucky Home," "Old Black Joe," "Camptown Races") is commemorated with a 97-tubular bell carillon and a small museum on the banks of the Suwannee. The carillon plays daily concerts, including his biggest hit, Florida's state song, whose correct title is "The Old Folks at Home."

The museum has memorabilia and dioramas on the theme of each song. It is hard to get a sense of the man here, probably because Foster was a native of Pittsburgh and never even visited Florida. But then, he never went to Ireland before writing "Jeanie with the Light Brown Hair." There are demonstrations of Florida crafts in the folk culture center.
🅰 196 A4 ✉ Off US 41, White Springs
☎ 904/397-2733 💲 $ ■

Beaches and more beaches:
The Panhandle boasts
history in Tallahassee and
Pensacola, but most visitors
flock to the emerald Gulf of
Mexico and the unbelievably
soft, white sand.

The Panhandle

**Sunbathing on
a Panhandle beach**

The Panhandle

THE PANHANDLE IS DIFFERENT FROM THE REST OF FLORIDA. DRIVE FROM Tallahassee to Pensacola and you see herds of cattle grazing in wide open spaces. Where the peninsula is famously flat, the landscape here is noticeably hilly. The highest point in the state, all of 345 feet above sea level, is northwest of DeFuniak Springs, up near the border with Alabama. In this long, narrow strip of land wedged between the Gulf of Mexico and the borders with Georgia and Alabama, palm trees are outnumbered by pine trees and enormous live oaks, dripping with Spanish moss.

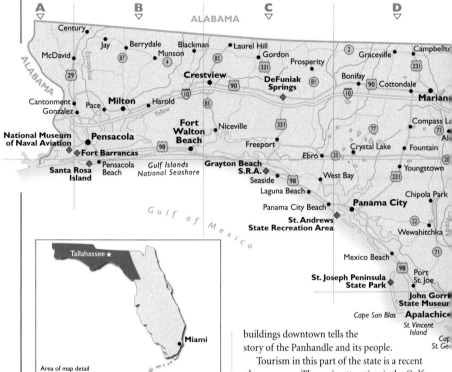

Tallahassee, the state capital, has the atmosphere of a small southern town, and the basis of the economy is government and education. Although St. Augustine rightly claims to be the oldest permanently settled community in North America, Pensacola traces its European roots right back to 1559, and the first Spanish attempt to set up a colony. In the 20th century, airplanes became a focus of the town, and a large museum on the naval air station tells the story of pilots and their aircraft. As for heritage, an unusual complex of museums and historic buildings downtown tells the story of the Panhandle and its people.

Tourism in this part of the state is a recent phenomenon. The main attraction is the Gulf shoreline. With the softest of white sand, rolling dunes, and emerald water, these beaches justify their claim to be among the best in the country. In recent years, they have become a favorite destination for college students from Northern states, who crowd into sprawling communities such as Grayton Beach, Fort Walton Beach, and Panama City.

In 1995, Hurricane Opal wreaked havoc along this coast. In retrospect, the storm created an opportunity to improve the design of buildings along the coastline and bring in

Visitors come to the Panhandle to get away from it all.

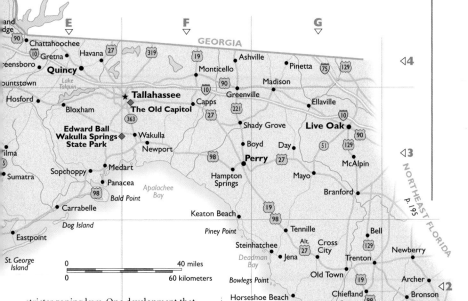

stricter zoning laws. One development that stands out for the quality of its design is Seaside. This vibrant, forward-looking project is more than just a resort, it is a new town whose architecture reflects traditional regional styles.

The region has its share of eccentric places to visit: DeFuniak Springs, with its reminders of a great educational movement; Cedar Key, whose heyday a century ago was built on the manufacture of pencils; Apalachicola, where the refrigerator first saw the light of day; and Wakulla Springs, an icy-clear pool that is home to some of Florida's largest alligators.

Do remember that west of Apalachicola, Florida is on Central, rather than Eastern standard time, out of line with the rest of the state. Many an appointment has been missed by those who forget that they are crossing from one time zone to another. ■

Tallahassee

Above: The New Capitol towers above Florida's first seat of government. Opposite: Tallahassee is proud of its canopy roads—historic routes radiating from the city.

LONG BEFORE EUROPEANS SETTLED IN FLORIDA, Tallahassee was the site of Anhaica, capital of the Apalachee. Spanish adventurer Hernando de Soto captured the village in 1539, and celebrated the first Christmas in North America. When Florida gained statehood in 1845, this site became the capital, halfway between the twin capitals of the territory, St. Augustine and Pensacola. From the 22nd-floor observatory of the New Capitol Building, you can see the seven hills of this city, Florida State University, Florida Agricultural and Mechanical University (F.A.M.U.), and the small downtown. Radiating outward are the canopy roads, shaded by live oak trees hung with Spanish moss.

Tallahassee

🅰 217 F3

Visitor information

✉ Capitol Complex, 400 S. Monroe St. & Apalachee Pkwy.

☎ 850/413-9200

Old Capitol

☎ 850/487-1902

New Capitol

☎ 850/488-6167

It is worth making a visit to the **Old Capitol.** With its red-and-white-striped awnings, this is a Southern belle of a capitol building, as charming as the 1978 **New Capitol,** nearby, is characterless. Saved from demolition, it was stripped of its 20th-century additions and restored to its 1902 glory. Now it is a museum of Florida's political history.

The old Supreme Court, Senate, House of Representatives, and Governor's Office are all open to the public, along with galleries of exhibits presenting an excellent overview of the people and events that shaped the state.

Take time to read the reproductions of contemporary documents and newspaper reports. In the House of Representatives chamber, the three semicircular rows of seats look almost like school desks. In the Supreme Court, the atmosphere is as weighty as it was when judgments were given on cases ranging from labor disputes to racial discrimination. No punches are pulled in this museum: Everything is put on record.

(*Continued on p. 222*)

A walk around Tallahassee

This walk through downtown Tallahassee reveals some of the colorful characters and important events in the past 150 years of the city's history. Wear comfortable shoes, since the route goes up and down steep hills.

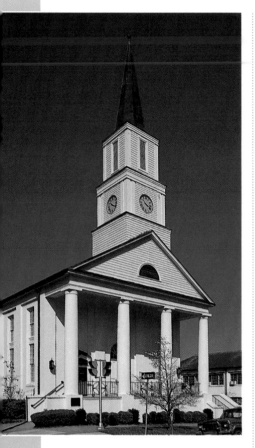

The Greek Revival First Presbyterian Church (1838) was renovated in the 1980s.

Start on the west side of the New Capitol Building, where the five flags reflect the historic allegiances of Florida. Walk down the steps to South Duval Street; turn right on Pensacola Street and go uphill, then turn left on to South Adams Street.

At **City Hall ❶**, the stone monument records that Tallahassee was laid out in 1824. This was Wayne Square, the original market-place, dubbed "rascals' yard" because of its pillory. The early 1980s saw the renovation of downtown buildings such as **Gallie's Hall ❷**, opposite. Built in 1874, the upper floor was an opera house, the venue for one of only two activities in Tallahassee, according to locals. The other was going to church.

Continue along Adams Street, and at the corner of West College Avenue and Adams Street look west to the **Florida State University** campus, half a mile away on another hilltop. Established in 1857, its main building stands on the site of the town gallows, a reminder to the seminary students of the "best and worst that mankind is capable of."

Walk down on West College Avenue, looking across Kleman Plaza to the new gray and blue **Capital Cultural Center.** Turn right on Martin Luther King Jr. Boulevard and continue to Park Avenue. When the **Old City Cemetery ❸** (*Park Ave., Tel 850/488-3901*) was dedicated in 1829, it was on the edge of the city. Near the southeast corner, the low headstones mark the graves of Confederate soldiers who died in the battles of Olustee and Natural Bridge. Farther along the West Park Avenue side, just before South Macomb Street, are the graves of black soldiers who fought on the Union side.

Walk up the middle of the **Chain of Parks,** pausing on the corner of North Bronough Street. Now converted to offices, the Gothic brick building was **St. James Colored Methodist Episcopal Church ❹.** Four separate pleasantly shady green parks stretch up the hill to North Monroe Street. Continue to the corner of North Duval Street. Typical of mansions from the 1830s, **The Columns ❺** is the oldest building still standing in Tallahassee, although it was moved from the site where it was put up by a Georgian banker, William "Money" Williams. The story that he put a nickel into every brick may have started because each brick cost five cents. The nickel didn't exist in the 1830s!

Walk to the corner of North Adams Street to the **First Presbyterian Church ❻** (*110 N.*

Adams St., Tel 850/222-4504). Rifle slits in the basement walls supposedly allowed worshipers to protect themselves from Indian attacks during the Seminole Wars of the mid-1800s. This is the oldest church still in use in Tallahassee. Continue along Park Avenue to North Calhoun Street, nicknamed "Gold Dust Street" for the wealthy families who lived in grand mansions.

Walk across the park to 301 East Park Avenue and the **Knott House** ❼ (*301 E. Park Ave., Tel 850/922-2459, guided tour only*). Since 1865, May 20 has been a special day for the black community of Tallahassee. It was on

the steps of this house that Gen. Edward McCook of the Union Army read out the Emancipation Proclamation. The Knott family moved into the house in the 1920s and the house has been restored to its 1920s' appearance. Take time to go inside this home of Louella Knott, the eccentric wife of a state politician who wrote poems to her furniture. ∎

This re-created period room in the Knott House Museum retains a 1920s ambience—a perfect setting for writing and composing poetry.

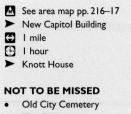

Ⓜ See area map pp. 216–17
▶ New Capitol Building
↔ 1 mile
🕐 1 hour
▶ Knott House

NOT TO BE MISSED
● Old City Cemetery
● The Columns
● First Presbyterian Church
● Knott House

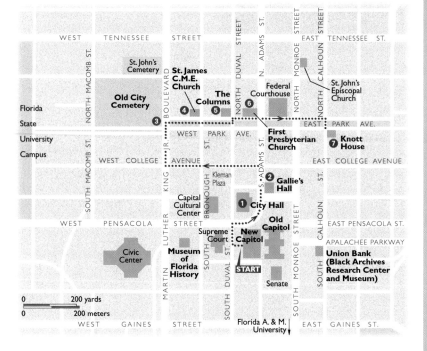

**Black Archives
Research Center
& Museum**

✉ Union Bank Bldg.,
corner of Apalachee
Pkwy. & S.
Calhoun St.

☎ 850/487-3803

**Startling displays
in the Black
Archives
Research Center
& Museum help
today's Floridians
come to terms
with the past.**

(*Continued from p. 218*)
In recent years, recognition has been given to the role African Americans have played in the development of Florida (see pp. 26–27 & p. 33). The **Florida Black Heritage Trail** covers over a hundred sites, including several in Tallahassee. The booklet is published by Florida Heritage (*Florida Dept. of State, 500 S. Bronough St., Tallahassee 32399-0250, Tel 850/487-2344*).

There are two branches of the **Black Archives Research Center & Museum.** The older one at the Florida A&M University Campus is mainly for research into black history worldwide.

A separate downtown museum is just east of the Old Capitol, in the Union Bank. Opened in 1996, the downtown branch tells the story of the blacks and whites in Florida.

Space here is very limited, so exhibits are rotated regularly. You may see a "talking drum," an African method of communication that was forbidden on plantations. There are posters, prints, and old newspapers, such as the copy of *The National Anti-Slavery Standard* from April 30, 1864. Reporting on the Battle of Olustee, it notes that the battle cry of the 54th Massachusetts Colored Infantry, "Three cheers for old Mass. and $7 a month," was as sarcastic as it was patriotic. Despite a promise of equal pay, the Union Army paid black soldiers less than their white comrades. Most chilling of all is the *Amistad*-like leg chain and key from a 17th-century slave ship, and the leaflets and posters published by the Ku Klux Klan.

Union Bank is well worth a visit in its own right. Dating from 1841, it is the oldest surviving bank building in Florida. After the Civil War, it became the Freedman's Bureau Bank, whose clients were emancipated slaves.

Two blocks west from the Capitol Complex is the **Museum of Florida History** (*500 S. Bronough St., Tel 850/488-1484*). From the end of the Ice Age 12,000 years ago to 20th-century tourism, this museum covers all aspects of Florida's history.

The chronicle of the Native Americans ranges from the burial rites of ancient peoples, such as the site at Windover (see p. 181), to the sad story of the Seminole, who fought to keep their lands in the 19th century. The Civil War, "orange fever" (the boom-to-bust cycle of the citrus industry), and "Tin Can Tourism" are intriguing exhibits reflecting the hows and whys of modern Florida. ∎

Wakulla Springs State Park

THANKS TO THE AQUIFERS IN FLORIDA'S LIMESTONE, THE state abounds with springs, whose crystal-clear water bubbles up and out to form rivers.

At Wakulla, a state park since 1986, the freshwater springs are among the world's largest and deepest. From 185 feet below the surface, more than 600,000 gallons of water gush out every minute, all at a constant 68–70°F. The name translates as "strange and mysterious waters"; add in dense vegetation and tall cypress trees and you have a jungle-like setting just right for shooting movies such as *The Creature from the Black Lagoon* (1954), *Airport '77* (1977), and six 1930s Johnny Weismuller Tarzan films. There are ample opportunities for wildlife spotting here, and nature trails to take you through the park.

Explore the springs for 30 minutes in a glass bottom boat, or take the one mile cruise down the Wakulla River and back aboard a pontoon boat. Along the route, you will pass the site of the Tarzan movies, and usually spot ibis, turtles, and deer as well as innumerable alligators. You can swim here, but you have to be an experienced cave diver to explore the underwater cavern system that has been mapped for some 11,000 feet.

Wakulla Lodge, the former home of financier Edward Ball and now a hotel and restaurant, has a 650-pound, 11-foot 2-inch, mounted alligator in the lobby known as Old Joe. ■

Edward Ball Wakulla Springs State Park

🅰 217 E3

✉ 15 miles south of Tallahassee, Fla. 267

☎ 850/922-3633

$ $

Sunbathing alligators and turtles (top) and a pontoon tour boat (bottom) at Wakulla Springs State Park

Apalachicola

Apalachicola

216 D2

Visitor information

✉ Chamber of
Commerce,
99 Market St.

☎ 850/653-9419

**John Gorrie
State Museum**

✉ 46 6th St.

☎ 850/653-9347

🕐 Closed Tues.–Wed.

💲 $

**St. George Island
State Park**

☎ 850/927-2111

Shrimpers
contribute to
Apalachicola's
seafood industry.

A RIVER, A BAY, AND A SMALL, SLEEPY TOWN ALL BEAR THE
name Apalachicola. Seafood is the main industry, with one in five of the
nation's oysters coming from the broad bay locked in by the long, sandy
barrier of St. George Island. Oyster boats still moor at the Eastpoint
waterfront, and the local radio station is WOYS Oyster Radio.

A walking tour of the charming
historic downtown is a good way
to learn about the boom times
when fishing, cotton, sponges, and
timber brought trade via the
harbor. Shipping lost out to the
railroad in the early 19th century,
but the buildings recall busier
times. The Chamber of Commerce
will supply a walking tour map.

Wooden buildings with wraparound verandas hark back to earlier
days. Just such a building is the 1909
Gibson Inn (*Market St. and Ave. C,
Tel 850/653-2191*), restored in the
1980s. Also, do not miss **Raney
House** (*128 Market St.*) built in
1838 in the Greek Revival style.

Dr. John Gorrie (1803–1855), a
pioneer of refrigeration, is honored
in the **John Gorrie State
Museum.** However, this small
museum in Gorrie's house does little
to bring his interesting story to life
and also has general exhibits about
the town.

Apalachicola's waters are protected by barrier islands. It is linked by a
bridge to the largest, **St. George
Island.** White beaches and abundant wildlife attract visitors, and
there is an increasing number of
holiday houses. At the eastern end
of the island, **St. George Island
State Park** preserves more than
9 miles of dunes. ■

Seaside
🏕 216 C3
Visitor information
✉ Fla. 30A
☎ 850/231-2201

Grayton Beach State Recreation Area
✉ Fla. 30A, off US 98
☎ 850/231-4210

Seaside is a planned community of wooden frame houses.

Seaside

IN TERMS OF DEVELOPMENT, FLORIDA HAS IT ALL: FROM the best to the worst. Seaside is one of the most innovative of all planned communities, a new town with an old-fashioned look. There are brick-paved lanes and narrow sandy alleyways, white picket fences and porches for sitting and chatting to neighbors. Indeed, "neighborhood" is at the heart of the concept that founder Robert Davis turned into reality in the 1980s.

Ever since the worldwide acclaim for *The Truman Show*, the 1998 film starring Jim Carrey, movie-tourists have flocked to Seaside. They come to see Seahaven, the backdrop to the surreal plot. What they discover is an experiment in town planning. As one resident points out, "This is like a New England village. People know each other, people have businesses here as well as homes."

Take time to wander and observe how Davis has created a community, rather than a vacation resort. Unlike the current vogue for private, gated developments, Seaside stands on a public road; residents have to cross the road to get to the white, sandy beach and blue-green waters of the Gulf of Mexico.

Less than 2 miles west of Seaside, **Grayton Beach State Recreation Area** has one of the nation's top-rated beaches. The sands are white and the clear water is popular with swimmers. ■

"...each Seaside house will continue the regional building tradition and will contribute to giving Seaside's neighborhoods the coherence, cohesion, and strong sense of place that characterize such towns as Charleston, Savannah, Nantucket and Cape May."
—Seaside Urban Code, 1982

Sand & beaches

Beaches are one of Florida's greatest attractions, with about 1,100 miles of sandy shore along the 1,800 miles of coastline. According to Stephen J. Leatherman, Director of the Laboratory for Coastal Research at the University of Maryland, Florida has more good beaches than any other state. Nicknamed Dr. Beach, he has been rating beaches across the nation for several years, and Florida always vies with Hawaii for top honors in the lists. As well as looking for obvious qualities such as cleanliness, safety, access, and sunshine, Dr. Beach also assesses the softness of the sand and the warmth of the water.

In the 1998 report, St. Joseph Peninsula State Park rated highly because "the snow-white sand from the beach had been blown by onshore winds into the anchoring sea oats to produce some of the largest sand dunes in Florida…the aquamarine water is crystal clear…the surf is normally low, making for excellent swimming." Other commendations included Caladesi Island, Cape Florida, Fort DeSoto Park, and St. George Island. A previous national winner was St. Andrews State Recreation Area, with the "finest white sand in the world."

Florida's beaches have an intriguing variety of sand. On the Atlantic, the sand is downstream from the mountains of the Carolinas, so the textures are rougher and rockier than those of the Gulf. The Panhandle and the beaches from Clearwater to Sarasota consist of shimmering, fine-grained quartz sand, whereas farther south along the Gulf shore, coral sand and shell hash provide the pinkish sand.

Erosion has long been a problem, so "nourishment" programs are widespread, with dredgers and giant vacuum pumps sucking sand out of the bays and back onto the beaches. The cost is enormous: one million dollars a square mile, but for resorts such as Miami Beach, the vacationer dollar justifies the cost. As ever, man plays with nature. Miami's naturally fine shell and coral sand has been replaced with rougher-textured sand, which packs down harder and so lasts longer. Where beaches are a major vacationer attraction, towns experiment with ways to protect the sand. Some go for massive concrete jetties or walls, others prefer the more picturesque and conservation-friendly wooden groins and piers. There seems to be no system that is foolproof or everlasting.

The fragile dunes, and the communities that now lie behind them, need a helping hand from nature to save them from the massive waves and wind induced by hurricanes. Sea oats, a grass that can withstand salt-laden winds, flourish on the windward flank of the dunes, helping to bind the sand together. In fact, the more sand is piled up on the sea oats, the deeper the plants dig in their roots.

Watch for wildflowers such as the sea oxeye and the beach sunflower, which both display yellow flowers. Once the yellow flowers of the prickly pear cactus die off, the characteristic edible red fruit grows and ripens. Although the scrubby sea grape is attractive to both humans and raccoons, thanks to its berries which make tasty jelly, the small black fruit on the beach berry is strictly for wildlife, for whom it is a valuable source of food, year-round. As the saw palmetto is home to small rodents, the spiky plant also attracts snakes hunting for dinner, while its white flowers are particularly attractive to honey bees. ∎

Left: Cars are still allowed to drive on the firm sand of Daytona Beach.
Right: Some of the finest sand and best beaches are on the Gulf Coast.

Pensacola

Pensacola

🗺 216 B4

Visitor information

✉ 1401 E. Gregory St.

☎ 850/434-1234

Historic Pensacola Village

✉ 200 E. Zaragoza St.

☎ 850/595-5985

🕐 Closed Sun.

💲 $

IN 1559, DON TRISTAN DE LUNA Y ARELLANO ARRIVED in what is now Pensacola from Mexico with 500 soldiers and 1,000 civilians. A few years later, after storms, starvation, and rebellion, the settlement was abandoned. Two centuries later, Pensacola became the capital of the British West Florida territory. Although the old shipyard was abandoned in 1911, this is still a Navy town. The United States' first-ever naval air station is still a working base, home to the Blue Angels display team and also a popular airplane museum.

Pensacola has many visible traces of its colonial past. The street names reflect Spanish rule, while the grid system of streets dates from the brief period under the British flag.

Within the 26-block Seville Historic District down by the waterfront is **Historic Pensacola Village,** a complex of museums, architecturally important houses, and archaeological sites. At the hub is an imposing Renaissance Revival building, once City Hall and now the **T. T. Wentworth, Jr. Florida State Museum** (*330 S. Jefferson St., Tel 850/444-8905*). Wentworth amassed a collection that has all the eccentricity of a Ripley's

Believe It or Not! museum, with everything from a massive mounted Kodiak bear to a crumb from Thomas Edison's birthday cake.

More edifying are the historic houses that demonstrate how life has been lived in the city: Some are furnished with fine antiques, others reflect age-old crafts such as weaving. One of the most interesting is **Julee Cottage** (1805). Named in honor of Julee Paton, a freed slave, it contains a small tribute to African-American life in West Florida. It is pleasant to stroll through the shaded streets, following the self-guided tour pamphlet, but this area really comes to life on

The F44 Corsair, a combatant in World War II battles in the Pacific, is on display at the National Museum of Naval Aviation.

one of the two daily guided tours (*Tel 850/444-8905*).

In 1997 almost a million visitors flocked to see the naval aircraft and memorabilia at the **National Museum of Naval Aviation,** located on the Naval Air Station, 8 miles from downtown. The *Top Gun*-style F14 Tom Cat at the entrance is one of 130 planes, all with a tale to tell. The joke in the early days was that the Navy was only comfortable with these new-fangled aircraft as long as they were called boats: hence the Curtiss Flying Boat. Early models are frighteningly flimsy: The A-1 Triad looks more like a contraption than a plane, with its two flimsy seats and a steering wheel. More substantial is the JN-4 Curtiss "Jenny." After World War I, this reliable work-horse was sold off inexpensively to the hundreds of newly qualified pilots, generating innumerable Waldo Peppers. Lucky Lindbergh was among those barnstormers.

Present-day heroes are also well represented. The *Magic of Flight* movie at the IMAX cinema has the popular Blue Angels display team.

Also on the air station is **Fort Barrancas,** the third structure on this site (earlier forts were built by the British, in 1763, and the Spanish, in 1797). From its superb position, high above the narrow entrance to Pensacola Bay, you can see **Fort Pickens** across the water. To get there by car, take the Pensacola Bay Bridge from down-town to Gulf Breeze, then Fla. 399 onto **Santa Rosa Island.** At the west end of the island is the fort where Apache leader Geronimo was held (1886–88) and, humiliatingly, turned into a tourist attraction. Both forts offer excellent regular guided tours. Much of the beautiful beach on Santa Rosa Island is part of the **Gulf Islands National Seashore,** which protects over 50

miles of coastline in West Florida. For information stop at the visitor center at **Naval Live Oaks** (*1801 Gulf Breeze Pkwy., US 98, Tel 850/9342600*). Here a small exhibition explains why live oak trees were important in 18th- and 19th-century shipbuilding. Outside are nature trails through some of the 1,000 acres of woodland. ■

National Museum of Naval Aviation
✉ 1750 Radford Blvd., Pensacola Naval Air Station
☎ 850/452-3604

Fort Pickens
✉ Gulf Islands National Seashore, Santa Rosa Island
☎ 850/934-2600
💲 $

Fort Barrancas
✉ Navy Blvd., Pensacola Naval Air Station
☎ 850/455-5167
💲 $

Top and left: Pensacola's heritage, preserved in the Seville Historic District

More places to visit in the Panhandle

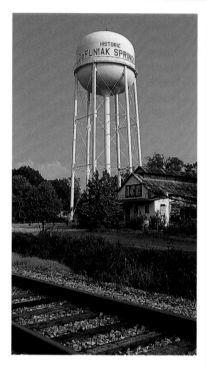

Top: Pelicans are only visitors to this abandoned, offshore hut at Cedar Key. Above: Water tower at DeFuniak Springs

CEDAR KEY

Set in the Gulf of Mexico at the end of a 3-mile causeway, Cedar Key has changed little since 1896, when a hurricane blew away its sawmills. The cedar wood used in a billion lead pencils was shipped out of this tiny port.

Only 800 people live here year-round, swelling to 1,200 in winter. Come here to experience what locals describe as Old Florida. There are no broad beaches, no movie theater, and no fast food outlets. Here the visitor attractions include the **Cedar Key Historical Society Museum** (*609 2nd St., Tel 352/543-5549*), which has interesting exhibits and sells a walking map of the historic area.

Cedar Key Scrub State Preserve is ideal for birdwatchers, who know that the surrounding islets are right on the migratory routes.

⚠ 217 G1 ☎ 352/543-5600

DEFUNIAK SPRINGS

DeFuniak Springs was the winter home of the New York Chautauqua—a popular movement around the turn of the century famous for its lyceum and entertainment series. Once radio and movies became popular, the movement lost its momentum and purpose. The town began as a stop along the Louisville and Nashville Railroad, developed around Open Pond, a spring-fed, near-circular lake.

The lake was, and still is, the town's focal point, surrounded by handsome Victorian houses with gables and verandas. Dominating what looks like a college campus is the shimmering, white wooden 1909 **Hall of Brotherhood.** With its 40 elegant, Greek-style columns representing each of the then-40 states, its auditorium seated 4,000 for lectures. During office hours, visitors can see inside the Hall of Brotherhood, where the Chamber of Commerce is housed.

Self-guided tour pamphlets trace the architectural highlights of this quiet town.

⚠ 216 C4 ✉ Visitor information, 2760 Freeport Rd. S., DeFuniak Springs ☎ 850/892-4300 ∎

Travelwise

**License plates on
Marathon Key**

TRAVELWISE INFORMATION

PLANNING YOUR TRIP

Florida must offer more vacation options than any other region in the world. With tourism the number one industry, the whole state is geared to attracting visitors. The Sunday newspapers all across America have ads in their travel sections for Florida, including flights, car rentals, and accommodations, with a host of add-ons such as entry to theme parks, short cruises, or good, old-fashioned sight-seeing. It is one of the most popular spots for package deals whether you are from Chicago, New York, or St. Louis. These packages tend to be competitively priced, offering considerable value for money.

More and more repeat visitors to the Sunshine State are discovering the freedom of individual travel, exploring the less publicized areas, staying perhaps at the numerous bed-and-breakfast inns that have sprung up in recent years. Some even organize unusual (for Florida) programs for cycling from inn to inn.

If you follow the advice of Florida natives that "the real Florida begins where the roads end," then you will enjoy boating. Florida is a paradise for yachters, and even the most inexperienced sailors can cruise the calm and shallow waters of Pine Island Sound and Charlotte Harbour, near Fort Myers. Then there are the specialist vacations for tennis players and golfers for which Florida is famous. Again the packages to tempt you are many and varied.

Remember that in southern Florida, hotel and condo prices drop dramatically in the summer months; in the north of the state, however, prices tend to stay the same all year.

CLIMATE

In the past decade or so, Florida has developed into a year-round destination. In southern Florida, the winter months are the most popular for visitors as there is little rain and sunny, warm days. This so-called "season," running from December to April, is when most cultural and festival activities take place. In the summer and fall (June to October), the weather is hot and humid (over 90°F.), with heavy rain storms in the afternoon. The hurricane season runs from June 1 to November 30. More often than not, the path of the storm passes across southern Florida: Miami, the Keys, and the Naples area (see pp. 118–19). The weather in northern Florida is different. Winters are mild, with pleasant days and cool evenings: good golfing weather. Summers are hot and humid.

WHAT TO TAKE

The dress code is casual. Although residents like to put on a jacket and tie for a formal evening out, few visitors need to pack them. In any case, there will always be a shop nearby if you want to splurge on, say, a new dress for a concert. In winter, a sweater, jacket, or wrap is useful in the evening, but in summer, even the lightest clothing can seem too heavy when outdoors. Clothes that cover legs and arms are a godsend when there are bugs around. Remember that air-conditioning can be chilly, so an extra layer is useful. Lightweight rainwear and extra footwear are also useful. All year round, insect repellent is essential for outdoor attractions.

There is an overload of information available about the Sunshine State, one of the world's most popular destinations. The only difficulty is distinguishing between the hype and the reality. For more information, call 1-888-7FLA-USA.

USEFUL WEBSITES

Florida has a comprehensive and up-to-the-minute website covering a vast range of interests and activities, including attractions, recreation parks, events calendar, lodging, campgrounds, and even current weather conditions:

www.flausa.com

Other sites worth exploring once you know where you will visit include:

Bradenton Area Convention & Visitors Bureau:
www.floridaislandbeaches.org

Central Florida (Polk County) Convention & Visitors Bureau:
www.cfdc.org/tourism

Daytona Beach Area:
www.daytonabeach.com

Florida Keys & Key West:
www.fla-keys.com

Greater Fort Lauderdale Convention & Visitors Bureau:
www.sunny.org

Greater Miami Convention & Visitors Bureau:
www.miamiandbeaches.com

Kissimmee-St. Cloud Convention & Visitors Bureau:
www.floridakiss.com

Lee Island Coast (Fort Myers Beach, Sanibel, & Captiva Islands): www.leeislandcoast.com

Marco Islands & the Everglades:
www.marcoislandeverglades.com

Orlando Tourism Bureau:
www.go2orlando.com

Palm Beach County Convention & Visitors Bureau:
www.palmbeachfl.com

St. Petersburg/Clearwater Area Convention & Visitors Bureau: www.stpete-clearwater.com

Sarasota Convention & Visitors Bureau: www.state.sarasota.fl.us

GETTING AROUND

Air
There are always attractive offers for flights to the Sunshine State, but it is important to make reservations well in advance if your travel plans coincide with major holidays. Depending on your final destination, it is worth considering nearby, alternative airports at busy periods. An example would be Orlando/ Sandford instead of Orlando International.

Among the important airports are Daytona Beach, Fort Lauderdale-Hollywood, Gainesville, Jacksonville, Key West, Miami International, Melbourne, Orlando, Palm Beach, St. Petersburg-Clearwater, Sarasota-Bradenton, Southwest Florida International (at Fort Myers), Tampa, Panama City, Pensacola, and Tallahassee.

All major airports are serviced by efficient airport transfer operators. As well as taxi services, shuttle services from the terminals to nearby downtown hotels are clearly indicated. Reservations are only required for the service to the airport. Limousine services are also available to nearby towns. All rental car companies have detailed maps of cities, to help visitors.

Car
The major car rental companies have outlets all over the state. Prices are very competitive, but be wary of low introductory prices that spiral upward when all the extras, such as liability coverage and state tax, have been added in.

Alamo Tel 800/327-9633
www.goalamo.com

Avis Tel 800/331-1212
www.avis.com

Budget Tel 800/527-0700
www.drivebudget.com

Dollar Tel 800/800-4000
www.dollarcar.com

Hertz Tel 800/654-3131
www.hertz.com

Thrifty Tel 800/367-2277
www.thrifty.com

Bus
Greyhound Lines (Tel 800/232-2222) has a comprehensive network linking all the major Florida destinations.

Train
Amtrak's Silver Service (Silver Palm, Silver Star, Silver Meteor) from the Northeast runs three daily trains between New York, the Carolinas, and Florida. The journey from the Big Apple to the Big Orange takes the best part of 24 hours, stopping at major destinations such as Jacksonville, Daytona, Orlando, Tampa, West Palm Beach, Fort Lauderdale, and Miami.

The daily Amtrak Auto Train carries passengers and their cars from Lorton, Virginia (near Washington, D.C.), to Sandford, near Orlando. (Tel 800/USA-RAIL)

PRACTICAL ADVICE

Safety
Florida's reputation for criminal activity tends to be in areas that no tourist would want to visit. Vacation time is no time, however, to drop your guard: Carrying a wallet in your back pocket is as tempting in Miami as it is in New York City. Use the same rules that you would back home. Always lock your car and never leave cameras and bags in view. Keep valuables in

the hotel safe during the day. Carry credit cards and travelers' checks, rather than large amounts of cash.

Taxes
A sales tax of 6–7% is added to all prices in shops, restaurants, and attractions.

Travelers with disabilities
Most area Convention & Visitors Bureaus have material helpful to travelers with disabilities. Many Florida beaches also offer Surf Chairs, wheelchairs designed for enjoying the beach. Again, the local tourist offices have details.

Wheelchair Getaways, Inc., covering South Florida rents vans and mini-vans equipped with wheelchair lifts and tie downs. Optional hand controls and power seats are available on select models. Each van has either a raised roof or lowered floor and can accommodate one or two wheelchairs (P.O. Box 20126, West Palm Beach, FL 33416, Tel 561/748-8414, Fax 561/641-3658).

EMERGENCIES

As ever, 911 is the number to call in case of police, ambulance, or fire emergency. If you are robbed, make sure that you call the police using the local non-emergency number. In order to claim insurance once you get home, you usually need a police report. If you have had a credit card or travelers' checks stolen contact the following numbers:

Credit cards
American Express 800/528-4800
Diners Club 800/234-6377
Discover 800/347-2683
MasterCard 800/826-2181
Visa 800/336-8472

Travelers' checks
American Express 800/221-7282
MasterCard 800/223-9920
Thomas Cook 800/223-7373
Visa 800/227-6811

HOTELS & RESTAURANTS

Florida has a wide range of accommodations and restaurants. The following selection includes places to stay and to eat that are within easy reach of the attractions listed earlier in this book. All have special character, so reservations are recommended.

As standards of facilities for those with disabilities can vary, it is important to call ahead and be sure that the hotel or bed-and-breakfast inn has what you need and expect. All hotels and restaurants have either valet parking or parking lots on or near the premises. Breakfast is sometimes included in bed-and-breakfast inns. Large hotels and resorts offer special packages for families, golf/tennis, and long stays. In addition, hotels in the Orlando area have packages that include admission to the theme parks.

LATIN AMERICAN MENU READER

Ingredients with Spanish names are used not only in Caribbean and Latin American restaurants; Several Floridian/New Florida-style chefs also use them as part of their style of regional cooking. Here are some of the more common words:

adobo: marinade with garlic and sour orange juice (Cuba)
arepa: cheese/corn pancake (Colombia)
arroz con leche/pollo: rice pudding/chicken and rice
asado: roasted
azúcar: sugar
batido: fruit shake, made with condensed milk
boliche: meat sandwich (Cuba)
bolo: beef sandwich (Cuba)
bollo: bread roll
bollos: black-eyed pea fritters (Cuba)
boniato: sweet potato/yam
buche: small cup of strong Cuban coffee, like an espresso
café carajillo: coffee with a shot of brandy
café con leche: very milky coffee
café cortadito: coffee with splash of milk
café cubano: sweetened, strong black coffee
calabaza: pumpkin from West Indies
carambola: another name for star fruit
cebolla: onion
chayote: type of squash
chicharrón: pork crackling
chipotle: smoked jalapeño
chimichurri: marinade/sauce (Argentina)
chorizo: spicy pork sausage
(a bit like salami)
churrasco: barbecue/tenderloin (Nicaraguan style)
congri: red beans and rice (Cuba)
empañadas: deep fried turnovers with spicy meat filling
emparedado: sandwich
flan: crème caramel dessert
gazpacho: chilled tomato soup
griots: Haitian fried pork chunks
guacamole: spicy avocado dip
guarapo: sugarcane juice
helado: ice cream
jalapeño: pepper
lechón: suckling pig
lonchería: snack bar
mariquitas: like potato chips, but green plantains
media noche: Cuban BLT with layers of roast pork, cheese, ham, mustard, and pickle
mojito: rum, lime, and mint spritzer
mojo: garlicky Cuban-style marinade, with sour oranges and limes
moros y cristianos: black beans and rice
natilla: cinnamon custard (Cuba)
pan: bread
pan suave: sweet roll (Cuba)
pastelito: meat pie (Nicaragua)
picadillo: spicy beef hash (Cuba)
plátano: cooking banana
queso: cheese
ropa vieja: shredded beef stew with peppers, garlic, and sherry
salsa: sauce, usually spicy
sangria: wine and fruit juice cooler
sapote: fruit that tastes like chocolate pudding
serrano: dried ham
sofrito: spicy tomato ketchup (Cuba)
tamales: snack in a corn husk
tapas: hors d'oeuvres
tres leches: meringue/cake dessert, using three types of milk (Nicaragua)
vaca frita: deep-fried shredded beef
yuca: cassava root

PRICES

HOTELS
An indication of the cost of a double room without breakfast is given by $ signs

$$$$$	Over $200
$$$$	$150–199
$$$	$100–$149
$$	$50–$99
$	Under $50

RESTAURANTS
An indication of the cost of a three-course dinner without drinks is given by $ signs

$$$	Over $35
$$	$20–$35
$	Under $20

MIAMI & MIAMI BEACH

DOWNTOWN 33130

🏨 **MIAMI RIVER INN**
$$
118 S.W. SOUTH RIVER DR.
TEL 305/325-0045
FAX 305/325-9227
Just across the Miami River from downtown, five century-old clapboard houses have been turned into a New England-style bed-and-breakfast. Don't be put off by the East Little Havana location.
🛏 40 ⊕ 🅰 All major cards

COCONUT GROVE 33133

🏨 **GRAND BAY HOTEL**
$$$$$
2669 S. BAYSHORE DR.
TEL 305/858-9600
FAX 305/858-1532
From the windows of this hotel, Coconut Grove is just a

sea of green. Expensive, sophisticated, and modern setting, with a recently remodeled restaurant.

ⓘ 178 🔁 🅢 🌊 🔽
🅢 All major cards

🏨 GROVE ISLE CLUB AND RESORT
$$$$
4 GROVE ISLE DR.
TEL 305/858-8300
FAX 305/858-5908
Drive over the bridge and onto the small island, and this comfortable hotel is right on Biscayne Bay. Plenty of sports facilities make this attractive for families as well as small executive conferences.

ⓘ 50 🔁 🅢 🌊 🔽
🅢 All major cards

🍴 THE GROVE ISLE
$$
4 GROVE ISLE DR.
TEL 305/858-8300
Nowhere else in Miami has a waterside setting like this, with dolphins and pelicans for entertainment. There is an indoor dining area, but the best place to eat is outside, on the tented terrace. Enjoy the modern American cuisine.

🍴 100 🅢 All major cards

🍴 CAFÉ TU TU TANGO
$
COCOWALK, 3015 GRAND AVE.
TEL 305/529-2222
From this second-floor vantage point, you can watch the busy life on Grand Avenue and CocoWalk. A mock artist's loft with imaginative fast food, this is a good place to take children.

🍴 250 🅢 AE, MC, V

🍴 NEWS CAFÉ
$
2901 FLORIDA AVE.
TEL 305/774-6397
A branch of the old established one on South Beach, serving classic American coffee shop food. Just off the main hub of Coconut Grove, and full of

locals, who come in anytime, day or night.

🍴 250 🅢 All major cards

CORAL GABLES 33134

SOMETHING SPECIAL

🏨 THE BILTMORE HOTEL
A historic landmark, this hotel opened in 1926. The guestbook includes movie stars and royalty. Worth a visit to swim in the largest hotel swimming pool in America. Johnny Weismuller of Tarzan fame once performed in water shows here. A full range of resort activities are offered, from tennis and golf to spa treatments.
$$$$
1200 ANASTASIA AVE.
TEL 305/445-1926
FAX 305/913-3159

ⓘ 275 🔁 🅢 🌊 🔽
🅢 All major cards

🏨 PLACE ST. MICHEL
$$
162 ALCAZAR AVE.
TEL 305/444-1666
FAX 305/529-0074
This 70-year-old flavor of France in the heart of downtown Coral Gables is perfect for those tired of the noise of South Beach. Comfortable, well run Stuart's Bar is a local haunt.

ⓘ 27 🔁 🅢 🅢 All major cards

🍴 NORMAN'S
$$$
21 ALMERIA AVE.
TEL 305/446-6767
The best restaurant in Miami, this is the place to discover what South Florida's New World cuisine is all about. Try the seven-course degustation menu.

🍴 200 🕐 Closed Sun. L & D 🅢 All major cards

🍴 CAFFÉ ABBRACCI
$$$
318 ARAGON AVE.
TEL 305/441-0700
Modern Italian food in an elegant setting. As in other upscale restaurants in the Gables, diners dress up for a highly sophisticated night out.

🍴 150 🕐 Closed Sat., Sun. L 🅢 All major cards

🍴 RESTAURANT ST. MICHEL
$$$
HOTEL PLACE ST. MICHEL,
162 ALCAZAR AVE.
TEL 305/444-1666
Intimate and romantic, with a white piano, this is a change from the minimalistic decor of so many trendy restaurants. Sample the fine modern cooking with the focus on fish and tropical ingredients.

🍴 100 🅢 All major cards

SOUTH BEACH, MIAMI BEACH 33139

🏨 THE TIDES
$$$$$
1220 OCEAN DR.
TEL 305/604-5000
FAX 305/604-5180
The most luxurious hotel on Ocean Drive has quotes from Oscar Wilde in the lobby and a telescope at the window of each room, ready for spotting cruise ships out on the ocean. Restaurant Twelve Twenty (see p. 236) in the lobby has expensive but top-quality French food.

ⓘ 45 🔁 🅢 🌊 🔽
🅢 All major cards

🏨 IMPALA
$$$$
1228 COLLINS AVE.
TEL 305/673-2021
FAX 305/673-5984
An oasis of refinement in trendy South Beach, with an entrance hidden away down a garden path. Spiga is the excellent modern Italian restaurant in the

---

🅢 Air-conditioning 🈯 Indoor/🌊 Outdoor swimming pool 🔽 Health club 🅢 Credit cards

original lobby.

⬤ 17 **⊟** **⑤** **⬥ All major cards**

🏨 OCEAN FRONT HOTEL
$$$$
1230 OCEAN DR.
TEL 305/672-2579
FAX 305/672-7665
This hotel has been completely renovated and now has deep comforts and a French Riviera atmosphere all due to the French owners, managers, and food.

⬤ 27 **⊟** **⑤** **⬥ All major cards**

SOMETHING SPECIAL

🏨 THE MARLIN

What other hotel has a recording studio on the premises? Guests include famous names such as Mick Jagger, U2, and Aerosmith, as well as Oliver Stone. Funky ambience, hi-tech gadgets, and kitchenettes for those who want to be alone.

$$$$
1200 COLLINS AVE., MIAMI BEACH, 33139
TEL 305/604-5000
FAX 305/673-9609

⬤ 13 **⊟** **⑤** **⬥ All major cards**

🏨 INDIAN CREEK HOTEL
$$
2727 INDIAN CREEK DR.
TEL 305/531-2727
FAX 305/531-5651
A short drive up Miami Beach from South Beach, this hotel is on the creek, not the ocean. Comfortable and welcoming with pleasant Pancoast restaurant. Gym facilities nearby.

⬤ 61 **⊟** **⑤** **⬥ All major cards**

🍴 NEMO
$$$
100 COLLINS AVE.
TEL 305/532-4550
What started out as a local spot has been discovered by

others. The Sunday brunch is one of the best anywhere and desserts are always praised.

⬛ 160 **⬥ AE, MC, V**

🍴 PACIFIC TIME
$$$
915 LINCOLN RD.
TEL 305/534-5979
Jonathan Eismann is one of the top chefs in the city, so make reservations to sample his Pan-Asian cooking here. Most fun is to be had sitting at the counter with views straight into the kitchen. P.T. Next Door is the café, under the same ownership, next door.

⬛ 150 **🕐 Closed L**
⬥ All major cards

🍴 TWELVE TWENTY
$$$
1220 OCEAN DR.
TEL 305/604-5000
Elegant and expensive, this lobby restaurant at The Tides brings modern versions of French classics to South Beach. Fabulous desserts by a top pastry chef who is, of course, French.

⬛ 120 **⬥ All major cards**

🍴 LES DEUX FONTAINES SEAFOOD RESTAURANT
$$
1230 OCEAN DR.
TEL 305/672-7878
At the Ocean Front Hotel, choose between the terrace, where you can watch the people go by along Ocean Drive, or the indoor French-style brasserie, with its wood paneling and mural. The seafood platter and bouillabaisse (fish soup) are outstanding. Jazz evenings.

⬛ 200 **⬥ All major cards**

🍴 SOUTH BEACH BRASSERIE
$$
910 LINCOLN RD.
TEL 305/534-5511
With movie actor Michael Caine a co-owner, this place

attracts visitors hoping for a glimpse of the star as well as locals who stop at the bar for tapas after work. The menu ranges from British-style bangers and mash (sausage and mashed potatoes) to elaborate salads.

⬛ 250 **⬥ All major cards**

🍴 11TH STREET DINER
$
1065 WASHINGTON AVE.
TEL 305/534-6373
In a railroad dining car shipped down from Pennsylvania, this diner attracts everyone from families during the day to nightclubbers. Sandwiches, full meals, breakfast.

⬛ 70 inside **⬥ All major cards**

🍴 BIG PINK
$
157 COLLINS AVE.
TEL 305/532-4700
Opened in 1996, this is big, noisy, and informal, serving everything from spaghetti and meatballs for kids to salmon teriyaki, all carefully prepared on the premises. Televisions in each corner are tuned to the business channel.

⬛ 200 **⬥ AE, MC, V**

🍴 VAN DYKE CAFÉ
$
LINCOLN RD.
AT JEFFERSON AVE.
TEL 305/534-3600
Breakfast is available anytime from 8 a.m. until 2 a.m. at what is a favorite meeting place for locals. Tables also outdoors on the pedestrian-only Lincoln Road mall. Sandwiches, omelettes, and salads. Jazz nightly.

⬛ 150 **⬥ All major cards**

🍴 WOLFIE'S
$
2038 COLLINS AVE.
TEL 305/538-6626
A tradition on Miami Beach and the best place for a quick fix of Jewish specialties. Big portions in an old-fashioned

family-restaurant setting. The Celebrity Room has photos of showbiz legends.

🛏 250 💳 MC, V

EVERGLADES & THE KEYS

FLAMINGO 33034

🏨 FLAMINGO LODGE
$$
FLAMINGO, EVERGLADES NATIONAL PARK
TEL 941/695-3101
FAX 941/695-3921
Rather old-fashioned and motel-like, but a great place to stay. Right in the national park, this is the best starting point for boating and fishing trips into the mangroves.

ℹ 125 ❄ 🌊 💳 All major cards

🍴 FLAMINGO DINING ROOM
$
FLAMINGO, EVERGLADES NATIONAL PARK
TEL 941/695-3101
Eat breakfast, lunch, or dinner while looking out on Florida Bay and numerous keys. During the summer, when this restaurant is closed, and at public holiday time, the Buttonwood Patio is open for simple meals from Thursday to Monday.

🛏 100 🕐 Closed May–Oct.
💳 All major cards

BIG PINE KEY 33043

🏨 BARNACLE BED & BREAKFAST
$$
LONG BEACH RD., US 1
TEL 305/872-3298
FAX 305/872-3863
With a two-story atrium and a rooftop deck, this bed-and-breakfast is quiet, comfortable, and only 33 miles from Key West. Handy for snorkeling, swimming, and the Key deer preserve.

ℹ 4 ❄ 💳 MC, V

ISLAMORADA 33036

🏨 CHEECA LODGE
$$$$
US 1, MM 82
TEL 305/664-4651
FAX 305/664-2893
An upscale luxury resort catering to fisherpeople, who can charter a boat or try their luck from the 525-foot pier. For non-fisherpeople, there are tennis courts, a 9-hole golf course and a scuba-diving center. If you would like an ocean view, ask for a room on the fourth floor.

ℹ 203 ❄ ❄ 🌊
💳 All major cards

KEY LARGO 33037

🏨 JULES' UNDERSEA LODGE
$$$$$
51 SHORELAND DR.
TEL 305/451-2353
FAX 305/451-4789
The only underwater hotel in the world. Scuba dive down to your quarters, dine on lobster or steak, and spy on the late-night fish world. An expensive experience, but one that is not to be forgotten.

ℹ 2 ❄ 💳 All major cards

🏨 HOLIDAY INN RESORT
$
US 1
TEL 305/451-2121
FAX 305/451-5592
Moored in the marina is *The African Queen*, the boat that starred in the classic Humphrey Bogart movie of the same name. Good base for exploring the nearby coral reef. Modern rooms and excellent views. Restaurants.

ℹ 132 ❄ ❄ 🌊 🏋
💳 All major cards

KEY WEST 33040

🏨 THE GARDENS HOTEL
$$$$
526 ANGELA ST.
TEL 305/294-2661
FAX 305/292-1007

A high standard bed-and-breakfast, set in lush botanical gardens, this is an expensive experience, but one that is well worth it for a special occasion.

ℹ 17 ❄ 🌊 💳 AE, MC, V

🏨 LITTLE PALM ISLAND
Set on a private island reached by boat, this resort is the epitome of exclusivity, with individual thatched cottages, a gourmet restaurant, and a staff to indulge every request. Plenty of activities available, but guests can also sit back and do nothing at all.

$$$$$
US 1, MM 28.5,
LITTLE TORCH KEY, 33042
TEL 305/872-2524
FAX 305/872-4843
ℹ 30 ❄ 🌊 🏋
💳 All major cards

🏨 MARRIOTT'S CASA MARINA RESORT
$$$
1500 REYNOLDS ST.
TEL 305/296-3535
FAX 305/296-3008
The last resort hotel built for the Florida East Coast Railroad (after Flagler's death), this grande dame retains much of its glamour of yesteryear, even though it is now part of the Marriott chain. Popular with families.

ℹ 311 ❄ ❄ 🌊
💳 All major cards

🏨 SIMONTON COURT
$$$
320 SIMONTON ST.
TEL 305/294-6386
FAX 305/293-8446
Once a cigar factory, this complex has nine characterful buildings set in large L-shaped gardens. Choose from four swimming

pools, including one specially lit at night. For adults only.

ⓘ 26 ⬜ ⬜
Ⓐ AE, MC, V

SOMETHING SPECIAL

🏨 THE MARQUESA

Two small swimming pools and lush tropical landscaping make this an idyllic spot in the bustling heart of Key West. Expect luxurious furnishings and one of the best restaurants in town, Café Marquesa (see this page).

$$$
600 FLEMING ST.,
KEY WEST, 33040
TEL 305/292-1919
FAX 305/294-2121
ⓘ 27 ⬜ ⬜ Ⓐ All major cards

🏨 ISLAND CITY HOUSE HOTEL
$$
411 WILLIAM ST.
TEL 305/294-5702
FAX 305/294-1289
The gardens here are larger than many in town, and the three buildings offer a choice of furnishings. One of the few bed-and-breakfasts in town that is suitable for families as well as couples.

ⓘ 24 ⬜ ⬜ Ⓐ All major cards

🏨 THE MERLIN
$$
811 SIMONTON ST.
TEL 305/296-3336
FAX 305/296-3524
Rooms vary in size but all are comfortable; one is accessible by wheelchair, with a second bedroom upstairs. The informality reflects the casual atmosphere of Key West.

ⓘ 18 ⬜ ⬜ Ⓐ AE, MC, V

🏨 BANANA BAY RESORT AND MARINA
$
2319 N. ROOSEVELT BLVD.
TEL 305/296-6925
FAX 305/296-2004
The emphasis is on sports activities in this small, modern resort a short drive from the historic district of Key West. Set on the Gulf, it has a pool, fitness center, and a dive shop.

ⓘ 30 ⬜ ⬜ ⬜ Ⓐ All major cards

🍴 CAFÉ MARQUESA
$$$
600 FLEMING ST.
TEL 305/292-1244
In The Marquesa hotel (see box this page). Stylish modern dishes using plenty of tropical food with piquant flavors are the specialty of chef Susan Ferry. Watch her staff prepare your meal in the open-to-view kitchen. Expensive, but just right for a romantic occasion.

🍽 50 🕐 Closed L daily
Ⓐ All major cards

🍴 LOUIE'S BACKYARD
$$$
700 WADDELL AVE.
TEL 305/294-1061
Several top-class chefs, including Norman van Aken, have kick-started their careers at this classy restaurant where diners sit out under the famous mahoe tree. Innovative cooking using Caribbean ingredients.

🍽 150 🕐 Closed L summer
Ⓐ All major cards

🍴 CAFÉ DES ARTISTES
$$
1007 SIMONTON ST.
TEL 305/294-7100
The French name emphasizes regional dishes with a Gallic twist. The lively paintings by local artists, contrasting with naïve Haitian art, are all part of the experience in the house that once belonged to Al Capone's accountant.

🍽 100 🕐 Closed L
Ⓐ AE, MC, V

PRICES

HOTELS
An indication of the cost of a double room without breakfast is given by $ signs
$$$$$ Over $200
$$$$ $150–199
$$$ $100–$149
$$ $50–$99
$ Under $50

RESTAURANTS
An indication of the cost of a three-course dinner without drinks is given by $ signs
$$$ Over $35
$$ $20–$35
$ Under $20

🍴 MANGOES
$$
700 DUVAL ST.
TEL 305/292-4606
Modern food in one of the prime spots for people-watching on Key West's main thoroughfare. With tables in two gardens and one indoor room, this does not feel like a large restaurant.

🍽 300   Ⓐ All major cards

🍴 CAMILLE'S
$
703 DUVAL ST.
TEL 305/296-4811
Best known as a breakfast and lunch place, this tiny restaurant has funky furnishings and a well-priced, varied menu. A local hangout.

🍽 24   Ⓐ All major cards

🍴 HALF SHELL RAW BAR
$
LANDS END VILLAGE,
231 MARGARET ST.
TEL 305/294-7496
The sort of seafood restaurant everyone looks for. Overlooking the fishing boats, with the specials chalked on a board. Expect plenty of work peeling your own shrimp. Down-to-earth plastic tables, fun.

🍽 250   Ⓐ AE, MC, V

KEY   🏨 Hotel   🍴 Restaurant   ⓘ No. of bedrooms   🍽 No. of places   🕐 Closed   🛗 Elevator

MARATHON 33050

🍴 KEY COLONY INN
$
700 W. OCEAN DR., NEAR MM
53.5, KEY COLONY BEACH
TEL 305/743-0100
Conch chowder and stone
crabs (in season) feature on a
menu that also includes such
standards as veal Parmigiana,
steaks, and chicken.
🍽 180 🚫 AE, MC, V

**SOMETHING
SPECIAL**

🏨 COCOPLUM BEACH
& TENNIS CLUB
Set amid tropical gardens,
this is a small enclave of
tree houses with entrances on
the second floor, screened-in
porches, Jacuzzis. Perfect for
families, since each villa
sleeps six. Self-catering. Small
swimming pool, sandy beach.
$$$
109 COCOPLUM DR., TEL
305/743-0240
FAX 305/743-9351
🛏 20 villas 🆒 🏊
🚫 AE, MC, V

🍴 LEIGH ANN'S
COFFEE HOUSE
$
7537 OVERSEAS HIGHWAY
(US 1)
TEL 305/743-2001
A small, informal, local haunt
where mornings bring muffins
straight from the oven and
lunch could be homemade
soup and sandwiches.
🍽 20 🕐 Closed Sun. L & D
🚫 MC, V

NORTH OF MIAMI

FORT LAUDERDALE
33301

🍴 MARK'S LAS OLAS
$$$
1032 E. LAS OLAS BLVD.
TEL 954/463-1000
Mark Militello is one of the
finest innovative chefs in the
United States. You may not
have heard of his exotic
ingredients, but you can trust
him. A feast for the eyes as
well as the palate. Reservations essential.
🍽 120 🕐 Closed Sat., Sun.
L 🚫 All major cards

**SOMETHING
SPECIAL**

🏨 RIVERSIDE HOTEL
Dating from 1936, this
comfortable, well-run
hotel stands on the trendiest
street in the city, where locals
and visitors promenade,
window shop, and eat indoors
or out at sidewalk tables.
$$$
620 E. LAS OLAS BLVD.,
TEL 954/467-0671
FAX 954/462-2148
🛏 109 🆒 🔧 🏊
🚫 All major cards

LAUDERDALE-BY-
THE-SEA 33308

🏨 A LITTLE INN BY
THE SEA
$$
4546 EL MAR DR.
TEL 954/772-2450
FAX 954/938-9354
Swiss-run and a good
standard, this small hotel is
situated right on the beach.
A favorite with Europeans
as well as Americans, it is a
contrast to the larger hotels
along this stretch of Florida's
coast.
🛏 27 🆒 🏊
🚫 All major cards

PALM BEACH 33480

🏨 CHESTERFIELD HOTEL
$$
363 COCOANUT ROW
TEL 561/659-5800
FAX 561/659-6707
Within walking distance
of the famous Worth
Avenue shopping district, the
Chesterfield was built in 1926
but has completely up-to-date
comforts. The English
country house decoration
is reinforced by English-style
afternoon tea in the library.
There is live evening
entertainment at the
exclusive Leopard Lounge
and Supper Club.
🛏 55 🆒 🔧 🏊 🐾
🚫 All major cards

**SOMETHING
SPECIAL**

🏨 THE BREAKERS
With a history dating
back to 1896, this is
one of the most famous
hotels in Florida. Back to
its original glory—thanks
to multimillion dollar
refurbishment—its
improvements include a
full spa and impressive
children's activity programs.
$$$$
ONE SOUTH COUNTY RD.,
TEL 561/655-6611
FAX 561/659-8403
🛏 562 🆒 🔧 🏊
🐾 All major cards

🏨 PLAZA INN
$$
215 BRAZILIAN AVE.
TEL 561/832-8666
FAX 561/835-8776
A few blocks away from
Worth Avenue, this is a well-
priced hotel for this resort
town. Run by a former Indian
Army officer who is also
involved with the polo scene
in West Palm Beach. You can
enjoy an Indian buffet on
Friday night.
🛏 50 🆒 🔧 🏊 🚫 All
major cards

🍴 TA-BOO RESTAURANT
$$$
221 WORTH AVE.
TEL 561/835-3500
Named for the legendary
Worth Avenue eatery of the
1940s, Ta-Boo relies on skillful
grilling and imaginative salads.
A place to dress up for some

🆒 Air-conditioning 🏊 Indoor/🏊 Outdoor swimming pool 🐾 Health club 🚫 Credit cards

serious people watching in a fashion-conscious setting.
🔳 150 🔲 All major cards

🍴 SEAFOOD BAR
$
THE BREAKERS,
I SOUTH COUNTY RD.
TEL 561/655-6611
One of four restaurants at The Breakers (see p. 239), it is worth reserving one of the 24 tables that overlook the sea. Plenty of seafood, whether from the raw bar or cooked in delicate sauces.
🔳 125 🔲 All major cards

POMPANO BEACH 33060

🍴 DARREL & OLIVER'S CAFÉ MAXX
$$$
2601 E. ATLANTIC BLVD.
TEL 954/782-0606
A theatrical restaurant with modern American dishes prepared by Oliver Saucy. Bewildering combinations of ingredients leave guests wide-eyed with admiration. Reservations essential.
🔳 130 🕐 Closed L 🔲 All major cards

STUART 34994

🏨 THE HOMEPLACE
$$
501 AKRON AVE.
TEL 561/220-9148
FAX 561/221-3265
Suzanne and Michael Pescitelli are constantly improving their bed-and-breakfast home, built in 1913. Breakfast bananas, grapefruit, mangoes,, and starfruit come straight from their garden.
🛏 6 🔲 🔲 🔲 MC, V

SOUTHWEST FLORIDA

BONITA SPRINGS 33923

🍴 ROOFTOP
$$
25999 HICKORY BLVD.

TEL 941/992-0033
At the north end of Bonita Beach, the views over Estero Bay make this casual restaurant a popular spot. Steaks are cut to your liking, or choose your lobster from the tank. The seafood strudel has been a favorite for 20 years. Even more casual dining dockside in the Flying Fish Café.
🔳 225 🕐 Closed Mon. May–Nov. 🔲 MC, V

BRADENTON 34217

🏨 HARRINGTON HOUSE
$$$
5626 GULF DR.,
HOLMES BEACH
TEL 941/778-5444
FAX 941/778-0527
In a house dating from 1925, this is a New England-style bed-and-breakfast inn on the brilliant white sands of Holmes Beach. Set in a quiet, residential area, it is a hideaway for couples.
🛏 13 🔲 🔲 🔲 MC, V

FORT MYERS AREA

🏨 SOUTH SEAS PLANTATION
$$$$$
5400 PLANTATION RD.,
CAPTIVA ISLAND, 33924
TEL 941/472-5111
FAX 941/481-4947
One of the best known names in the area, this self-contained resort on 330 beautifully landscaped acres has golf and tennis, plus all the water sports. Spacious rooms. Popular with European families. Ask about special packages.
🛏 600 🔲 🔲 🔲 🔲 All major cards

🏨 SONG OF THE SEA
$$$$
863 E. GULF DR., SANIBEL ISLAND, 33957
TEL 941/472-2220
FAX 941/481-4947
Right on the beach, with wonderful views of sunsets,

this small bed-and-breakfast hotel contrasts with the larger places to stay on the island. Casual in atmosphere, it is good for families as well as couples.
🛏 30 🔲 🔲 🔲 All major cards

🏨 GRAND VIEW
$$
8701 ESTERO BLVD.
FORT MYERS BEACH, 33931
TEL 941/765-4422
FAX 941/765-4499
The name says it all: wide open views over the Gulf and Estero Bay. Right on Lovers Key, suites have good facilities, are well priced, and good both for families and couples who want a beach vacation.
🛏 75 🔲 🔲 🔲 🔲 All major cards

LONGBOAT KEY

SEE SARASOTA (p. 241)

NAPLES 34102

🏨 OLD NAPLES TRIANON
Opened in late 1997, this luxurious boutique hotel is right in Old Naples, a short walk from the elegant restaurants and stores of Fifth Avenue. The beach is just a few minutes away by automobile. Although breakfast is the only meal served, the buffet is one of the best.
$$
955 7TH AVE. S.,
TEL 941/435-9600
FAX 941/261-0025
🛏 58 🔲 🔲 🔲
🔲 All major cards

🍴 PAZZO
$$
853 5TH AVE. S.
TEL 941/434-8494
Call this "innovative Italian" as the chef draws on Asian

spices, Caribbean flavors, and Latin flair for this stylish eatery on Naples' fashionable boulevard. Sister restaurant two doors down is the more conventional Chops City Grill.

🛏 179 🕐 Closed L
🅰 All major cards

SANIBEL ISLAND

SEE FORT MYERS (p. 240)

SARASOTA AREA

🏨 BANANA BAY RESORT
$$
8254 MIDNIGHT PASS RD.,
SIESTA KEY, 34242
TEL 941/346-0113
FAX 941/349-4161
Watch herons catching fish from the windows of your suite at this well-priced, small complex in a quiet residential area on a lagoon. Strikingly decorated. Not far from stores and restaurants.

🛗 7 🅂 🏊 🅰 Not accepted

SOMETHING SPECIAL

🏨 THE COLONY BEACH & TENNIS RESORT

Don't be put off by the high-rise buildings on the eastern end of Longboat Key; this 40-year-old resort has low buildings surrounded by mature landscaping. Right on the beach, it is known for tennis programs catering to all ages on the 21 courts. One of the best restaurants in town is here (see Colony Dining Room, this page). Ask about special packages.

$$$$
1620 GULF OF MEXICO DR.,
LONGBOAT KEY, 34228
TEL 941/383-6464
FAX 941/383-7549
🛗 232 🈁 🅂 🏊 🅆
🅰 All major cards

🍽 COLONY DINING ROOM
$$$
1620 GULF OF MEXICO DR.,
LONGBOAT KEY
TEL 941/383-6464
Great views and great cooking don't usually go together, but they do here. Watch the sun go down over the Gulf, then enjoy modern American cooking, well presented and well served.

🛏 150 🅰 All major cards

🍽 MICHAEL'S ON EAST
$$$
1212 EAST AVE. S.
TEL 941/366-0007
This restaurant is located just south of Longboat Key. Owner Michael Klauber has a strong local following for his chic mix of Continental dishes and cool jazz. À la carte only. The wine list is outstanding.

🛏 148 🕐 Closed Sun. L & D May–Nov. 🅰 All major cards

SIESTA KEY

SEE SARASOTA (this page)

TAMPA & ST. PETERSBURG

CLEARWATER 33756

🏨 BELLEVIEW BILTMORE RESORT & SPA
$$$$
25 BELLEVIEW BLVD.
TEL 727/442-6171
FAX 727/443-6361
This Victorian resort, set among pines and oaks on a bluff, has benefited from a multimillion-dollar face-lift. With every sport under the sun, there is also a sense of the grandeur of days gone by in the Starlight Room, Tiffany Room, and Children's Dining Room.

🛗 292 🈁 🅂 🏊 🅆
🅰 All major cards

CRYSTAL RIVER 34429

🏨 PLANTATION INN AND GOLF RESORT
$$
9301 W. FORT ISLAND TRAIL
TEL 352/795-4211
FAX 352/795-1368
Bounded by the Crystal River, the 232 acres have 27 holes of golf, tennis courts, and a croquet lawn. The great attraction here is the chance to swim with the manatees, which live on its doorstep. Eat in the Plantation Room or the Den, a sports bar.

🛗 126 🈁 🅂 🏊 🅆
🅰 All major cards

ST. PETERSBURG 33701

SOMETHING SPECIAL

🏨 DON CESAR BEACH RESORT

Now more than 70 years old, the grand Pink Palace has a history packed with celebrities. Recent renovations have once more put the resort among Florida's leading destinations. The modern comforts, spas, and food combine well with old-fashioned service and atmosphere. Right on the beach.

$$$
3400 GULF BLVD., ST. PETE BEACH, 33706
TEL 727/360-1881
FAX 727/367-360
🛗 345 🈁 🅂 🏊 🅆

🏨 BAYBORO HOUSE
$$
1719 BEACH DR. S.E.
TEL/FAX 813/823-4955
The epitome of a bed-and-breakfast inn, this is a home away from home where the clock seems to have stopped 100 years ago. Only the street separates the house from the water.

🛗 4 🅂 🅰 MC, V

HURRICANE SEAFOOD RESTAURANT

$

807 GULF WAY
PASSE-A-GRILLE BEACH
TEL 727/360-9558

With four bars right across the road from the Gulf of Mexico, this is as much a spot to enjoy the sunset as to eat simply prepared fresh fish, crab cakes, and steamed shrimp.

🔅 250 🚫 AE, MC, V

TAMPA 33543

SADDLEBROOK RESORT

$$$

5700 SADDLEBROOK WAY
WESLEY CHAPEL
TEL 813/973-1111
FAX 813/973-1312

This is one of Florida's most impressive resort hotels, with 45 tennis courts. No wonder Wimbledon champion Pete Sampras is a regular here to practice. Golfers, too, come for the two championship courses. Luxury rooms, spa. Ideal for families.

🛏 790 🚻 🛗 🏊 📺
🚫 All major cards

COLUMBIA

$$

2117 E. 7TH AVE., YBOR CITY
TEL 813/248-4961

An institution since 1905, this echoing Spanish restaurant, with its elaborate tiling, is a four-generation family enterprise. Spanish bean soup, Cuban sandwiches, and the 1905 salad with its house dressing are all part of the legend. Flamenco dancing nightly.

🔅 1,660 🚫 All major cards

MISE EN PLACE

$$

442 W. KENNEDY BLVD.
TEL 813/254-5373

Despite its French name, this is an all-American bistro, serving everything from Creole grouper chowder to a classic Cuban sandwich,

and seafood risotto to tournedos of beef. Husband Marty Blitz cooks and wife Maryann is the hostess. On the outskirts of Hyde Park.

🔅 250 🕐 Closed Mon. D, Sat. L, Sun. L & D 🚫 All major cards

CAFÉ CREOLE

$

1330 E. 9TH ST., YBOR CITY
TEL 813/247-6283

Since the 1960s, the D'Avanza family have been serving the cooking of their home town, New Orleans, in this 19th-century brick building complete with balustrade. Busy and popular, a fun place to meet. Interesting wine list.

🔅 250 🕐 Closed Sat. L, Sun. L & D 🚫 All major cards

TARPON SPRINGS 34684

WESTIN INNISBROOK RESORT

$$

36750 US 19
TEL 727/942-2000
FAX 727/942-5576

Just inland from the Greek-influenced town of Tarpon Springs, the lodge accommodations are scattered over more than 1,000 groomed acres. Two restaurants. Idyllic for sports visitors with 4 golf courses, 11 tennis courts, and 6 swimming pools Free shuttlebus to the beach.

🛏 733 🚻 🛗 🏊 📺
🚫 All major cards

DINO'S RESTAURANT

$

610 ATHENS ST.
TEL 727/938-9082

A fun, ethnic restaurant in the Greek district of town, with authentic dishes as well as live music and dancing on Friday and Saturday nights. The Greek community crowd in for Sunday lunch.

🔅 110 🕐 Closed Tues.–Fri. L, Mon. L & D 🚫 AE, MC, V

PRICES

HOTELS
An indication of the cost of a double room without breakfast is given by $ signs
$$$$$ Over $200
$$$$ $150–199
$$$ $100–$149
$$ $50–$99
$ Under $50

RESTAURANTS
An indication of the cost of a three-course dinner without drinks is given by $ signs
$$$ Over $35
$$ $20–$35
$ Under $20

WESLEY CHAPEL

SEE TAMPA (this page)

YBOR CITY

SEE TAMPA (this page)

ORLANDO & THE THEME PARKS

MOUNT DORA 32757

LAKESIDE INN

$$

100 N. ALEXANDER ST.
TEL 352/383-4101
FAX 352/735-2642

At this lakeside town, famous for its antiques shops, this century-old hotel combines history with modern comforts. A New England atmosphere, with a cozy lounge and plenty of woodwork.

🛏 88 🛗 🏊 🚫 All major cards

BEAUCLAIRE RESTAURANT

$$

LAKESIDE INN,
100 N. ALEXANDER ST.
TEL 352/383-4101

The atmospheric restaurant in the historic Lakeside Inn (see above) is a pleasant place to spend a candlelit evening,

HOTELS & RESTAURANTS

where the menu has traditional favorites such as roast duck, crab cakes, and scallops.
🛏 200 🚫 All major cards

LAKE BUENA VISTA

🏨 DISNEY'S BOARDWALK INN
$$$$$
2101 N. EPCOT RESORTS BLVD., 32830
TEL 407/939-5100
FAX 407/939-5150
The Disney organization has a wide range of accommodations, all with a theme. The BoardWalk reproduces the old inns of the eastern seaboard. Bedrooms are large, easily sleeping a family of five. Handy for Epcot (by boat or footpath) or Disney-MGM (by boat). Take a bus to the other attractions.
🛈 378 🔋 🌀 🏊 🏋
🚫 All major cards

🏨 HOTEL ROYAL PLAZA
$$$
1905 HOTEL PLAZA BLVD., 32830
TEL 407/828-2828
FAX 407/827-6338
This is a well-priced, 17-story hotel in Walt Disney World Village. As well as all the standard facilities such as restaurants, saunas, and four floodlit tennis courts, there is free and regular transportation to the theme parks.
🛈 394 🔋 🌀 🏊 🚫 All major cards

🏨 PERRIHOUSE BED AND BREAKFAST INN
$$
10417 CENTURION CT.
FLA.. 535, 32836
TEL 407/876-4830
FAX 407/876-0241
On Disney's doorstep, this is the minnow among the whales, an enterprising, friendly, family-run bed-and-breakfast. Ideal for families with small children.
🛈 6 🌀 🏊 🚫 AE, MC, V

LAKE WALES 33853

🏨 CHALET SUZANNE
$$$
3800 CHALET SUZANNE DR.
(OFF US 27)
TEL 941/676-6011
FAX 941/676-1814
The Chalet, as locals call it, is an institution. Dating back to 1931, the interior is an eclectic collection of vacation souvenirs: English and Persian tiles, Italian altar angels, a Norwegian bar. The rooms themselves are comfortable, but ask for one with a walk-in shower for extra convenience. (See restaurant, below)
🛈 30 🌀 🏊 🚫 All major cards

🍴 CHALET SUZANNE
$$$
3800 CHALET SUZANNE DR.
(OFF US 27)
TEL 941/676-6011
When astronauts from nearby Cape Canaveral took Chalet Suzanne soup (freeze dried) into space, the business also went into orbit. Dishes, however, are quite traditional, served by waitresses in pseudo-dirndls.
🛏 150 🚫 All major cards

MAITLAND 32810

🏨 HOMEGATE STUDIOS AND SUITES
$$
1951 SUMMIT TOWER BLVD.
TEL 407/659-0066
FAX 407/659-0067
Just off I-4, this complex of apartments is designed for long stays. Clean, modern, and bright, with practical kitchens.
🛈 134 🔋 🌀 🏊 🏋
🚫 All major cards

WINTER HAVEN 33884

🏨 BEST WESTERN ADMIRAL'S INN
$
5665 CYPRESS GARDENS BLVD.
TEL 941/324-5950
FAX 941/324-2376
A well-positioned hotel on

the doorstep of Cypress Gardens, featuring straightforward modern rooms with good facilities, and an extra large swimming pool.
🛈 157 🔋 🌀 🏊 🚫 All major cards

WINTER PARK 32789

🏨 PARK PLAZA
$$
307 PARK AVE. S.
TEL 407/647-1072
FAX 407/647-4081
Overlooking City Park, this 1920 hotel has a European air, but the lively young staff makes it a welcoming place to stay. Peaceful rooms. Handy for museums and Orlando itself, but best suited to adults. (See Park Plaza Gardens, below)
🛈 27 🔋 🌀 🚫 All major cards

🍴 PARK PLAZA GARDENS
$$$
307 PARK AVE. S.
TEL 407/647-1072
Run as a separate business from the hotel (see Park Plaza, above), this is a popular meeting place for locals who enjoy light lunches and more formal dining in the evening.
🛏 200 🚫 All major cards

🍴 PANERA
$
118 W. FAIRBANKS AVE.
TEL 407/645-3939
The pride and joy of this casual, noisy restaurant is its bread: sourdough, rye, nine grain, and lots more. The accompanying soups, salads, and sandwiches are carefully prepared and popular.
🛏 160 🚫 All major cards

HOTELS & RESTAURANTS

CASSADAGA 32706

🍴 LOST IN TIME CAFÉ
$
355 CASSADAGA RD.
TEL 904/228-2323
A casual place for lunch in the Cassadaga Hotel. Find it opposite the bookstore that is also the information center for the Cassadaga Spiritualist Camp.
🍴 40 🕑 Closed D
🃏 MC, V

SOMETHING SPECIAL

🏨 INN AT COCOA BEACH
The personality of manager Amy Donaghy makes this small, modern hotel facing the water a special spot. Country-style pine furniture, fresh flowers, and books in the bedrooms. Watch a space shot from your balcony at nearby Kennedy Space Center.
$$$
4300 OCEAN BEACH BLVD., COCOA BEACH, 32931
TEL 407/799-3460
FAX 407/784-8632
🛏 50 🔄 🃏 🖼
🃏 AE, MC, V

COCOA BEACH 32931

🍴 CAFE MARGAUX
$$$
222. BREVARD AVE.
COCOA VILLAGE
TEL 407/639-8343
One of the best places in town. Expect creative French cooking and Mediterranean touches to traditional French dishes. Interesting wine list.
🍴 75 🕑 Closed Tues.
L & D 🃏 All major cards

🍴 PARADISE ALLEY CAFÉ
$$
234 BREVARD AVE.
COCOA VILLAGE
TEL 407/635-9032
A fun, casual place to dine next to the Playhouse. Every day seven or eight specials are offered, often seafood and often blackened. Wines available by the glass.
🍴 45 🕑 Closed Mon.–Wed. D, Sun. L & D
🃏 DC, MC, V

DAYTONA BEACH 32114

🏨 LIVE OAK INN BED AND BREAKFAST
$$
448 S. BEACH ST.
TEL 904/252-4667
FAX 904/254-1871
Behind a white picket fence, these two 19th-century houses look appropriately old-fashioned. Two rooms, however, pay tribute to the town's love affair with speed: the Harley Room and the Bill France Room.
🛏 13 🔄 🃏 🖼 🃏
🃏 AE, MC, V

SOMETHING SPECIAL

🏨 THE VILLA
Filled with antiques, this could be a film set if it weren't a bed-and-breakfast. The swimming pool is in a small but lovely garden. Jim Camp is an experienced host.
$$
801 N. PENINSULA DR., DAYTONA BEACH, 32118
TEL/FAX 904/248-2020
🛏 4 🃏 🃏 🃏 MC, V

🍴 LIVE OAK INN RESTAURANT
$$
448 S. BEACH ST.
TEL 904/252-4667
In a romantic and unhurried atmosphere, chef Tom Papa serves American cuisine with Caribbean, Californian, and Italian influences. This is part of the inn (see entry, this page), but under separate management.
🍴 42 🕑 Closed Sat. & Sun. L, Sun.–Wed. D 🃏 AE, MC, V

NEW SMYRNA BEACH

🏨 LITTLE RIVER INN
$$
532 N. RIVERSIDE DR., 32168
TEL 904/424-0100
This 100-year-old house opened as a bed-and-breakfast in 1997. Manatees and blue heron have been spotted in the river, rocking chairs await on the porch. Victorian decor.
🛏 6 🃏 🃏 All major cards

🏨 NIGHT SWAN INTRACOASTAL BED & BREAKFAST
$$
512 S. RIVERSIDE DR., NEW SMYRNA BEACH, 32168
TEL 904/423-4940
FAX 904/427-2814
On the mainland side of the Indian River, views from the windows are of sailboats, and occasionally of dolphins traveling up and down the Intracoastal Waterway. Highly rated for standards of comfort and a warm welcome.
🛏 15 🃏 🃏 AE, MC, V

🏨 RIVERVIEW HOTEL
$
103 FLAGLER AVE., NEW SMYRNA BEACH, 32169
TEL 904/428-5858
FAX 904/423-8927
On the eastern bank of the Indian River, the Intracoastal Waterway, this bed-and-breakfast inn has tennis, swimming, and golf nearby. The restaurant on site is Riverview Charlie's (see p. 245).
🛏 18 🃏 🃏 🃏 AE, MC, V

NORWOOD'S SEAFOOD RESTAURANT
$$
400 2ND AVE.
TEL 904/428-4621
Near the bridge over the Intracoastal Waterway, this is a big, bustling place to eat. Menu has American standards, from fish to steaks.
🪑 230 AE, MC, V

RIVERVIEW CHARLIE'S
$
101 FLAGLER AVE.
TEL 904/428-1865
Part of the Riverview Hotel (see p. 244) that overlooks the water, this casual restaurant serving good seafood is suitable for children as well as couples.
🪑 200 AE, MC, V

VERO BEACH 32963

DISNEY'S VERO BEACH RESORT
$$$$
9250 ISLAND GROVE TERRACE
FLA. A1A
TEL 407/934-7639
FAX 561/234-2030
Located right on the beach, this well-run resort has the feel of a lodge in a national park. There are plenty of activities on offer, but best of all is a Turtle Walk during the sea turtle nesting season (usually May, June, and July). Groups for the Turtle Walk are limited in size. Call ahead for details and to book your place.
ℹ 115 All major cards

DRIFTWOOD RESORT
$$
3150 OCEAN DR.
TEL 561/231-0550
FAX 561/234-1981
This is a delightful surprise among the high rises along the coast. The Driftwood really was built from timbers and planks washed ashore at the turn of the century. Guests can stay for as little as one night at what is now an attractive time-share on the ocean.
ℹ 100 units All major cards

SEA TURTLE INN
$
835 AZALEA LN.
TEL 561/234-0788
FAX 561/234-0717
This friendly, two-story inn is small but practical, with microwaves, refrigerators, and toasters in each room. Also offers laundry facilities. One block from the ocean.
ℹ 20 MC, V

NORTHEAST FLORIDA

AMELIA ISLAND

SOMETHING SPECIAL

AMELIA ISLAND WILLIAMS HOUSE
Fernandina Beach is a delightful town, known for bed-and-breakfasts, but this is truly special. Two houses have been luxuriously furnished with antiques and unusual fabrics. A place for special occasions and romantic anniversaries.
$$$
103 9TH ST., FERNANDINA BEACH, 32034
TEL 904/277-2328
FAX 904/321-1425
ℹ 8 MC, V

AMELIA ISLAND PLANTATION
$$$$$
6800 FIRST COAST HWY., 32035
TEL 904/261-6161
FAX 904/277-5159
Known as one of the best golf resorts in the United States, the Plantation also has a Racquet Park with 25 courts. Ideal for families, there is also a broad beach, horseback riding, and nature trails.
ℹ 520 All major cards

FLORIDA HOUSE INN
$$
20 S. 3RD ST., 32034
TEL 904/261-3300
FAX 904/277-3831
One of the state's oldest hotels, the building dates back to 1857. Recent renovations have upgraded the decor. Guests over the years have included Gen. Ulysses S. Grant and the Rockefellers.
ℹ 14 AE, MC, V

BEECH STREET GRILL
$$$
801 BEECH ST., FERNANDINA BEACH, 32034
TEL 904/277-3662
Despite recent expansion, the quality of the cooking and service has remained as high as ever. Daily blackboard specials include fresh fish, cooked impeccably, with homemade sauces and chutneys. Reservations essential.
🪑 210 Closed L
 AE, MC, V

JOE'S 2ND STREET BISTRO
$$$
14 S. 2ND ST., FERNANDINA BEACH, 32034
TEL 904/321-2558
Joe Robucci is the chef, who cooks everything from spicy shrimp tamales to antelope sirloin with a port and mustard sauce. Try the home-baked bread. Fine wine list.
🪑 92 Closed L, Mon. D
 All major cards

FERNANDINA BEACH

SEE AMELIA ISLAND
(this page)

GAINESVILLE 32601

SOMETHING SPECIAL

🏨 MAGNOLIA PLANTATION BED & BREAKFAST INN

First-timers feel at home immediately, returning guests think of it as staying with friends. Having totally renovated the century-old house, the Montalto family enjoy sharing it with others. Antiques, plenty of comforts, and a lovely garden behind.
$$
309 S.E. 7TH ST.
TEL 352/375-6653
FAX 352/338-0303
ⓘ 6 🛗 🚫 MC, V

🏨 SWEETWATER BRANCH INN
$$
625 E. UNIVERSITY AVE.
TEL 352/373-6760
FAX 352/371-3771
Right on one of the main thoroughfares of town, this inn's atmosphere is businesslike, although perfectly welcoming. The quieter rooms are at the back, overlooking the garden.
ⓘ 6 🛗 🚫 AE, MC, V

🍴 HARRY'S
$$
110 S.E. FIRST ST.
TEL 352/372-1555
The chef comes from New Orleans, so there's Cajun-style cooking with rice, jambalaya, red beans, and sausage. Quite spicy. Informal atmosphere.
🔲 200 🚫 AE, MC, V

JACKSONVILLE 32204

🏨 PLANTATION-MANOR INN
$$
1630 COPELAND ST.
TEL 904/384-4630
FAX 904/387-0960
With massive columns and a wraparound veranda, this is a grand example of a Southern mansion with an interior to match.
ⓘ 9 🛗 🚫 AE, MC, V

🏨 SABAL PALM INN
$$
115 5TH AVE. S.
TEL 904/241-4545
FAX 904/241-2407
This newly restored bed-and-breakfast inn is straight out of Old Florida. With elegant rooms, a broad balcony, and veranda. A few steps from the sandy beach. Golf courses nearby.
ⓘ 5 🛗 🚫 MC, V

🍴 CAFÉ ON THE SQUARE
$$$
1974 SAN MARCO BLVD.
TEL 904/399-4848
Opposite the Fountain of the Lions, in the middle of San Marco Boulevard. Choose between the upstairs restaurant and the lively downstairs bar/bistro with live music. Both serve enterprising entrées such as almond ginger-crusted salmon.
🔲 200 🕐 Closed L, & Sun.
🚫 All major cards

🍴 CAFÉ CARMON
$$
1986 SAN MARCO BLVD.
TEL 904/399-4488
People watchers like to linger over coffee and desserts, which are a specialty at this café. Located in an enclave of stores and galleries, including a good bookstore and an old-fashioned movie house.
🔲 95 🚫 All major cards

🍴 RIVER CITY BREWING COMPANY
$$
835 MUSEUM CIRCLE
TEL 904/398-2299
Next door to the Museum of Science and History. You can eat outside by the river or indoors, where huge windows look across the water to the Jacksonville skyline. Ale is brewed on site. Food is American—hamburgers and the like.
🔲 200 🚫 All major cards

MICANOPY 32667

🏨 HERLONG MANSION
$$
CHOLOKKA BLVD.
TEL/FAX 352/466-3322
It is a special treat to stay in this fine example of a beautiful Southern mansion. Ask about the fascinating history of the house and family.
ⓘ 12 🛗 🚫 MC, V

🏨 SHADY OAK
$$
203 CHOLOKKA BLVD.
TEL 352/466-3476
FAX 352/466-9233
A modern bed-and-breakfast above stores right in the center of the village. Wide verandas plus contemporary stained glass made by the owner in the studio behind.
ⓘ 7 🛗 🚫 MC, V

OCALA 34471

🏨 SEVEN SISTERS INN
$$
820 S.E. FORT KING ST.
TEL 352/867-1170
FAX 352/867-5266

PRICES

HOTELS
An indication of the cost of a double room without breakfast is given by $ signs
$$$$$ Over $200
$$$$ $150–199
$$$ $100–$149
$$ $50–$99
$ Under $50

RESTAURANTS
An indication of the cost of a three-course dinner without drinks is given by $ signs
$$$ Over $35
$$ $20–$35
$ Under $20

You can't miss this very large, pink-painted Victorian house, with gables and veranda. Inside, rooms are very comfortable but are densely decorated. Breakfast is formal, with unusual hot dishes.
🆑 8 🅲 🅲 AE, MC, V

PONTE VEDRA BEACH

SEE ST. AUGUSTINE

ST. AUGUSTINE

🏨 WORLD GOLF VILLAGE RESORT HOTEL
$$$
500 S. LEGACY TRAIL, 32092
TEL 904/940-8000
FAX 904/940-8008
This hotel is a stroll away from the new Golf World Hall of Fame. Guests here have privileges at the challenging new course. Expect modern, practical rooms. It has a restaurant and is 10 miles from St. Augustine.
🆑 301 🔁 🅲 🅲 🅲 🅲 All major cards

🏨 CARRIAGE WAY BED & BREAKFAST
$$
70 CUNA ST., 32084
TEL 904/829-2467
FAX 904/826-1461
Bill and Diane Johnson are experienced hosts who like nothing better than helping guests get the best out of St. Augustine. Rooms are comfortable, with Victorian-style furnishings.
🆑 9 🅲 🅲 AE, MC, V

🏨 CASA DE SOLANA
$$$
21 AVILES ST., 32084
TEL 904/824-3555
FAX 904/824-3316
Since the Casa de Solana was built in 1763, this very comfortable bed-and-breakfast can claim the title of "oldest accommodation in the state." The four suites

here are luxurious with antiques; each suite has its own sitting room. Named for Don Manuel Solana, it opened to guests in 1983.
🆑 4 🅲 🅲 AE, MC, V

🏨 KENWOOD INN BED & BREAKFAST
$$
38 MARINE ST., 32084
TEL 904/824-2116
FAX 904/824-1689
St. Augustine has numerous bed-and-breakfast places, but this is one of the few with a swimming pool. Eccentric atmosphere with old-fashioned plumbing. Set on a quiet side street within walking distance of all the sites, this is a relaxing place to stay.
🆑 14 🅲 🅲 🅲 MC, V

🍴 LA PARISIENNE
$$
60 HYPOLITA ST.
TEL 904/829-0055
More formal than most restaurants in town, this is considered a special occasion place. French-style food such as steak-frites, homemade soups, and French pastries.
🆑 49 🕐 Closed Mon. & Tues. D 🅲 AE, MC, V

🍴 GYPSY CAB COMPANY
$
828 ANASTASIA BLVD.
TEL 904/824-8244
A modern, varied menu with a bit of everything, although Gypsy chicken is the favorite with regulars.
🆑 90 🕐 Closed Mon.–Fri. L 🅲 All major cards

🍴 KING'S FORGE
$
12 AVENIDA MENENDEZ
TEL 904/829-1488
Variety is the key here. There is a deck outside overlooking the water and the Castillo de San Marcos, a front balcony, an upstairs bar at sunset, and indoor dining down-stairs. Steak, sandwiches,

and salads are on offer.
🆑 220 🅲 All major cards

THE PANHANDLE

CEDAR KEY 32625

🏨 ISLAND HOTEL
$
2ND & B. STS.
TEL 352/543-5111
FAX 352/543-6949
Built in 1859 of seashell tabby with oak supports and sloping wooden floors, this inn has a wraparound, two-story veranda and a good restaurant. Rooms are plain but comfortable. A getaway place on an island at the end of a 3-mile-long causeway.
🆑 13 🅲 🅲 MC, V

HAVANA 32333

🍴 NICHOLSON FARMHOUSE RESTAURANT
$$
3.5 MILES W. OF TOWN ON FLA. 12
TEL 850/539-5931
The Nicholson family has lived here since 1828, but the restaurant business is only a decade old. Known for steaks: nine cuts, cooked six ways from rare to burned. BYO wine and beer.
🆑 600 🕐 Closed Sun. & Mon. 🅲 All major cards

PENSACOLA 32501

🏨 NEW WORLD INN
$$
600 S. PALAFOX ST.
TEL 850/432-4111
FAX 850/432-6836
Near the historic district, this small hotel was once a box factory. Now part of a complex with a lunchtime restaurant and conference hall. The comfortable bedrooms are businesslike rather than romantic.
🆑 16 🅲 🅲 All major cards

🅲 Air-conditioning 🅲 Indoor/🅲 Outdoor swimming pool 🅲 Health club 🅲 Credit cards **KEY**

HOTELS & RESTAURANTS

🍴 MR. MANATEE'S
$
619 S. PALAFOX ST.
TEL 850/434-0001
Sit outdoors and watch
the moored boats, or
indoors in the large, busy
restaurant. Try the pasta,
seafood, and salads.
🔢 200   🚫 AE, MC, V

QUINCY (NORTH OF TALLAHASSEE) 32351

🏨 MCFARLIN HOUSE
$$
305 E. KING ST.
TEL 850/875-2526
The Faubles are a young
couple who rescued and
renovated this stunning
century-old house. Only 20
minutes from Tallahassee, this
is off the beaten track but is
a fine place to stay.
🛏 9   🚫   🚫 All major cards

SEASIDE 32459

🏨 JOSEPHINE'S FRENCH COUNTRY INN
$$$
101 SEASIDE AVE.
TEL 850/231-1940
FAX 850/231-2446
In the upscale resort of
Seaside, all accommodations
are self-catering—except for
this inn, which looks more
Southern mansion than
French auberge. A relaxing,
very comfortable place to
stay, with an intimate
atmosphere.
🛏 11   🚫   🚫   🚫 MC, V

🏨 SEASIDE
$$$
FLA. 30A
TEL 850/231-4224
FAX 850/231-2293
A variety of accommodations
is available throughout this
mock-Victorian resort
development. Choose from
cottages or penthouse
apartments. Use of the town's
M&M gym for energetic
guests.
🛏 250   🚫   🚫   🚫 All
major cards

🍴 BUD & ALLEY'S
$$$
FLA. 30A
TEL 850/231-5900
Right on the beach, this is
the fun spot in this demure
town. The barman was a
stand-in for Jim Carrey in *The
Truman Show*. At sunset, the
roof-deck bar is the place
to be. The inventive menu
features modern American
cooking.
🔢 197   🕐 Closed Tues.
🚫 MC, V

🍴 JOSEPHINE'S RESTAURANT
$$$
101 SEASIDE AVE.
TEL 850/231-1940
In the romantic dining room
of Josephine's French Country
Inn (see entry, this page),
specialties include seafood
chowder and crab cakes.
Many vegetables and herbs
are organic, and come from
local farms.
🔢 22   🕐 Closed L
🚫 MC, V

TALLAHASSEE 32301

🏨 GOVERNORS INN
$$$
209 S. ADAMS ST.
TEL 850/681-6855
FAX 850/222-3105
A short walk from the
state capitol buildings,
rooms here are named for
former governors of Florida.
With a mix of antiques and
reproduction furniture, this
caters to business executives
as well as vacationers.
🛏 40   🚻   🚫
🚫 All major cards

🍴 ANDREW'S SECOND ACT
$$$
228 S. ADAMS ST.
TEL 850/222-3444
This is a classy, serious
restaurant in the state
capital. The frequently-
changing menu features
seafood, pasta, and salads.
You will find it across from

the Governors Inn and
above Express, the big, busy
bar and informal restaurant
that serves salads and
sandwiches.
🔢 100   🕐 Closed Sat. L
🚫 All major cards

WAKULLA SPRINGS 32305

🏨 WAKULLA SPRINGS LODGE
$$
550 WAKULLA PARK DR.
TEL 850/224-5950
FAX 850/561-7251
Reminiscent of a lodge in the
national parks of the West,
this establishment overlooks
the famous springs in the
state park. Simple comforts in
old-fashioned rooms add up
to a historic experience. The
park entrance fee is waived
for hotel guests.
🛏 27   🚻   🚫   🚫 All major
cards

YANKEETOWN 34498

🏨 IZAAK WALTON LODGE
$
1 63RD ST.
TEL 352/447-2311
FAX 352/447-3264
Set in woods just inland from
the Gulf, this lodge is about
as far as you can get from
theme parks, sandy beaches,
and glitz. In a remote hamlet
on the Withlacoochee River,
the spacious, 75-year-old
wooden lodge is dedicated
to fishing. Rooms are simple;
the separate men's and
women's bathrooms are old-
fashioned. All of this would
add up to a real Old Florida
experience if it weren't for
the unexpectedly high
standard of cooking that
draws diners from as far
away as St. Petersburg.
🛏 9   🕐 Closed L & Mon. D
🚫 In some rooms
🚫 AE, MC, V

SHOPPING IN FLORIDA

Millions of visitors to Florida enjoy spending time shopping. Unlike some parts of the world, however, there is not a tempting range of handmade local crafts or colorful markets.

Most of the shopping is in vast, air-conditioned malls, which often double as exercise venues for mall walking in the early mornings. Some towns have a reputation as antiques centers. While many visitors enjoy spending an afternoon looking for a bargain, these are rarely the haunts of serious collectors.

Some cities and resorts have long been known for specialty shops, but recent years have seen moves to restore and revive the old business districts of many towns. Gradually, cafés, galleries, clothing, and gift shops are making a comeback.

MIAMI & MIAMI BEACH

Aventura Mall
19505 Biscayne Blvd., Aventura
Tel 305/935-1110
Recently renovated, this mall has once again become an attractive place to shop. There are more than 200 stores here, including Macy's, Lord & Taylor, and Bloomingdale's, plus specialty stores and restaurants.

Bayside Marketplace
401 N. Biscayne Blvd., Miami
Tel 305/577-3344
Built to revitalize downtown Miami, this informal Bahamian-style shopping, dining, and entertainment complex on the water has 150 stores. Street performers and evening music make this a lively venue.

Bal Harbour Shops
9700 Collins Ave., Bal Harbour
Tel 305/866-0311
Saks Fifth Avenue and Florida's largest Neiman Marcus are balanced by Chanel, Tiffany, and Louis Vuitton in this upscale shopping development set amid tropical gardens.

CocoWalk
3015 Grand Ave.
Coconut Grove
Tel 305/444-0777
The focal point of the young outdoor scene in Coconut Grove, with a large movie theater and small shops and cafés. Eating, drinking, and music continue until the wee hours.

Lincoln Road Shopping District
Lincoln Rd., Miami Beach
Tel 305/673-7010
Twelve blocks of this street have been made pedestrian-only, creating a lively atmosphere. Art galleries and studios, restaurants, and concert halls complement some 200 individual shops. Farmers' market and antiques stands in season.

Miami International Arts and Design District
N.E. 36th–N.E. 41st Sts., between N.E. 2nd Ave. and N. Miami Ave.
Closed Sat.–Sun.
One square mile filled with furniture, antiques, and accessory stores as well as fashion outlets. This is revitalizing a rundown area; get good directions.

Falls Shopping Center
US 1 and S.W. 136th St., Miami
Tel 305/255-4570
As well as 100 well-known names, this mall has cafés, restaurants, and movie theaters. Anchored by Bloomingdale's.

Streets of Mayfair
2911 Grand Ave.
Coconut Grove
Tel 305/448-1700
The Mediterranean/Spanish plaza in Coconut Grove has been totally renovated and is now more inviting than before, with small shops, restaurants, and night spots.

La Gloria Cubana de E.P.C
1106 S.W. 8th St., Miami
Tel 305/858 4162
Closed Sun.
In this small workroom, cigars are made in the Cuban way, in the heart of Little Havana. You can watch the cutting and wrapping of cigars, then buy a Double Corona, Corona Gorda, Corona, Panetela, or Torpedo.

EVERGLADES & THE KEYS

FLORIDA CITY

Florida Keys Factory Shops
250 E. Palm Dr. (S.W. 344th St.)
Tel 305/248-4727
This factory outlet center has 60 popular brand name stores, 30 minutes south of Miami.

KEY WEST

Like any seaside town, Key West has its share of T-shirt and souvenir shops. Savvy shoppers know, however, that it also has a wide choice of art galleries and clothing. Duval Street is the main street of the historic district; the farther south you go, the more upscale are the stores. Other streets worth checking out are Fleming and Simonton.

Key West Island Books
513 Fleming St., Key West
Tel 305/294-2904
A first-rate, traditional bookstore with a wide range of titles. Particularly useful for books about Key West, as well as works by authors who have lived, or still live, here. There are also used and rare volumes.

NORTH OF MIAMI

BOCA RATON

In the heart of Boca Raton, Mizner Park is named for the early 20th-century architect/developer Addison Mizner. Like a small village, it has restaurants, small shops, and an eight-screen movie theater. It also is the home of the

International Museum of Cartoon Art (see p. 102).

DELRAY BEACH

Atlantic Avenue
Tel 561/278-0424. Closed Sun.
This road retains brick sidewalks and old-fashioned street lights. Shopping ranges from jewelry to antiques and from gift shops to art galleries.

FORT LAUDERDALE

Sawgrass Mills
W. Sunrise Blvd. at Flamingo Rd., Sunrise
Tel 954/846-2350
Nine miles west of town is the famous mall that claims the title of world's largest outlet mall. Sawgrass Mills has expanded to 300 manufacturers' outlets, retail outlets, and name brand discounters as well as children's entertainment, video walls, and food courts. Shuttle buses run to and from Fort Lauderdale and Miami.

Las Olas Riverfront
Tel 954/480-4942
Opened in 1998, this is a complex of stores, restaurants, night spots, and movie theaters right in downtown. For those who like to shop and promenade in a traditional setting, Las Olas Boulevard is the trendy place to be. Lined with flowering trees and shrubs, this is a delightful enclave of specialty stores, restaurants, and art galleries.

As well as Las Olas Boulevard, there are art galleries in Hollywood, Deerfield Beach, and Pompano Beach. There are some 50 in all, showing paintings, sculpture, ceramics, photographs, and glass. Listings from Cultural Affairs Division, Broward County (Tel 954/357-7457).

The Galleria
E. Sunrise Blvd. (N of downtown, between Fla. A1A and Federal Hwy.)
Tel 954/564-1015

An upscale collection of stores ranging from Brooks Brothers and Cartier to Neiman Marcus and Saks Fifth Avenue.

PALM BEACH

Worth Avenue
Tel 561/659-6909. Closed Sun.
This is one of the world's most famous shopping streets. Stretching from South Ocean Boulevard to Cocoanut Row, the four blocks offer names that claim to rival Manhattan or Beverly Hills. There are more than 200 specialty shops, upscale department stores, art galleries, and gourmet restaurants.

SOUTHWEST FLORIDA

ELLENTON

Gulf Coast Factory Shops
5461 Factory Shops Blvd.
Tel 941/723-1150
Caribbean-style setting for Florida's largest outlet center for designer names at discount prices. Some 200 stores, plus restaurants and children's playground.

SARASOTA

Palm Avenue, just off Main Street in downtown Sarasota, has been nicknamed "Interior Designers' Row" because of its numerous galleries, antiques shops, and specialty stores.

St. Armand's Circle
Tel 941/388-1554
Built by John Ringling so that his wife had no need to go to Palm Beach. Just over the causeway from the mainland on St. Armand's Key. Exclusive galleries, stores, and restaurants.

TAMPA & ST. PETERSBURG

TAMPA

Old Hyde Park Village
Tel 813/251-3500
Two miles west of downtown

Tampa, this is a historic enclave and a very relaxing place to shop, with some 60 stores including names such as Polo/Ralph Lauren and Mondi. Sidewalk cafés add to the old-fashioned ambience.

YBOR CITY

The historic square has a bit of everything, from antiques and crafts to small specialty shops. A century ago, this area was known for cigar factories, and you can still watch them being made in the traditional way at **Gonzalez y Martinez Cigar Company,** then buy some to take with you (2025 E. 7th Ave., Tel 813/247-3249).
On weekends, the open-air **Ybor Market** is a favorite late-night spot. Expect food, shops and a Caribbean atmosphere (1632 E. 7th Ave., Tel 813/231-2720, closed Mon.–Fri.).

ST. PETERSBURG

Downtown St. Petersburg is undergoing a revival. From Ninth Street East to Tampa Bay is an eclectic mixture of stores, museums, galleries, and restaurants. Two areas for antique hunters are **Fourth Street Antique Alley,** where 60 dealers are under one roof (1535 4th St. N., Tel 727/823-5700) and the **Gas Plant Antique Arcade,** with 80 dealers on four floors of collectibles (1246 Central Ave., Tel 727/895-0368).

ORLANDO & THE THEME PARKS

MOUNT DORA

A lakeside town that exemplifies the best of small-town America, Mount Dora has about 50 art galleries, antiques shops, and gift boutiques. Year-round, between 200 and 500 dealers put out their wares in the well-known **Renninger's Twin Markets** on Saturdays and Sundays (Tel 352/383-8393).

ORLANDO

Church Street Station
Tel 407/422-2434
Part of the revitalization of downtown Orlando. This four-block complex has shopping as well as theme restaurants, live music, and dancing.

Disney's Village Marketplace
Lake Buena Vista
Tel 407/824-4321
Everything you ever wanted from the realm of Disney. It is the biggest Disney shopping experience in the world.

WINTER PARK

A total contrast to theme parks and malls, this upscale residential area north of Orlando is the home of the Morse Museum of American Art on Park Avenue (see p. 154). Also on **Park Avenue** are numerous shops selling fine jewelry and antiques, gifts and clothes. There is a wide choice of restaurants. (Tel 407/644-8281)

COCOA VILLAGE

Tel 407/631-9075
Just off Fla. 520, the tree-lined streets and historic buildings of this old-fashioned village make it a delightful place to spend time. There are arts and crafts shops, gourmet food stores, and clothing boutiques. Also events and festivals throughout the year.

Ron Jon Surf Shop
4151 N. Atlantic Ave. (Fla. A1A)
Cocoa Beach
Tel 407/799-8888
The most famous surf goods store in the world, this is open 24 hours a day, 365 days a year. Since opening in 1963, it has expanded and now has two acres of swimwear, surfboards, and related goods.

COCOA BEACH

Harvey's Groves
3811 N. Atlantic Ave. (Fla. A1A)
Tel 407/783-8640

Indian River oranges are known for their thin skin and juiciness. Since 1924, Harvey's Groves have grown and sold Florida citrus. Also branches in Melbourne, Titusville, and South Rockledge.

DAYTONA BEACH

Let's Talk Antiques
140 N. Beach St.
Tel 904/258-5225
This lively and funky antiques mall is devoted to affordable collectibles, with sections devoted to everything from housewares to clothing.
As well as a café, there is an auction house where themed auctions are held every Monday at 6 p.m.

NORTHEAST FLORIDA

GAINESVILLE

Oaks Mall
6419 Newberry Rd. (I-75)
Tel 352/331-4411
One of the largest shopping centers in north-central Florida, with five major department stores, 160 specialty shops, and numerous movie theaters and restaurants. A special feature is the measured mile-long indoor walking course.

Alachua County Farmers Market
Corner of US 441 and N.W. 34th St. (Fla. 121)
Tel 352/392-1845 (ext. 416)
Closed Sun.–Wed. & Fri., p.m. Thurs. & Sat.
Locally produced fare is the guarantee of this market, to the north of Gainesville. Farmers sell not just fruit and vegetables but also herbs, honey, and plants.

JACKSONVILLE

Historic areas such as **San Marco** on the south side of the St. Johns River and **Riverside** and **Avondale** on the north bank are good for small specialty stores and galleries. Right on the

river, **Jacksonville Landing** is a modern complex of stores, restaurants, and entertainment venues. (Tel 904/353-1188)

JACKSONVILLE BEACH

Worth Antiques Gallery
1316 Beach Blvd.
Tel 904/249-6000
Antique hunters should head for this gallery, with one of the largest collections of European, American, and Asian furniture and objets d'art.

ST. AUGUSTINE

The historic district has plenty to tempt the shopper. Around the plaza near the cathedral are art galleries and gift shops.

St. Augustine Outlet Center
Outside of town, I-95 exit 95
Tel 904/825-1555
An upscale mall, with some 100 brand-name stores.

THE PANHANDLE

HAVANA

Cannery
12 miles N of Tallahassee on US 27
Tel 850/539-3800
The small village of Havana boasts a reputation as an antiques center. Start at the Cannery, an old factory building given over to antiques dealers, and artists' studios and galleries.

TALLAHASSEE

Bradley's Country Store
Centerville Rd.
12 miles NE of Tallahassee
Tel 850/893-1647
Proud to be old-fashioned, this family business has been going for 70 years and is known for traditional smoked sausages. They sell 70,000 pounds of sausage links a year, seasoned to Grandma Mary's secret recipe. Also sells and ships grits and cornmeal.

ENTERTAINMENT/BOOKS ABOUT FLORIDA

You are never far from some sort of live entertainment in Florida. Throughout the winter season, visitors can expect to see the great names of rock, pop, country, and jazz at venues all over the Sunshine State. Many concerts are outdoors. However, in recent years, a number of impressive, purpose-built concert halls have been erected. Staging performances of classical music, ballet, and opera, these reflect the growing demand for more high-brow culture. Always check the local newspapers to see who is in town.

MIAMI & MIAMI BEACH

Greater Miami has a thriving cultural scene. The major companies include the Greater Miami Opera, the New World Symphony, and the Miami City Ballet, which also performs across southern Florida.
In Miami, the major venues are:
Jackie Gleason Theater of the Performing Arts
(sometimes known as TOPA)
1700 Washington Ave.
Miami Beach
Tel 305/673-7300
Gusman Center for the Performing Arts
174 E. Flagler St.
Tel 305/372-0925
Dade County Auditorium
2901 W. Flagler St.
Tel 305/545-3395
Colony Theater
1040 Lincoln Rd., Miami Beach
Tel 305/674-1026
Coconut Grove Playhouse
3500 Main Hwy.
Coconut Grove
Tel 305/442-4000

EVERGLADES & THE KEYS

KEY WEST

Key West has a lively theater scene in the winter season.
Waterfront Playhouse
Mallory Dock
Tel 305/294-5015
The Red Barn Theatre
319 Duval St.
Tel 305/296-9911
Tennessee Williams Fine Arts Center
5901 W. College Rd.
Tel 305/296-1520

NORTH OF MIAMI

FORT LAUDERDALE

Broward Center for the Performing Arts
201 S.W. 5th Ave.
Tel 954/468-3326
This 52-million-dollar multitheater complex presents music, drama, and more.

PALM BEACH

Raymond F. Kravis Center for the Performing Arts
701 Okeechobee Blvd.
West Palm Beach
Tel 561/659-0331 (Philharmonic), 561/835-4141 (Regional Arts Foundation)
The major cultural magnet for the area. The venue for the Miami City Ballet, Florida Philharmonic Orchestra, Palm Beach Opera, Palm Beach Pops, and the Regional Arts Foundation, which share this spectacular building with a fountain and reflecting pool.

SOUTHWEST FLORIDA

SARASOTA

Sarasota Opera
61 N. Pineapple Ave.
Tel 941/366-8450
Four operas presented during February and March.

Sarasota Concert Band
73 Palm Ave. S., #224
Tel 941/955-6660
Fifty professional players present monthly concerts through the winter season at the Van Wezel

Performing Arts Hall (see below).

Florida West Coast Symphony
709 N. Tamiami Trail.
Tel 941/953 4252
From Sept.–June, this orchestra has a full range of symphonic and chamber music events.

Florida State University Center for the Performing Arts
5555 N. Tamiami Trail
Tel 941/351-8000
The Sarasota Ballet of Florida and the Asolo Theatre put on works of a high standard each year from January through April.

Van Wezel Performing Arts Hall
777 N. Tamiami Trail
Tel 800/826-9303
This stunning example of modern architecture on Sarasota's bayfront has regular concerts, dance performances, and theater productions.

TAMPA & ST. PETERSBURG

Tampa Bay Performing Arts Center
1010 N. MacInnes Place, Tampa
Tel 813/229-7827
Right on the water, this striking modern building has four theaters, hosting everything from Broadway shows to experimental theater, as well as opera, dance, and classical music.

Tampa Theater
711 Franklin St., Tampa
Tel 813/274-8981
Built in 1926 as a movie palace, this is a beautiful setting for concerts and special events. There is also a special program of movies, ranging from Hollywood classics to arts films.

Florida International Museum
100 2nd St. N., St. Petersburg
Tel 727/821-1448
Huge venue for international blockbuster exhibitions.

ORLANDO & THE THEME PARKS

LAKE WALES

Black Hills Passion Play
Tel 813/676-1495
The company winters here, in the natural amphitheater surrounded by orange groves. Two-hour performances run from mid-February through mid-April.

SPACE & SPEED

DAYTONA BEACH

Peabody Auditorium
600 Auditorium Blvd.
Tel 904/255-1314
Home of the Daytona Beach Symphony and Daytona Beach Civic Ballet. Every two years, the 2,500-seat hall is packed for the visit of the London Symphony Orchestra during the Florida International Festival.

NORTHEAST FLORIDA

GAINESVILLE

Center for the Performing Arts
315 Hull Rd., at S.W. 34th St.
University of Florida campus
Tel 352/392-2787
Built in 1992, this 1,800-seat hall has performances across the spectrum of the arts.

JACKSONVILLE

Times-Union Center for the Performing Arts
300 Water St.
Tel 904/632-3373
In 1997 the Robert E. Jacoby Symphony Hall opened as the home of the Jacksonville Symphony Orchestra.

ST. AUGUSTINE

St. Augustine Amphitheater
Fla. A1A S.
(3 miles from downtown)
Tel 904/471-1965

This outdoor performing space hosts everything from Shakespeare to folk festivals.

THE PANHANDLE

MONTICELLO

Courthouse Square
Tel 850/997-5552 (Chamber of Commerce)
This small town has a grandiose 1890 opera house, where Shakespearian plays, concerts, and dance are all presented in restored grandeur.

TALLAHASSEE

Civic Center
Tel 850/413-9200 (CVB)
The Civic Center, which holds 14,000, attracts major names such as Elton John and Barry Manilow, as well as Broadway musicals. Florida State University and Florida A&M present their student productions of dance, drama, and music here.

BOOKS ABOUT FLORIDA

Classics
Travels of William Bartram (1791). A trained naturalist, Bartram traveled through the southeast of what is now the United States in the late 18th century.

Palmetto Leaves (1873) by Harriet Beecher Stowe. The author of *Uncle Tom's Cabin* wintered near Jacksonville.z

The Everglades: River of Grass (1947) by Marjory Stoneman Douglas. This book helped to alert fellow Americans to the importance of the Everglades. Compulsory and compulsive.

A Naturalist in Florida (1994) and *The Everglades* (1973), both by Archie Carr. Personal and graphic "celebrations of Eden".

History and environment
The Commodore's Story (1930) by Ralph Munroe and Vincent

Gilpin. Memoirs of the pre-railroad days.

Florida's Flagler (1949) by Sidney W. Martin. A portrait of the man who turned Florida into a tourist destination.

Birds of Florida (1971) by George S. Fichter. Useful for first-time birdwatchers.

Papa Hemingway in Key West (1972) by James McLendon. The Nobel prize-winning author's life in the Keys, warts and all.

Osceola (1973) by William and Ellen Hartley. A record of the brave Seminole leader who defied the U.S. Army.

Florida's Fantastic Fauna and Flora (1977) by Leslie Fletcher. Keep this handy, along with binoculars.

Some Kind of Paradise (1989) by Mark Derr. Reflections on the environmental destruction of Florida.

The Seminoles of Florida (1993) by James W Covington. Tracing the history of the tribe.

The New History of Florida (1996) by Michael Gannon and others. A serious but entertaining account of turbulent times.

Novels & other books
To Have and To Have Not (1936) by Ernest Hemingway. Set in the Keys during the Depression.

Their Eyes were Watching God (1937) by Zora Neale Hurston. There is an autobiographical subtext in Hurston's novel. Florida's best-known black writer was born in Eatonville, near Orlando.

The Yearling (1938) by Marjorie Kinnan Rawlings. A classic children's book about a boy and a fawn.

The Right Stuff (1979) by Thomas Wolfe. Classic, modern account of astronauts and the space race.

OUTDOOR RECREATION/ SPORTS & ACTIVITIES

There are several ways to explore natural Florida. Many people do it on their own, camping out at the splendid campgrounds. But for those who appreciate a little organization, there are tour operators that can help you make the best of your foray into the outdoors. Golf, fishing, and diving are some of the most popular sports in Florida. There are more golf courses here than in any other state and water sports are readily available.

Florida's festivals usually happen in the cooler months but the actual dates can vary from year to year. Visitors are recommended to check with visitor information offices for dates.

There is good fishing all over Florida: out on the ocean, from the shore and piers, and on freshwater inland lakes. All anglers need a license. The **Florida Marine Patrol** (Tel 904/488-5757) checks up from time to time. Certain species have seasons and there are also size and bag limits. Licenses are readily available at many marinas and bait and tackle stores.

It is easier than ever to enjoy Florida's great outdoors. There are more than 140 state parks, staffed by knowledgeable rangers who lead regular walks. For a booklet giving full details of all the parks, contact the Department of Environmental Protection Park Information, Mail Station, # 535, 3900 Commonwealth Blvd., Tallahassee, 32399-3000, Tel 904/488-9872.

Over the last 20 years, a network of trails has been established in Florida. The designated greenways allow canoeists, hikers, cyclists, and horseback riders access to some 40 pathways along canoe trails covering 1,000 miles of waterways. Information from the **Florida Professional Paddlesports Association,** P.O. 1764, Arcadia 34265. For a map and information on Florida's greenways contact the **Florida Department of Environmental Protection,** Office of Greenways and Trails,

Blair Stone Rd., MS-795, Twin Towers, Room 156, Tallahassee 32399-2400, Tel 850/488-3701.

Useful websites:
Florida Game & Freshwater Fish Commission
www.state.fl.us/gfc/fishing
Florida Fishing and Boating
www.fishandgame.com

MIAMI & MIAMI BEACH

All Florida Adventure Tours
8263-B S.W. 107 Ave.
Miami, 33173
Tel 800/33-TOUR3
Florida-wide with bus tours themed on nature, history, ecology, and culture.

Style Ventures
2300 Ponce De Leon Blvd.
Miami 33134
Tel 305/444-8428
Personalized tours of the Greater Miami area are available from Style Ventures, which can take you around in a luxurious, specially built minibus.

EVERGLADES & THE KEYS

ISLAMORADA

Holiday Isle Dive Shop/ Capt. Scuba
84001 Overseas Hwy., 33036
Tel 305/664-4145 or
800/327-7070
As well as PADI scuba instruction, scuba and snorkel trips are offered twice daily.

KEY LARGO

Sharky's Dive Center
Overseas Highway, MM 106,
33037
Tel 800/935-DIVE
Using a high-speed catamaran, guests dive and snorkel at Pennekamp Park.

KEY WEST

Conch Bike Express
930-B Eaton St.
Tel 305/294-4318
Locals and visitors alike bicycle around Key West. This company delivers the bikes to your hotel and collects them at the end of your stay. Includes rescue service.

Dry Tortugas National Park Ferry
Tel 800/634-0939
The *Yankee Freedom* leaves Key West at 8 a.m. each morning for the Dry Tortugas. There is time on site for swimming, snorkeling, and also exploring Fort Jefferson.

Key West Air Service
5603 College Rd.
Tel 305/292-5201
A faster and more expensive way to get to the Dry Tortugas National Park is by seaplane.

NORTH OF MIAMI

CLEWISTON

Billie Swamp Safari
HC 61 Box 46, 33440-9772
Tel 800/617-7516
Near Ah-Tah-Thi-Ki Museum, you can book swamp buggy ecotours and airboat rides in the Everglades.

FORT LAUDERDALE

In this city of canals and waterways, why not travel by boat? **The Water Taxis of Greater Fort Lauderdale** (Tel 954/467-6677), a fleet of yellow boats, connect the Center for the Performing

Arts, classy stores of Las Olas Boulevard, restaurants, night spots, and the Convention Center. They also offer guided tours of the historic New River.

JUPITER

Canoe Outfitters of Florida
8900 W. Indiantown Rd.
33478-5402
Tel 888/272-1257
Canoe and kayak rentals, with guided or self-guided tours along the scenic Loxahatchee River, with 500-year-old cypress trees and rare wildlife.

SOUTHWEST FLORIDA

BRADENTON

Canoe Outpost
18001 US 301 S., Wimauma
Tel 941/634-2228
This company has trips on 28 miles of the Little Manatee River, designated an Outstanding Florida Waterway. A chance to see the wilderness up close.

Everglades Bicycle Tours
6003 Green Blvd., Naples
Tel 941/455-7211
An unusual way of exploring South Florida's world-famous wilderness is by bicycle. The tour company provides transportation, guides, bicycles, and binoculars so you get the best out of your time in the Everglades.

FORT MYERS

Thomas Edison invented an electric boat. A reproduction of the launch, the *Reliance,* carries visitors from Fort Myers Yacht Basin down the Caloosahatchee River to the waterfront Edison and Ford Winter Estates (see pp. 120–21). Entertaining tales from the captain complete the experience (Tel 941/334-7419).

PUNTA GORDA

King Fisher Fleet
1200 W Retta Esplanade
33950-5317
Tel 941/639-0969
Choose between back bay fishing in Charlotte Harbor and deep-sea fishing on the Gulf of Mexico.

SANIBEL ISLAND

Canoe Adventures
2058 Wild Lime Dr.
Tel 941/472-5218
This is the best way to see wildlife. Mark "Bird" Westall, as his nickname suggests, is an expert on birds as well as other local wildlife.

SARASOTA

Charter Boat Freedom
6214 Hawkins Rd., 34241-9369
Tel 941/925-1871
Veteran fishing guide Ed Hurst leads novice and seasoned anglers to redfish, snook, and tarpon using light tackle spin and flyfishing techniques.

TAMPA & ST. PETERSBURG

TAMPA

Tampa Town Ferry
801 Channelside Dr.
Tel 813/223-1522
Tampa is rediscovering its river. This ferry links sights such as the Florida Aquarium, the Convention Center, and the Performing Arts Center, as well as offering hour-long cruises.

Canoe Escape
9335 E. Fowler Ave.
Thonotosassa (NE of Tampa)
Tel 813/986-2067
Explore the Hillsborough River as it flows through a 16,000-acre wilderness park, paddling downstream with a Canoe Escape craft. Drop-off and pick-up service, whether you choose a two-hour trip or a full day on the river. Plenty of wildlife, including alligators and

pileated woodpeckers, owls and herons.

TREASURE ISLAND
Far Horizons Charter Boat
9610 Gulf Blvd., 33706
Tel 727/367-7252
Professional fishing instruction, with bait and tackle provided for sport and deep-sea fishing.

ORLANDO & THE THEME PARKS

LAKE WALES

Southland Scenic Water Tours
5000 Fairmont St., Lake Wales
33853-6945
Tel 941/439-5898
Canoe and kayak tours on Lake Kissimmee and the Kissimmee River available from two hours to two days. Customized backcountry ecowater tours.

WINTER PARK

There are 17 lakes in this area, of which five are linked by canals. As you cruise along the water, past Rollins College and beautiful old mansions, the guide explains the history of the town and points out exotic plants and trees. **Scenic Boat Tours'** (Tel 407/644-4056) hour-long cruises leave on the hour from 10 a.m.–4 p.m. Their dock is on Lake Osceola, at the eastern end of East Morse Boulevard.

Captain Dana's Fishing and Scenic Tours
923 Beard Ave., 32789-1817
Tel 407/645-5462
Boating or fishing on central Florida's rivers reveals alligators, and osprey and other bird life.

SPACE & SPEED

ORMOND BEACH

Back Country Charter Service
270 Greenwood Circle, 32174-5241

OUTDOOR RECREATION

Tel 904/672-8929
Backcountry fishing trips from
Matanzas Inlet to Mosquito
Lagoon. License included for
spinning, casting, and fly rods.
Artificial and live bait.

TITUSVILLE

Osprey Outfitters
132 S. Dixie Ave., 32796
Tel 407/267-3535
Go back to nature in a kayak,
paddling the Econlockhatchee,
one of the few remaining wild
rivers in Florida, or the waters
around the Merritt Island
National Wildlife Refuge. Birdwatchers are almost guaranteed
to add to their life lists. Half-day
and full-day trips are offered.

NORTHEAST FLORIDA

AMELIA ISLAND

Kayak Amelia
1925 S. 14th St., 32034
Tel 904/321-0697
Kayak lessons and guided tours
are available here. This is the way
to see the islands, waterways,
and wildlife.

GAINESVILLE

Boulware Springs Park
off S.E. 15th St. (trailhead)
Walkers, cyclists, and horseback
riders take advantage of the
17-mile Gainesville to
Hawthorne Rail Trail through
the Lochloosa Wildlife Area.
The lush forest is broken by
lakes and prairie vistas.

Holbrook Travel
3540 N.W. 13th St.
Gainesville, 32609
Tel 352/377-7111
Tours of natural Florida by
canoes and kayaks, horses and
bicycles, even photographic
tours, from the northern part
of the state to the Everglades.

River Run Campground
Outside Ichetucknee Springs
State Park entrance, NE of
Gainesville on US 27

Tel 904/935-1086.
Ichetucknee Springs State Park
Tel 904/497-4690
"Tubing the Tuck" is a favorite
summer pastime of locals in the
area. Anyone can do it—just
rent an inner tube and go into
Ichetucknee State Park. Here, in
peak season, a tram connects
the put-in and take-out areas.
Fun and inexpensive. River Run
Campground is a good place to
rent tubes.

Sante Fe Canoe Outpost
High Springs, W of Gainesville
Tel 904/454-2050
Runs canoe trips down the
Sante Fe and Ichetucknee
Rivers. Choose from a tour
of three hours to three days.

JACKSONVILLE

Hornblower Marine Services
Tel 904/241-9969
There is no bridge over the
St. Johns River linking Mayport
and Fort George Island. Instead,
Hornblower runs the historic
ferry, which makes the regular
eight-minute crossing, enabling
drivers on Fla. A1A to continue
their journeys north or south.

O'BRIEN

**Ichetucknee Family
Grocery & Campsites**
CR 238/Old Ichetucknee Rd.
Rte. 1, Box 1576, O'Brien, 32071
Tel 904/497-2150
This store rents canoes, kayaks,
rafts, and tubes for floating down
the spring-fed Ichetucknee River.

OCALA

Several thoroughbred farms
welcome visitors to see horses
in training. Call ahead to confirm
time and directions.
Hooper Farm
Tel 352/237-2104
**Meadowbrook of the Ocala
Jockey Club**
Tel 352/591-1212
**Ocala Breeder's Sales Co.
and Training Center**
Tel 352/237-2154

Florida Kayak Fishing
3323 S.E. 2nd St., 34471
Tel 352/624-1878
Specialists in kayak fishing, fly
fishing, flats fishing, bass fishing,
and ecotours. Also instruction.

ST. AUGUSTINE

Tour St. Augustine
P.O. Box 860094, 32086
Tel 904/471-9010
Takes groups on guided walks
through the historic district of
the United States' oldest
permanent settlement. At night,
the "Ghostly Experience" is a
lantern-lit stroll, with plenty of
thrilling stories.

WHITE SPRINGS

**American Canoe
Adventures**
10315 S.E. 141st Blvd.
32096-2437
Tel 904/397-1309 or
800/624-8081
Canoe, kayak, and raft trips
on the Suwannee River from
Fargo, Georgia, to Suwannee
River State Park in Florida.

THE PANHANDLE

DESTIN

Charter Boat Silver Lining
641 Pompano Ave., 32548
Tel 850/243-7304
Destin is famous for its sport
fishing. Fully equipped with 40
rods and the latest electronic
technology, *The Silver Lining*, a
46-foot vessel, is licensed for
up to 16 passengers.

TALLAHASSEE

The capital of Florida is famous
for its canopy streets, where oak
trees dripping with Spanish moss
arch across and meet above the
streets. There is a total of 60
miles in all, radiating from
downtown. The "Canopy Roads
and Country Lanes" booklet is
available from the CVB, 200 W.
College Ave., 32302, Tel
850/413-9200.

Historic Tallahassee Tours
610 W. Call St., # 3, 32304
Tel 850/222-4143
Take a walking, driving, or
carriage tour with a guide
who brings to life the colorful
past of the state's capital.

St. Mark's Trail
Tel 850/922-6007
The trail is 16 miles long and
straight and flat, so it attracts
thousands of cyclists along what
was the railroad track between
Tallahassee and St. Mark's. Also
good for in-line skating and
horseback riding.

DeFuniak Springs
A pamphlet available from the
visitor information center in the
Chautauqua Auditorium traces a
self-guided walk around the lake.
It includes details of the more
interesting buildings and houses
of this century-old town, which
hosted the famous Chautauqua
Institute. Walton County
Chamber of Commerce, 95 W.
Circle Dr., Tel 850/892-3191.

SPORTS & ACTIVITIES

GOLF

No state has more places to
play golf than Florida. With
some 1,100 courses, there is
rarely any difficulty in getting a
tee time. The variety is endless.
Some are flat and edged with
water, others are links-type
courses by the seaside.

Golf clinics and instructional
schools abound, especially at
the grand resorts. What is
more, many of the world's
leading professionals call Florida
home, from Greg Norman to
Nick Price and from Ray Floyd
to Gene Sarazen. The PGA,
LPGA, Senior PGA, and Nike
tours all have tournaments
here. The so-called fifth major,
the Players' Championship is
played at TPC Sawgrass, Ponte
Vedra Beach.

Green Fees
$ Under $50
$$ $50–$100
$$$ More than $100

MIAMI & MIAMI BEACH

MIAMI

The Biltmore Golf Club
$
1210 Anastasia Ave.
Coral Gables
Tel 305/460-5366
With mature banyan and live
oaks, this long-established
course is open daily.
Par 71, 6,642 yds.

**Don Shula's Hotel and Golf
Club**
$
15255 Bull Run Rd., Miami Lakes
Tel 305/820-8106
This championship course has a
teasing executive par 3.
Par 72, 7,055 yds.

Doral Golf Resort and Spa
$$
4400 N.W. 87th Ave., Miami
Tel 305/591-6453
Home of the PGA Doral/Ryder
Open and known for the famous
Blue Monster.
Blue: Par 72, 7,125 yds.

Miami National Golf Club
$
6401 Kendale Lakes Dr., Miami
Tel 305/382-3935
Three nine-hole public courses
are manned by PGA pros.
Par 36, 3,445 yds.

EVERGLADES & THE KEYS

KEY WEST

Key West Golf Club
$
6450 E. College Rd., Stock Island
Tel 305/294-5232
With a Rees Jones designed
18-hole championship course.
Beware the 143-yard, par 3
Mangrove Hole, played over a
field of intertwined mangroves.
Par 68, 6,500 yds.

NORTH OF MIAMI

BOCA RATON

Boca Raton Resort and Club
$$$
501 E. Camino Real
Tel 561/447-3000
Two championship golf courses,
the Resort Course and Country
Club Course, complement the
luxury facilities of the celebrity
resort.
Par 71, 6,150 yds.

PALM BEACH

Palm Beach Golf Getaway
Tel 800/465-1547
Handles reservations at hotels
and tee times for a dozen
courses in the county. The
choice ranges from Atlantis
Country Club to Winston Trail
Country Club.

The Breakers
$$
1 S. County Rd.
Tel 561/655-6611
The oldest 18-hole course
in the state. Short, but tight
fairways, small greens.
Par 70, 6,017 yds.

Palm Beach Gardens
$$$
PGA National Resort and Spa
1000 Ave. of the Champions
Tel 561/627-2000
Jack Nicklaus recently renovated
the Champion Course, one of
five championship courses.
Par 72, 7,200 yds.

STUART

**Champions Club at
Summerfield**
$
3550 S.E. Summerfield Way
Tel 561/221-7601
Designed by Tom Fazio, this
public course has been
recognized by the Audubon
Society for its harmonious
coexistence with the local
wildlife.
Par 72, 7,022 yds.

SPORTS & ACTIVITIES

SOUTHWEST FLORIDA

BRADENTON

Tee Times USA
Tel 904/439-0001
Provides a central reservation service for the Bradenton area, with no reservation fee. Guaranteed tee times.

Legacy Golf Club at Lakewood Ranch
$
8255 Legacy Blvd.
Tel 941/351-6514
This is a chance to play one of Arnold Palmer's newer courses. Par 72, 7,123 yds.

David Leadbetter Golf Academy
$$$
5500 34th St. W.
Tel 941/755-1000
Leadbetter has coached grand-slam winners such as Nick Faldo and Nick Price, but his method is available to all, from beginners to grizzled veterans. Everything from individual lessons to five-day courses. Part of the Bollettieri Sports Academy.

CAPTIVA ISLAND

South Seas Plantation
$
South Seas Plantation Rd.
Tel 800/CAPTIVA
This course, which along with the resort takes up the northern part of Captiva Island, may only have nine holes but is fun and not tricky. Ideal for vacationers. Par 36, 2,978 yds.

NAPLES

Naples Beach Hotel and Golf Club
$$
851 Gulf Shore Blvd. N.
Tel 941/261-2222
The oldest course in Naples, which hosts the South Florida PGA Open.
Par 72, 6,497 yds.

Lely Flamingo Island Club
$$
8002 Lely Resort Blvd.
Tel 941/793-2223
Designed by Robert Trent Jones, this course has friendly, wide fairways but tricky greens.
Par 72, 7,171 yds.

Pelicans Nest
$$
4450 Bay Creek Dr.
Tel 941/597-3232
With thick woodlands and swamps, the Hurricane and Seminole courses are in tune with nature. Designed by Tom Fazio.
Par 72, 6,940 yds.

SANIBEL ISLAND

Dunes Golf and Tennis Club
$$
949 Sand Castle Rd.
Tel 941/472-3355
Nature lovers will enjoy this Mark McCumber-designed course, where the back nine snakes through a wildlife preserve of 75 glorious acres.
Par 70, 5,600 yds.

SARASOTA

Bobby Jones
$$
Off Beneva, N of Fruitville
Tel 941/955-8097
The British style, with small greens and open terrain, and the American target golf, with holding greens, are offered.
Par 70, 6,467 yds.

VENICE

Plantation Golf and Country Club
$$$
500 Rockley Blvd.
Tel 941/497-1494
Two courses here provide a real test, thanks to a design reminiscent of Scottish links, with subtly shaped greens.
Par 73, 6,862 yds.

TAMPA & ST. PETERSBURG

CLEARWATER

Belleview Biltmore Resort and Spa
$$
25 Belleview Blvd.
Tel 727/442-6171
One of Florida's most famous courses, dating from 1925 and designed by legendary Donald Ross.
Par 72, 6,675 yds.

TAMPA

Saddlebrook Resort
$$
5700 Saddlebrook Way
Wesley Chapel
Tel 813/973-1111
Arnold Palmer designed the two 18-hole courses at this 480-acre resort northeast of Tampa. Set on rolling terrain with lagoons and tall cypress trees, they provide a stern test. Professional instruction at the Arnold Palmer Golf Academy.
Par 71, 6,469 yds.

Innisbrook Resort
$
US 19, Tarpon Springs
Tel 727/942-2000
The well-known Copperhead course is a real test of length and strength at this popular resort offering several sports.
Par 71, 7,087 yds.

ORLANDO & THE THEME PARKS

HAINES CITY

Grenelefe Golf and Tennis Resort
$$
3200 Fla. 546
Tel 941/422-7511
Ron Garl designed the South course, with large greens, pretty views, and lots of water. The East course is the toughest, its holes carved out of the pines, oaks, and palm trees. The West was designed by Robert Trent Jones, Sr., with long holes, rolling

fairways, and small greens.
Par 72, 7,325 yds

KISSIMMEE

Orange Lake Country Club
$$
8505 Irlo Bronson Memorial
Hwy.
Tel 407/239-1050
The subtle combination of sand,
trees, and water makes this an
attractive alternative to the
power courses nearby.
Par 72, 6,800 yds.

LAKE BUENA VISTA

Walt Disney World
$$$
P.O. Box 10,000, 32830
Tel 407/WDW-GOLF
Six 18-hole championship
courses. The landscaping is as
well groomed as the theme parks.
Par 72, 7,203 yds.

ORLANDO

International Golf Course
$$
6351 International Golf Club Rd.
Tel 407/239-6909
This course, designed by Joe
Lee, favors the good shotmaker,
with few water hazards.
Par 72, 6,750 yds.

Faldo Golf Institute by Marriott
$
11501 International Dr.
Tel 888/GO FALDO
This nine-hole course is
devoted to teaching players
and improving their game.
Video swing analysis at the
Ron Garl-designed course is
part of the package.
Par 32, 2,400 yds.

Hyatt Regency Grand Cypress Resort
$$$
1 N. Jacaranda
Tel 407/239-1234
Four courses, all designed by
Jack Nicklaus, bring the best
out of players in this luxury
resort. The New Course is
Jack's version of St. Andrews

Old Course in Scotland.
Par 72, 6,773 yds.

SPACE & SPEED

DAYTONA BEACH

Gold Daytona Beach
Tel 904/239-7076
Coordinates golf packages
for the area.

LPGA International
$$
300 Champions Dr.
Tel 904/274-3880
One of the newest courses in
this area, this is the home course
of the Ladies' Professional Golf
Association. Hosts the richest
event on the tour, the Sprint
Championship.
Par 72, 7,000 yds.

NORTHEAST FLORIDA

AMELIA ISLAND

Amelia Island Plantation
$$$
4700 Amelia Island Pkwy.
Tel 904/277-5908
Set on 1,250 acres, the
Plantation is recognized as
one of the best courses in the
United States. Play Ocean Links,
with its new back 9, the longer
Oak Marsh, or the toughest,
Long Point.
Par 72, 6,775 yards.

PONTE VEDRA BEACH

Ponte Vedra Inn and Club
$$
200 Ponte Vedra Blvd.
Tel 904/285-6911
Located in the sandy dunes,
both the Lagoon Course
and the Ocean Course are
reminiscent of Scotland thanks
to their links-style layout.
Par 72, 6,618 yds.

Tournament Players Club at Sawgrass
$$$
110 TPC Blvd.
Tel 904/273-3235

One of only 19 tournament
players' clubs in the United
States. Hosts the annual Players'
Championship each March, with
the world's best golfers. The
second course is the Valley
Course.
Par 72, 6,937 yds.

ST. AUGUSTINE

Radisson Ponce de León Resort
$
4000 US 1
Tel 904/829-5314
Blending in with the curve of the
coastline, this is another example
of a Scottish-style links course.
Par 72, 6,823 yds.

The Slammer and the Squire
$$
3370 International Golf Pkwy.
Vistana Resort at World Golf
Village (10 miles from St.
Augustine)
Tel 904/940-6000
This course pays tribute to two
of the legends of the game. Sam
Snead and Gene Sarazen helped
to design and build the course.
Par 72, 6,800 yds.

THE PANHANDLE

DESTIN

Sandestin Beach Resort
$
5500 US 98E
Tel 850/267-8144
There is plenty of water to
worry about on these links on
the Gulf of Mexico, including
canals, marshes, and lagoons.
Par 72, 7,000 yds.

GREENVILLE

Tartaruga Creek Golf and Village
$
US 2
Tel 850/997-0036
Set amid rolling countryside,
this relatively new course has
a Mediterranean look about it.
Par 72, 6,900 yds.

PENSACOLA

Lost Key Golf Club
$$
625 Lost Key Dr., Perdido Key
Tel 850/492-1300
New course designed by Arnold Palmer with plenty of water and sand. Snakes through an Audubon Sanctuary on Perdido Key. Par 72, 6,800 yds.

TENNIS

Florida can claim a number of international legends. Chris Evert grew up in the Fort Lauderdale area, and Pete Sampras, Andre Agassi, and Jim Courier trained in Florida. Tennis courts are everywhere. However, it is the vacation resorts and tennis camps, which include instruction, competitions, and unlimited court time, that appeal to aficionados.

The United States Tennis Association, Florida Section, has more information on the sport in the Sunshine State. (Tel 954/968-3434)

MIAMI & MIAMI BEACH

KEY BISCAYNE

International Tennis Center
Tel 305/365 2300
The Lipton Championship is actually played on public courts in Crandon Park. You, too, can play here. High-class instruction.

Pembroke Pines
Pembroke Lakes Racquet Club
Tel 954/431-4146
These public courts have professional instructors on hand.

NORTH OF MIAMI

BOCA RATON

Boca Pointe Racquet Club
7144 Boca Point Dr.
Tel 561/391-5100

DELRAY BEACH

Delray Beach Tennis Center
201 W. Atlantic Ave.
Tel 561/243-7360

PALM BEACH GARDENS

PGA National Health and Racquet Club
600 Ave. of Champions
Tel 561/627-4444

PLANTATION, NEAR FORT LAUDERDALE

Veltri Tennis Center
Tel 954/452-2530
These public courts have professional instructors on hand.

SOUTHWEST FLORIDA

BRADENTON

Nick Bollettieri Tennis Academy
5500 34th St. W.
Tel 941/755-1000
Monica Seles and Andre Agassi are among the alumni of one of the most famous schools of all. Part of a wide-ranging academy that includes not just tennis but also golf, soccer, baseball, and even the arts.

SARASOTA

Colony Beach and Tennis Resort
1620 Gulf of Mexico Dr.
Longboat Key
Tel 941/383-6464
One of the United States' leading tennis resorts. 21 courts.

TAMPA & ST. PETERSBURG

TAMPA

Saddlebrook Resort
5700 Saddlebrook Way
Wesley Chapel
Tel 813/973-1111
Pete Sampras practices here, northeast of downtown. Known for its Harry Hopman Program, the resort features 45 courts,

including grass and red clay surfaces.

ORLANDO & THE THEME PARKS

The resorts at Walt Disney World have a wide range of tennis facilities, most illuminated at night. (Tel 407/934-7639)

PALM COAST

Palm Coast Players Club
300 Clubhouse Dr.
Tel 904/446-6360
Halfway between Daytona Beach and St. Augustine, this club has 12 clay, 4 hard, and 2 grass courts available. Ten of these are illuminated for night play.

NORTHEAST FLORIDA

AMELIA ISLAND

Amelia Island Plantation
3000 First Coast Hwy.
Tel 904/277-5104
Known for the Bausch and Lomb Championships. This April fixture is one of the top events on the women's tour. 27 courts.

PONTE VEDRA BEACH

ATP-Tour International Headquarters
200 ATP-Tour Blvd.
Tel 904/285-6400
This is a training center for professional players as well as the nerve center of tournaments worldwide. Amateurs can learn at the ATP Academy.

Marriott at Sawgrass Resort
1000 TPC Blvd.
Tel 904/285 7777
Next door to the ATP-tour headquarters, this is the official hotel of the tour. Guests can use eight courts here, but also have privileges at the ATP's 11 courts (see above). Clinics and lessons available.

DIVING

Scuba divers can enjoy miles of underwater playgrounds around Florida. The clear water is studded with human artifacts. Best known is the bronze statue of Christ 25 feet down in the underwater John Pennekamp state park (see pp. 82–83). Among the well-known sunken Spanish galleons still visible on the seabed are the *Atocha* and the *Margarita,* 30 miles off Key West, only two among the thousands that lie off the Florida coast. They end up looking like some sort of avant-garde sculpture, as well as forming artificial reefs that attract fish, lobsters, and oysters. Many have been scuttled deliberately to provide easily acccessible dive sites only minutes from the shore.

Among the modern warships is the U.S.S. *Massachusetts,* a 350-foot battleship that sank off Pensacola in 1927; off the Lower Keys is the massive 610-foot *Wilkes-Barre,* a World War II cruiser missing only its gun turrets. Off Panama City, a T-33 trainer jet lies in 75 feet of water a few yards from the U.S.S. *Strength,* a World War II minesweeper. Sixty-five feet below the surface, divers in the Jacksonville area can visit the watery grave of the *Casa Blanca,* a Navy landing craft that looks ready to roll into action on the ocean floor.

For listings of dive shops and excursions, see pp. 254–57.

FESTIVALS

MIAMI & MIAMI BEACH

The rich ethnic population in Miami ensures that there are flamboyant festivals in the area almost every month of the year.

JANUARY
Orange Bowl (New Year's Day)
Celebrations include parades and the second oldest college football bowl game in the nation, as well as a host of international sports events. Most of these concentrate on young talent: Winners of the international tennis tournament are recognized as stars of the future.
Redland Natural Arts Festival (early Jan.)
Thousands flock to the festival at the Fruit and Spice Park in Homestead.
Art Deco Weekend (mid-Jan.)
During this festival stands line the whole of Ocean Drive as South Beach celebrates the architecture and design that have made it internationally famous.
Taste of the Grove (mid-Jan.)
For more than 15 years, restaurants in Coconut Grove have shown off their culinary skills during this festival held at Peacock Park.
Key Biscayne Art Festival (late Jan.)
Attracts some 200 artists from around the world. The annual event is on Crandon Boulevard.

FEBRUARY
Black Heritage Month (all month)
Celebrations take place throughout Greater Miami.
Miami International Film Festival (early Feb.) is now well-established and provides a good excuse to enjoy the oldest movie theater in Miami, the Gusman Center for the Performing Arts.
Coconut Grove Arts Festival (mid-Feb.)
On Bayshore Drive. Rated one of the top arts festivals in the United States and boasting an ever-increasing audience.
Calle Ocho Festival (late-Feb.–early March)
A celebration of the Hispanic community, takes over Eighth Street between 4th and 27th Avenues in the heart of Little Havana. Expect plenty of food and music. All part of Carnaval Miami, a week-long party with street parades and a million party-goers.

MARCH
Italian Renaissance Festival (late March)
This annual event has a perfect setting at the Villa Vizcaya Museum and Gardens.

JUNE
Miami/Bahamas Goombay Festival (early June)
Downtown Coconut Grove resounds to the rhythms of Caribbean music. Also food and dance.
Florida Dance Festival (mid-June)
Lovers of dance head for the Colony Theater in the Art Deco District of Miami Beach for this annual event.

AUGUST
Reggae Festival (early Aug.)
Miami's strong Caribbean connections come to the fore with the annual festivities at Bayfront Park.

DECEMBER
King Mango Strut (early Dec.)
A tongue-in-cheek take-off of Miami's famous Orange Bowl celebrations. Join the residents of Coconut Grove for this irreverent celebration.
Indian Arts Festival (end Dec.)
For the last 20 years, this festival has put the spotlight on the Native American artisans at the Miccosukee Indian Village, 30 miles west of Miami on the Tamiami Trail.

EVERGLADES & THE KEYS

FEBRUARY
Key West's Old Island Days (mid-Feb.)
A chance to go inside private houses and gardens.

JULY
Hemingway Days Festival (end July)
Dozens of square-jawed, white-haired gents turn up for the Look-alike Contest that is the highlight of the festival.

OCTOBER
Fantasy Fest (mid-Oct.)
This is when Key West turns into one big party. Expect the most extravagant of costumes in the parades.

Key West Theater Festival (mid-Oct.)
The kick-off to the thriving theater season.

NORTH OF MIAMI

JANUARY
Las Olas Art Fair (early Jan.)
Las Olas Boulevard, the trendy street of stores, restaurants, and galleries in Fort Lauderdale, stages this festival.

FEBRUARY
Florida Renaissance Festival (all month)
Snyder Park in Fort Lauderdale is the scene of the medieval and Renaissance-themed events.
Palm Beach Seafood Festival (mid-Feb.)
Currie Park in West Palm Beach is the venue for this event.

FEBRUARY–APRIL
The world's finest polo players and ponies are in action in and around Palm Beach for the season that climaxes with the **United States Open Polo Championship and Gold Cup**.

MARCH
Las Olas Art Festival
One of the nation's premier outdoor art celebrations. More than 250 artists from across the United States show their works. In support of the Museum of Art, this is a juried show.

APRIL
Delray Affair (mid-April)
Delray Beach hosts a wide-ranging festival of music, crafts, and arts.

MAY
Sunfest (early May)
Florida's largest music, art, and water festival takes place all along Palm Beach's downtown waterfront.

JULY/AUGUST
Summer Nights on the Avenue (Thurs. & Fri. nights)
Atlantic Avenue in Delray Beach is the place to be when street and block parties celebrate.

AUGUST
Bon Festival (mid-Aug.)
This annual event at the Morikami Museum in Delray Beach (see p. 103) re-creates the Japanese public holiday that honors ancestors with floating lanterns and fireworks. Japanese folk dancing, food, and games.

OCTOBER
Hollywood Jazz Festival
Jazz greats such as Dizzy Gillespie and Mongo Santamaria star in the annual festival that attracts musicians and fans from across the country. At Young's Circle, Hollywood.

OCTOBER/NOVEMBER
International Film Festival
Movie buffs flock to Fort Lauderdale for this showcase for 30 independently produced films. It also gives the audience a chance to meet the moviemakers.

NOVEMBER
Heritage Festival (early Nov.)
The South Florida Fairgrounds in West Palm Beach host the annual event.
Downtown Boca Festival of the Arts (early Nov.)
An annual outdoor juried art show in Boca Raton displaying the work of some 150 artists working in mixed media, photography, sculpture, pottery, and painting.

DECEMBER
Winterfest
In Fort Lauderdale, this is a series of star-studded events to celebrate the vacation season. The highlight of the festival is the Winterfest Boat Parade, with over 100 decorated vessels lighting up the Intracoastal Waterway.

SOUTHWEST FLORIDA

JANUARY
International Circus Festival and Parade
Sarasota's rich circus heritage combines with international circus talent.

FEBRUARY
Festival of the Arts (mid-Feb.)
Two hundred craftsmen and artists line Main Street in downtown Sarasota for this annual festival.
Marco Fine Art Juried Show (mid-Feb.)
For more than 25 years, artists have displayed their works at this show held at the Art League Grounds on Marco Island.
Medieval Fair (late Feb.– early March)
In Sarasota, the Ringling Museum of Art changes into a 14th-century European village, with 7 stages for plays and some 200 craftspeople showing their skills.

MARCH
Sailor Circus (dates vary)
Sarasota County's 50-year-old tradition of circus performances by 3rd- to 12th-grade students has come a long way from the original gymnastic classes. See them at this yearly show.
Sanibel Shell Fair (early March)
Sanibel Island is known for its shells, and each year this fair is a highlight for collectors.

Seafood Festival (mid-March)
Held in the elegant town of Naples.
Sarasota Jazz Festival (late March)
For nearly two decades, this festival has had star names such as Dave Brubeck.

APRIL
International Chamber Music Festival
Top class musicians in the Americas and from Europe perform in Sarasota's annual music festival.

The Florida Heritage Festival (all month)
Held in and around Bradenton, the festival commemorates the arrival of Hernando de Soto. The climax is a reenactment of the 1539 landing of the Spanish explorer at Shaw's Point, at the mouth of the Manatee River.

JUNE
Sarasota Music Festival
(early June)
For three weeks, this festival showcases international artists as well as talented music students from around the world. Chamber music is the focus.

TAMPA & ST. PETERSBURG

JANUARY
Feast of Epiphany (Jan. 6)
This is a major event in the Greek community of Tarpon Springs (see p. 150). Starting with morning services in St. Nicholas Greek Orthodox Cathedral, a procession leads to Spring Bayou, where 30 to 40 teenage boys dive into the water, hoping to be the first to bring up the cross. This tradition has continued since 1903.

FEBRUARY
Gasparilla Pirate Fest
(early Feb.)
Accompanied by hundreds of boats, a fully rigged pirate ship with a 700-strong crew sails across Hillsborough Bay from Ballast Point Pier to downtown Tampa. Pirates then parade along Bayshore Boulevard as part of this day-long event recalling the area's piratical past.

Fiesta Day (mid-Feb.)
Tampa's Latin Quarter, Ybor City, celebrates its Hispanic past with a street fair and concerts, arts and crafts. At night, illuminated floats form a glittering parade.

ORLANDO & THE THEME PARKS

JANUARY
Florida Citrus Festival and Polk County Fair (mid-Jan.)
Traditional country fair at Winter Haven's Citrus Festival Fairgrounds.
Battle of Townsend's Plantation and Civil War Festival (end Jan.)
The usually quiet town of Mount Dora echoes to the sounds of musket fire as locals dress up to reenact the events of the past.

FEBRUARY
Arts Festival (early Feb.)
Hundreds of artists come to Mount Dora to show off their works at this annual juried event. Well known as a high-quality event, it attracts thousands of visitors to the small downtown of this charming town.

MARCH
Bluegrass Festival
(early March)
Country music fans flock to the Silver Spurs Rodeo Grounds in Kissimmee for this annual event.
International Orchid Fair
(mid-March)
An alternative to Orlando's theme parks for garden lovers at the World of Orchids.
Winter Park Sidewalk Arts Festival (late March)
This is one of the most prestigious outdoor arts fairs in the nation. Over $50,000 in prizes in nine categories attracts some 250 artists. During the three days of art, music, and food, there are performances all day by world-class jazz musicians such as Herbie Hancock.

APRIL
International Fringe Festival
(late April)
More than 300 performers and theater companies entertain visitors to Orlando during this festival.

SPACE & SPEED

FEBRUARY–MARCH
Speed Weeks
For several weeks, Daytona fills with enthusiasts from all over the world for this annual happening at Daytona International Speedway. A variety of races and exhibitions for cars and motorcycles.

MARCH
Warbird Airshow (mid-March)
For more than 20 years, fans of classic airplanes have headed for Titusville for this airshow at the Space Coast Regional Airport, located on Fla. 405.

EASTER
Surfing Festival
For more than 30 years, the swimming season has opened with this event at Cocoa Beach Pier. As well as international male and female surfers, the event has concerts by top pop stars and all the fun of the fair.

APRIL
Melbourne Art Festival
Held on New Haven Avenue in historic downtown Melbourne, the festival has been a fixture on the calendar for more than a decade. A fine arts exhibition (250 artists) plus entertainment.
Indian River Festival
(late April)
The highlight of the festival is the raft race, where homemade rafts compete for awards varying from best-dressed crew to worst performance.

NORTHEAST FLORIDA

JANUARY
Jacksonville Craft Fair
(mid-Jan.)
The Jacksonville Fairground is the venue for the city's annual fair.

FEBRUARY
Florida Invitational Jazz Festival (early Feb.)
The campus of the University of

Florida in Gainesville is crammed with jazz enthusiasts from colleges all over the United States.

Battle of Olustee (mid-Feb.) The annual reenactment of the is a full-scale mock battle, with color ceremonies, more than 1,000 participants, and 28 artillery pieces. As well as the camps, there are demonstrations by medical units and even period church services.

APRIL
Springing the Blues Festival (early April)
Many of the nation's best-loved musicians congregate at the Seawalk Pavilion, Jacksonville Beach.

MAY
Isle of Eight Flags Shrimp Festival (early May)
Fernandina Beach is invaded by thousands of visitors, as it has been for more than 35 years. Party and eat Amelia Island's "pink gold"—the shrimp. Enjoy arts, crafts, and seafood galore at the home of the modern shrimping industry.

JUNE
Spanish Nightwatch Celebration and **Greek Landing Day Celebration** (late June)
In St. Augustine, the city's ethnic heritage is celebrated on two weekends. The Spanish Nightwatch Celebration includes music, military demonstrations, and cannon firing, and Greek Landing Day Celebration marks the arrival of the first colony of Greeks in the New World.

SEPTEMBER
Days In Spain/Founder's Day Fiesta (mid-Sept.)
The landing of Pedro Menéndez de Avilés (see p. 25) is part of the festival in the downtown historic area of St. Augustine. Spanish dancing and entertainment.

OCTOBER
Colonial Arts and Crafts Fair (early Oct.)
Quilting, rug-weaving, lace-making, and metalsmithing in the Spanish Quarter Village of St. Augustine.
Jeanie Auditions (early Oct.)
For nearly half a century, the songs of Stephen Foster have been brought to life by female vocalists in this competition with a music scholarship prize. The night before the contest, there is a ball, with guests in period dress. Both events are held at the Stephen Foster State Folk Culture Center, White Springs.

NOVEMBER–JANUARY
Nights of Lights Celebration
Beginning the Saturday before Thanksgiving, a million tiny white lights illuminate the outlines of historic buildings in the downtown and bayfront areas of St. Augustine for two months.

DECEMBER
Regatta of Lights (mid-Dec.)
St. Augustine's annual parade of boats along the Matanzas River.
Victorian Seaside Christmas (before Christmas)
The Victorian architecture of Fernandina Beach is decked out in its vacation finery for the annual event.

THE PANHANDLE

APRIL
Sandestin Wine Festival (mid-April)
The market at Sandestin has become a rallying point for wine lovers over the past decade.
Chautauqua Festival Day (mid-April)
DeFuniak Springs remembers the educational institution that put the town on the map a century ago.

MAY
Southern Shakespeare Festival (early May)
The festival in downtown

Tallahassee combines workshops and free outdoor performances with a medieval fair.

JUNE
Fiesta of Five Flags (early June)
Pensacola recalls the city's history under Spanish, English, French, Confederate, and United States rule.

JULY
Air Show
The nation's finest display team, the Blue Angels are the highlight of this month-long show over Pensacola Beach.

OCTOBER
The Indian Summer Seafood Festival (mid-Oct.)
Bessant Park at Panama City Beach has two days of eating and drinking in an event going strong for about 20 years.
Pensacola Interstate Fair (mid-Oct.)
This fair lasts ten days and is rated one of the biggest and most exciting in the country. Food, shows, rides, and plenty of fun.

NOVEMBER
Homecoming Show
The Blue Angels touring aerobatic display team comes back to the Naval Air Station in Pensacola this month and marks their return with this spectacular show.
Pensacola Jazzfest (early Nov.)
The old buildings around Seville Square echo to the rhythms of jazz. Plenty of star names.
The Great Gulf Coast Arts Festival (early Nov.)
More than 200 artists display their works in Pensacola at this annual juried art show of arts, crafts, and sculpture.

ILLUSTRATIONS CREDITS

Abbreviations for terms appearing below: (t) top; (b) bottom; (l) left; (r) right.

Cover: (tl), Eye Ubiquitous. (tr), Powerstock/Zefa. (bl), Pictures Colour Library. (br), Tony Stone Images. Spine: Powerstock/Zefa

1, Tony Stone Images. 2/3, Tony Stone Images. 4, Planet Earth/Geoff du Feu. 9, Peter Newark's American Pictures. 10, AA Photo Library/P Murphy. 11, Pictures Colour Library. 12/3, Catherine Karnow. 14, Catherine Karnow. 15, Catherine Karnow. 17, Tony Stone Images. 18/9, Tony Arruza. 20, Image Bank. 20/1, Image Bank. 22/3, Image Bank. 24/5, Peter Newark's Pictures. 26(t), Peter Newark's Pictures. 26(b), Peter Newark's Pictures. 27, Peter Newark's Pictures. 28, Peter Newark's Pictures. 29, Peter Newark's Pictures. 31 Jonathan Blair /National Geographic Image Collection. 32, Peter Newark's Pictures. 33(t), Bridgeman Art Library, London, Indian Man of Florida (lithograph) by John White (fl.c. 1570-93) (after) Private Collection. 33(b), Bridgeman Art Library, London, Indian Woman of Florida (lithograph) by John White (fl.c. 1570-93) (after) Private Collection. 34/5 Performing Arts Library/Clive Barda. 36, Tony Stone Images. 37, AA Photo Library/P Bennett. 38(t), Bridgeman Art Library, London, Portrait of Harriet Elizabeth Stowe (nee Beecher) (b/w photo) Private Collection. 38(b), Corbis. 39, Corbis/Kevin Fleming. 40/1, Historical Association of Southern Florida. 42(t), Ronald Grant Archive. 42(b), Ronald Grant Archive. 43, Image Bank. 46, AA Photo Library/P Bennett. 47, Gusman Center, Miami. 48, AA Photo Library/P Bennett. 49(t), Robin Hill. 49(b), Lanny Provo. 50/1, Robert Harding Picture Library. 52, AA Photo Library/P Bennett. 53, Robert Harding Picture Library. 54(t), AA Photo Library/P Bennett. 54(b), AA Photo Library/P Bennett. 55, Historical Association of Southern Florida, Miami News Collection. 56, Lowe Art Museum. 57(t), AA Photo Library/P Bennett. 57(b), Historical Museum of Southern Florida. 58, AA Photo Library/P Bennett. 59(t), AA Photo Library/P Bennett. 59(bl), AA Photo Library/J Davidson. 59(br), AA Photo Library/L Provo. 60/1, Allsport/Peter Taylor. 61(t), Allsport/Al Bello. 61(b), Allsport/Zoran Milich. 62, Catherine Karnow. 63(t), Mitchell Wolfson Jr. Collection, The Wolfsonian-Florida International University, Miami Beach, Florida. 63(b), Historical Museum of Southern Florida. 64, Sanford L. Ziff Jewish Museum of Florida. 65(t), Pictor International, London. 65(b), AA Photo Library/P Bennett. 67(t), Image Bank. 67(c), Robert Harding Picture Library. 67(b), AA Photo Library/P Bennett. 68, Catherine Karnow. 69(t), Catherine Karnow. 69(b), Catherine Karnow. 70, AA Photo Library/P Bennett. 71, AA Photo Library/J Davidson. 72, AA Photo Library/P Bennett. 73, Nature Photographers Ltd/P R Sterry. 74, Corbis/Patrick Ward. 76(t), Robin Hill. 76(b), Robin Hill. 77, Image Bank. 78, Image Bank. 79(t), Tony Stone Images. 79(b), Planet Earth/Doug Perrine. 80, AA Photo Library/J A Tims. 83, Catherine Karnow. 84(t), Tony Arruza. 84(b), Bruce Coleman Collection. 85, Planet Earth/Flip Schulke. 88, Pictures Colour Library. 89(t), Pictures Colour Library. 89(b), Audoben House Archives. 90, AA Photo Library/D Lyons. 91, AA Photo Library/P Bennett. 92, Robert Harding Picture Library. 95(t), Image Bank. 95(bl), AKG, London. 95(br), Hemmingway House. 96, Pictures Colour Library. 97, Image Bank. 98, Powerstock/Zefa. 100, Spectrum Colour Library. 101, Image Bank. 102, Marvel Entertainment Group, NY: Spider-Man TM and © 1999, Marvel Characters, Inc. All rights reserved. 103, Pictures Colour Library. 105(t), AA Photo Library/J A Tims. 105(bl), Flagler Museum Archives. 105(br), Flagler Museum. 106, Flagler Museum Archives. 106/7, Flagler Museum Archives. 107, Peter Newark's American Pictures. 108/9, Corbis/Vince Streano. 109, Bridgeman Art Library, London, The Agony in the Garden (Christ in the Garden of Olives), 1889 by Paul Gauguin (1848-1903), Norton Gallery, Florida. 110, Kevin Fleming 1999. 111, Image Bank. 113, Image Bank. 114, Tony Arruza. 115, Pictures Colour Library. 116, Tony Arruza. 117(t), AA Photo Library/J A Tims. 117(b), Dorling Kindersley Ltd/Dave King. 119(t), NASA/Science Picture Library. 119(b), E R Degginger/Science Picture Library. 120, Hulton Getty. 121, Tony Aruzza. 122, Pictor International, London. 123, Dorling Kindersley Ltd/Dave King. 125, Tony Stone Images. 128, Pictures Colour Library. 128/9, Pictures Colour Library. 130(t), Pictor International, London. 130(b), Florida State Archives. 131, Barlow Miniature Circus, 1948-1959, Collection of Ringling Museum of the Circus, Sarasota, Florida. 132, AA Photo Library/P Bennett. 133, Mote Marine Laboratory, Sarasota. 134(t), De Soto National Memorial, Brandenton, Florida/Robert Crain. 134(b), Mary Evans Picture Library. 135, Allsport/Al Bello. 137, Image Bank. 138, Pictures Colour Library. 139(t), Florida State Archives. 139 (b) AA Photo Library/J A Tims. 140(t) Robert Harding Picture Library. 140b, AKG, London. 141, © Busch Gardens. All Rights Reserved. 142, Museum of Fine Arts, St Petersburg. 143(t), St Petersburg Museum of History. 143 (b), Pictures Colour Library. 144, Bridgeman Art Library, London, The Disintegration of the Persistence of Memory, 1952-54 by Salvador Dalí (1904-89), Salvador Dalí Museum, Florida, © Salvador Dalí-Foundation Gala-Salvador Dalí/DACS 1999. 145, Tampa Bay Holocaust Museum. 146, Peter Newark's Pictures. 146/7, Images Colour Library. 148, AA Photo Library/P Bennett. 149, Tony Stone Images. 150, Tony Aruzza. 151, Pictures Colour Library. 152, Pictor International, London. 154, Orlando/Orange County Convention and Visitors Bureau. 155(t), AA Photo Library/T Souter. 155(b), Charles Hosmer Morse Foundation, Inc. 156/7, Image Bank. 157(t), © 1998 SeaWorld Adventure Parks, Inc. All Rights Reserved. 157 (b), © 1998 Universal Studios Escape. 159, © Disney Enterprises, Inc. 160, © Disney Enterprises, Inc. 160/1, © Disney Enterprises, Inc. 162, © Disney Enterprises, Inc. 163, © Disney Enterprises, Inc. 164, © Disney Enterprises, Inc. 165, © Disney Enterprises, Inc. 166, © 1998 SeaWorld Adventure Parks, Inc. 167, AA Photo Library/Tony Souter. 168/9 © 1997 Universal Studios Florida. 170, © 1997 Universal Studios Florida. 171, © 1997 Universal Studios Florida. 172, Tony Aruzza. 173, Cypress Gardens. 174, Peter Newark's

Pictures. 175, Pictures Colour Library. 176, courtesy of Florida Southern College. 177, Allsport/David Taylor. 178, Daytona Racing Archives. 180, Florida State Archives. 181, AA Photo Library/P Bennett. 183, Genesis Space Photo Library. 184(t), AA Photo Library/ T Souter. 184(b) US Astronaut Hall of Fame. 185, NASA/Genesis Space Photo Library. 186/7, Genesis Space Photo Library. 188, Corbis/Raymond Gehman. 189, Planet Earth/Doug Perrine. 190, Daytona Racing Archives. 190/1, Hulton Getty. 191, Daytona Racing Archives. 192, Daytona Racing Archives. 193(t) Robert Harding Picture Library. 193(b) The Museum of Arts and Sciences, Daytona Beach. 194, J Allan Cash Photolibrary. 195, Pictor International, London. 198, AA Photo Library/ P Bennett. 199, AA Photo Library/ P Bennett. 200, AA Photo Library/ P Bennett. 201(t), AA Photo Library/P Bennett. 201(b), AA Photo Library/ P Bennett. 202, Robert Harding Picture Library. 203, AA Photo Library/ P Bennett. 206, Pictor International, London. 207, AA Photo Library/ P Bennett. 209, Pictor International, London. 211, Majorie Kinnan Rawlings State Historic Site. 212/3, Tony Arruza. 213(t), Images Colour Library. 213(b), Powerstock/Zefa. 214, Olustee Battlefield State Historic Site. 215, Corbis/Nik Wheeler. 217, AA Photo Library/ P Bennett. 218, Tony Stone Images. 219, Image Bank. 220, Powerstock/Zefa. 221, AA Photo Library/ P Bennett. 222, AA Photo Library/ J Davidson. 223(t), AA Photo Library/ P Bennett. 223(b), AA Photo Library/ P Bennett. 224, Corbis/Richard Bickel. 225, Corbis/ Richard Bickel. 226, AA Photo Library/ P Bennett. 227, AA Photo Library/ P Bennett. 228, AA Photo Library/ J Davidson. 229(t), AA Photo Library/ P Bennett. 229(b), AA Photo Library/ P Bennett. 230(t) Dorling Kindersley Ltd/Dave King. 230(b) Tony Arruza. 231, AA Photo Library/ J A Tims.

The Yearling entry on p. 38: © Carl Hiaasen 1986. Reproduced by permission of the author c/o Rogers, Coleridge & White Ltd., 20 Powis Mews, London W11 1JN in association with International Creative Management, Inc., 40 West 57th St., New York, NY 10019. The publisher has made every effort to trace copyright holders and apologizes for any omissions.

Published by the National Geographic Society
John M. Fahey, Jr., *President and Chief Executive Officer*
Gilbert M. Grosvenor, *Chairman of the Board*
Nina D. Hoffman, *Senior Vice President*
William R. Gray, *Vice President and Director, Book Division*
David Griffin, *Design Director*
Elizabeth L. Newhouse, *Director of Travel Publishing*
Barbara A. Noe, *Associate Editor*
Caroline Hickey, *Senior Researcher*
Carl Mehler, *Director of Maps*
Joe Ochlak, *Map Coordinator*
Mary B. Dickinson, Kristin Edmonds, *Editorial Consultants*
Gary Colbert, *Production Director*
Ric Wain, *Production Project Manager*
DeShelle Downey, *Staff Assistant*

Edited and designed by AA Publishing (a trading name of Automobile Association Developments Limited, whose registered office is Norfolk House, Priestley Road, Basingstoke, Hampshire, England RG24 9NY. Registered number: 1878835).

Betty Sheldrick, *Project Manager*
David Austin, *Senior Art Editor*
Marilynne Lanng, *Editor*
Tom Reynolds, Keith Russell, *Designers*
Simon Mumford, *Senior Cartographic Editor*
Helen Beever, Nicky Barker-Dix, *Cartographers*
Richard Firth, *Production Director*
Liz Wells, *Picture Researcher*

Drives/Everglades walk maps: Chris Orr Assoc., Southampton, England
Cutaway illustrations drawn by Maltings Partnership, Derby, England
Fishes illustration by Ann Winterbotham
Shells illustration by Chris Orr Associates, Southampton, England

Library of Congress Cataloging-in-Publication Data
Arnold, Kathy.
The National Geographic traveler. Florida / Kathy Arnold and Paul Wade.
   p. cm.
   Includes index.
   ISBN 0-7922-7432-6
   1. Florida Guidebooks. I. Wade, Paul. II. Title. III. Title:
   Florida.
   F309.3.A75 1999
   917.5904'63--dc21   99-39976
                             CIP

Printed and bound by R.R. Donnelley & Sons, Willard, Ohio.
Color separations by Leo Reprographics, Hong Kong.
Cover separations by L.C. Repro, Aldermaston, U.K.
Cover printed by Miken Inc., Cheektowagea, New York.
Visit the society's Web site at http://www.nationalgeographic.com

The information in this book has been carefully checked and to the best of our knowledge is accurate. However, details are subject to change, and the National Geographic Society cannot be responsible for such changes or for errors or omissions. Assessments of sites, hotels, and restaurants are based on the author's subjective opinions, which do not necessarily reflect the publisher's opinion. The publisher cannot be responsible for any consequences arising from the use of this book.

THE NATIONAL GEOGRAPHIC TRAVELER

A Century of Travel Expertise in Every Guide

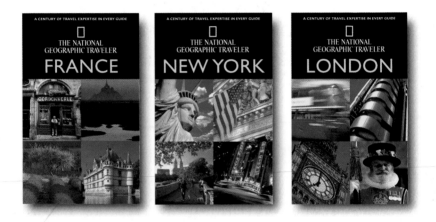

- **Australia** ISBN: 0-7922-7431-8
- **Canada** ISBN: 0-7922-7427-X
- **The Caribbean** ISBN: 0-7922-7434-2
- **Florida** ISBN: 0-7922-7432-6
- **France** ISBN: 0-7922-7426-1
- **Great Britain** ISBN: 0-7922-7425-3
- **London** ISBN: 0-7922-7428-8
- **Miami and the Keys** ISBN: 0-7922-7433-4
- **New York** ISBN: 0-7922-7430-X
- **Paris** ISBN: 0-7922-7429-6
- **Sydney** ISBN: 0-7922-7435-0

AVAILABLE WHEREVER BOOKS ARE SOLD